ENTERPRISE CLUSTERS AND NETWORKS
IN DEVELOPING COUNTRIES

EADI BOOK SERIES 20

Enterprise Clusters and Networks in Developing Countries

edited by

MEINE PIETER VAN DIJK
and
ROBERTA RABELLOTTI

FRANK CASS • LONDON

in association with

EADI   The European Association of Development Research
and Training Institutes (EADI), Geneva

First published in 1997 in Great Britain by
FRANK CASS & CO. LTD.
Newbury House, 900 Eastern Avenue,
London IG2 7HH

and in the United States of America by
FRANK CASS
c/o ISBS
5804 N.E. Hassalo Street
Portland, Oregon 97213-3644

Transferred to Digital Printing 2004

British Library Cataloguing in Publication Data

A catalogue record for this book
is available from the British Library

ISBN 0 7146 4333 5 (paperback)

Library of Congress Cataloging-in-Publication Data

Enterprise clusters and networks in developing countries / edited by
Meine Pieter van Dijk and Roberta Rabellotti.
   p.   cm. — (EADI-book series: 20)
   "In association with the European Association of Development
Research and Training Institutes (EADI), Geneva."
   Includes bibliographical references.
   ISBN 0-7146-4333-5 (pbk.)
   1. Business networks—Developing countries—Case studies.
I. Dijk, Meine Pieter van.   II. Rabellotti, Roberta.   III. Series.
HD69.S8E58   1996
338.8'09172'4—dc21   98-48445
                                                          CIP

Typeset by Regent Typesetting, London

Contents

Notes on Contributors

M.S.D. Bagachwa is associate research professor at the Economic Research Bureau and an Associate Dean of the Faculty of Arts and Social Sciences of the University of Dar es Salaam in Tanzania.

Michelle Bagella works at the Dipartimento di Economica e Istituzioni of the Università di Roma Tor Vergata in Rome, Italy.

Hanneke Dijkman is an economist from the Netherlands who worked for the University of Ougadougou (Burkina Faso) and is presently working for the Netherlands Development Association in Uganda.

Meine Pieter van Dijk is an economist at the Economic Faculty of Erasmus University, senior economist at the Institute for Urban and Housing Studies, both in Rotterdam, and Research Associate, CERES Research School, Utrecht, The Netherlands.

Dorothy McCormick is Senior Research Fellow at the Institute for Development Studies of the University of Nairobi, in Kenya.

Poul Ove Pedersen is director of the Centre for Development Research in Copenhagen, Denmark.

Carlo Pietrobelli works at the Dipartimento di Economica e Istituzioni of the Università di Roma Tor Vergata in Rome, Italy.

Roberta Rabellotti works at the Economics Department of the University of Padua, in Padua, Italy.

Arni Sverrisson works at the Research Policy Institute, University of Lund in Sweden.

Evert-Jan Visser worked as an economist at the Tinbergen Institute and the University of Amsterdam. He has recently joined the Foundation for Economic Research at Erasmus University in Rotterdam, the Netherlands.

1

Clusters and Networks as Sources of Co-operation and Technology Diffusion for Small Enterprises in Developing Countries

MEINE PIETER VAN DIJK
and ROBERTA RABELLOTTI

I. INTRODUCTION

After discussing alternative industrialisation strategies[1] and flexible specialisation,[2] the EADI working group on industrialisation in the Third World decided during the EADI conference in Berlin (September 1993) to delve more deeply into the factors determining the success of certain small enterprise clusters and networks. The underlying issue has always been how to increase employment and economic growth through small enterprise development.[3]

Most chapters in this collection look at the functions and advantages of clusters and networks. Different types of clusters and networks are described, and the diverse forms of external economies and co-operation effects derived from them are compared. The approach adopted in this volume is multidisciplinary. Economists use their microeconomic tools to analyse the economic advantages of clustering, geographers stress the importance of space, while, from a sociological perspective, interactions are analysed mainly as personal relationships based on trust. The integration of these different perspectives makes this volume an interesting witness of the fruitfulness of an interdisciplinary discussion.

In this introductory chapter we will define clusters and networks in a small enterprise context. The social basis for the positive effects of clustering and networking is trust, which is the central term used in Chapter 8 of the volume. The economic results of clustering and networks can be analysed in terms of external economies and co-operation effects, which are central in Chapters 2, 3 and 4. The concepts of trust, different types of economies and co-operation will be discussed in this chapter before the structure of the book is explained.

II. CLUSTERS, DISTRICT AND NETWORKS

In institutional economics a cluster of small enterprises is considered as a way of industrial organisation embracing both geographical and sectoral specialisation, competing with large and medium-scale enterprises. The spatial proximity of a group of firms specialised in making the same or similar products does bring benefits. More importantly, it is a major factor facilitating the division of labour among specialised producers, the emergence of suppliers, buyers and institutions aimed at providing specific services, the circulation of information about technology, the market and so on. The density, quality and type of these linkages are crucial to explaining the real economic advantages of clustering.

According to Marshall [*1890*], if a cluster is effectively characterised by, at least, some degree of division of labour, then it can be defined as an industrial district. Following the definition given by Rabellotti (in Chapter 3), a cluster matches the ideal-type of industrial district as described in the literature if the following key elements are satisfied:

– there is a strong, relatively homogeneous cultural and social background linking economic agents and creating a common and widely accepted behavioural code, sometimes explicit but often implicit;
– there exists an intense set of backward, forward, horizontal and labour market linkages, based both on market and non-market exchanges of goods, services, information and people;
– there is a network of public and private local institutions supporting the economic agents acting within the clusters.

Industrial districts and, sometimes, also geographical clusters of enterprises have as their social complement a network of entrepreneurs. Such a network (for example, of entrepreneurs from a similar region, tribe or profession) is often based on trust of one kind or another. The interesting thing is that networks may exist independently from physical clusters. Economic interaction can also take place in personal rather than spatial networks. The case studies presented in this book show that there are very different types of networks linking small entrepreneurs. Subcontracting networks are different from ethnic networks, which are again different from trader-run networks. In trader-run networks brokers and middlemen play an important role in organising small enterprise networks. They often take care of the financing, transport, insurance and distribution of the goods. They may be tied to suppliers through credit arrangements. These traders can also function in the transfer of new ideas about product design, quality and technologies to the producer.

Trade associations, defined as forms of collaboration between small entrepreneurs active in a similar branch, appear particularly to play a very clear role in countries such as Ghana and Kenya. Different forms of co-operation can be distinguished in Indonesia and Zimbabwe and, indeed, the role of traders in these networks is stressed by several authors in this book. Sandee [*1995*] provides a classification of clusters developed during his fieldwork in Indonesia. He distinguishes between clusters organised by traders, by institutions, by producers and by consumers. Sandee shows that different types of clusters also need different types of assistance, if the government wishes to develop these clusters.

The importance of networks and trust can particularly be observed in cases of credit and technology diffusion (see Bagachwa and Sverisson in Chapters 8 and 9). These are the most concrete examples of how a cluster can benefit a small entrepreneur. Dorothy McCormick (Chapter 6) notices that when quality becomes important, the relationship between producers and traders becomes more collaborative and personalised. It involves more elements of trust and stability. The same phenomenon has been documented in two Mexican footwear clusters by Rabellotti [*1995*].

III. TRUST

Trust is difficult to define in a scientific way. As stated by Gambetta [*1988*], in spite of the profusion of material emerging on the subject, trust still remains an 'elusive notion'. It can be described as a positive attitude towards somebody else, based on past experience, a common relation or background. The point that will be made is that trust is very important in all the networks and clusters. What is the basis for trust and how can trust be built? Going back to Sahlins' [*1972*] theories of exchange, economic relations may be placed at various points on a spectrum of reciprocities, including social and moral relations, and usually not regarded as economic at all. An industrial district then becomes a moral community 'where the limits to trust and self-interest are understood and backed up by public opinion, as they apply to different kinds of relationships: contracts, informal cooperation, competition' [*Holmstrom, 1994*].

Industrial districts, when looking at the relationships going on within them, can be seen as rather stable systems. They are characterised by well-established and accepted social norms, by frequent, long-term interactions among a large number of economic actors who know each other very well, and by the rapid and pervasive dissemination of information [*Rabellotti, 1995*]. In industrial districts one usually finds institutional arrangements, such as long-term trading relationships, long-lived organisations and well-functioning communication networks, through which the self-enforcement of co-operation takes place more easily [*Wilkinson and You, 1992*]. Within districts a reputation for fairness is highly valued, while the sanctions for enforcing the limits of commonly accepted business behaviour may be very heavy, the final

3

sanction being social exclusion from the community. Ultimately, in industrial districts, economic actors tend to value long-term benefits (duly discounted) more than short-term ones, and it is therefore credible that they may commit themselves to honesty and trustworthiness [*Platteau, 1994*].

Spatial proximity, an essential prerequisite for good information transmission and, consequently, for trust in industrial districts, is not a characteristic of networks. The question is therefore how can trust be built within networks? In the contributions to this volume, a number of networks based on family, friends, relatives, religions, ethnic origins are documented, providing a partial answer to this question.

However, as Platteau [*1994*] has remarked, the scale of these relationships is restricted by spatial proximity in the case of districts and by cultural, ethnic or religious proximity within networks. Therefore, if it is admitted that, outside clusters and networks, economic actors are normally opportunistic and information is imperfect, a problem of a lack of trust arises. This is typically a field where interdisciplinary research could help to gain more insight.

IV. EXTERNAL ECONOMIES AND CO-OPERATION EFFECTS

In a cluster, increasing flexibility within firms can be observed and increasing linkages with other firms often described [*Van Dijk, 1994*]. The result is a more pronounced division of labour and a simpler technology diffusion. Schmitz [*1992*] introduces the term 'collective efficiency' for the positive effects of working in a cluster, distinguishing between unplanned or incidental effects and planned or consciously pursued collective efficiency. Different types of economies and co-operative effects need to be distinguished to explain collective efficiency.

First of all, within clusters, economies of scale and scope are achieved by the participating enterprises. Economies of scale, as is well known, occur when the percentage increase in production is higher than the percentage increase in factors of production. Economies of scope are related to the advantages of producing several products at the same time, while using the same facilities (such as marketing, transport and financial services).

Then there are external economies which can be defined as unpaid, outside the market, side-effects of the activity of one economic agent on other agents. Formally, a production externality is a situation where the production function of a firm is not only directly affected by its market activities but also by the activities of other economic agents.[4] External economies therefore imply that market prices in a competitive market economy will not reflect marginal social costs of production. Hence a 'market failure' arises, meaning that the market economy cannot attain a state of efficiency on its own. Specifically, in an otherwise 'perfect' market economy, an economic agent producing external economies (positive external effects) for other agents would not extend his externality-generating activity to the point where marginal cost of production equals marginal social benefits of production.

The concept of external economies was first introduced by Marshall [*1890*] when he analysed industry production costs as a function of output:

> We may divide the economies arising from an increase in the scale of production of any kind of goods, into two classes – firstly, those dependent on the general development of industry; and secondly, those dependent on the resources of individual houses of business engaged in it, on their organisations and the efficiency of their management. We may call the former external economies, and the later internal economies [*1890: 266*].

Marshall described several examples of external economies: the increased knowledge about markets and technology accompanying the expansion of industrial output, the creation of a market for skilled labour, for specialised services and for subsidiary industries, the possibility of splitting the production process into specialised phases and, finally, the improvement of physical infrastructures such as roads and railways.

For individual firms, external economies essentially turn into cost reductions as a consequence of industry growth, that is, economies external to the firm, but internal to the industry. The analysis of these externalities remains firmly within the framework of a static analysis, as they refer to the allocative efficiency of given resources and express collective efficiency as a positive function of the district's size and of the density of interactions which occur within the cluster.

Remaining in a static framework, the Marshallian aggregation of a large number of small firms into one district also favours the reduction of transaction costs among economic actors operating therein. In situations characterised by high uncertainty, complexity and opportunism, transaction costs tend to be very high. In industrial districts, the reduction in transaction costs can be explained by geographical proximity and socio-cultural homogeneity. Economic actors tend to interact mainly with partners who are located in their own area, with whom they can have 'face-to-face' contacts. The stability of many of these relationships and the importance of building a reputation decrease the risk of opportunistic behaviour. In the districts a delay in delivery or bad quality production immediately becomes common knowledge and a bad reputation negatively influences future relationships. Moreover, in industrial districts, firms facing some problems with their partners may easily find a new enterprise able to satisfy their needs. This is possible because of the large concentration of similar firms in a small geographical area and the intense

5

diffusion of information which reduces costs involved in finding a suitable replacement partner.

A particularly emphasised sub-type of external economies are agglomeration economies. A distinction can be made between two types of agglomeration economies: localisation and urbanisation economies. Localisation economies are the advantages deriving from the spatial concentration of enterprises belonging to the same industry or sector; while urbanisation economies derive from the localisation in an urban area, typically endowed with generic infrastructures, information and labour market, available to every economic agent located there. Furthermore, cities are large markets, easily accessible to local enterprises, enjoying savings on transport and transaction costs.

The importance of urbanisation economies is stressed, for example, by Sullivan [*1990*], who writes that '*most of the clusters are not isolated from other activities, but are typically in cities*'. Ernste [*1992: 9*] stresses that these '*spatial agglomerations of linked production and service plants can develop over time into full fledged Marshallian districts*'. Cities generate substantial external agglomeration economies and are considered as incubators for new economic activities. Space and a certain infrastructure are required and environmental measures should be taken collectively [*Van Dijk, 1995*].

Moving from static to dynamic external economies, reference may again be made to Marshall [*1890*]. Some of his examples allude to the dynamic effects of industrial growth, which promote a kind of 'industrial atmosphere', capable not only of reducing the cost disadvantage of small firms compared to large ones, but of also helping them in their growth and innovation strategy. This is particularly obvious when he refers to external economies as being dependent on the '*general progress of industrial environment*'. Examples of dynamic externalities suggested by Marshall are the accumulation of skills, know-how and knowledge taking place in a spontaneous and socialised way within the district. Stewart and Ghani [*1991*] identify three types of dynamic external economies: changing attitudes and motivations, skill formation and changing knowledge about technologies and markets.

A further effect of dynamic external economies has been suggested by Camagni [*1991*], who stresses the role played by the districts in the reduction of uncertainty in innovation processes, due to imperfect information, difficulties in precisely defining the effects of innovative decisions, and problems in controlling the reactions and behaviour of economic actors. According to Camagni, the local environment performs the function of gathering and screening information through informal interchanges between firms, and a process of collective learning through the mobility of skilled labour force, customer–supplier interchanges and imitation processes.

Co-operation effects differ from external economies because the latter are the spontaneous by-product of economic activities undertaken within the districts, while the former are the result of explicit and voluntary co-operative behaviour among economic actors. Examples of the products of co-operative behaviour, enforced by self-interest and induced by the existence of a critical mass of norm-followers, are co-operation on process or product innovations between the producers and their suppliers,[5] the diffusion of information and the collective learning effects among groups of firms linked, for instance, by family ties or friendship. Co-operative effects may be either static or dynamic, therefore enhancing the system's efficiency, and its innovation and growth potentiality.

We can conclude that clusters and networks may bring about several collective effects that contribute to collective efficiency. The identification of these effects in emerging countries is an important requirement for understanding if, and how, it is possible to enhance collective efficiency with policy interventions.

V. ORGANISATION OF THE BOOK

The first part of the book comprises contributions which discuss, with different emphases, the concepts of clusters, external economies and co-operation, presenting empirical evidence from African, Latin American and Italian cases. In Chapter 2, Pedersen discusses three concepts used in relation to clusters of enterprises: collective efficiency, economies of agglomeration and transaction costs. He argues that the collective efficiency achieved through clustering depends on the structure of the cluster and on its links with the rest of the economic system. Two different types of clusters, namely the vertically specialised industrial cluster and the horizontally specialised market town, are introduced to explain why African clusters are often seen as characterised by little collective efficiency.

A comparison of the collective efficiency in two Italian footwear districts and two footwear clusters in Mexico is presented in Chapter 3 by Rabellotti. The chapter investigates backward, forward, horizontal, labour and institutional linkages among the economic agents acting in the four clusters, and then classifies the economic effects deriving from them, distinguishing between external economies and co-operation effects.

Visser looks in Chapter 4 at the importance of spatial clustering for the performance of small-scale industrial firms in Lima. He finds that the firms in the cluster are doing relatively well, however, not because of the significance of the vertical division of labour or subcontracting. Inter-firm division of labour and vertical specialisation seem to be incipient, while the role of local institutions still has little significance. He concludes that the migrants in the

7

cluster show a strong desire to become successful, to be able to show their family back home that they have not failed.

The second part of the book is focused on the discussion of the relevance of the concepts of districts and networks, particularly in marginal cases: among women economic activities or among very small informal businesses.

In Chapter 5, Dijkman and Van Dijk use the flexible specialisation concept to study the dynamics of small enterprises run by women in Ouagadougou. They consider the term a step forward in small enterprise research, since characteristics such as innovative mentality, skills and co-operation are related to each other. Even if the women are not aware that they work according to this paradigm, a number of them display the advantages of being flexible and specialised. With such a framework, one may discover different aspects of the reality of small enterprises from the classical small enterprise studies. They have found a very dynamic small enterprise sector with skilled, creative and innovative entrepreneurs trying to develop their business. In particular, women use their networks and benefit from clusters and mutual co-operation. Creating conditions for this kind of development is a challenge for many third world countries. Specialisation is important for small enterprises. Dijkman and Van Dijk conclude that there are also female entrepreneurs who are successful because they have diversified their businesses. Flexibility is an asset and needs to be promoted, even if it means aiming for diversification in certain cases. Entrepreneurs find their optimum by moving from niche markets to broader markets and back. Moving to other locations is an important part of the dynamics of small enterprises and should also be encouraged by urban authorities.

In Chapter 6, McCormick describes an industrial district in Nairobi, specialising in the garment industry. She finds that the individual businesses resemble one another in their relations with supply, labour and product markets, often based on ethnic, gender or educational links. Nevertheless, poor conditions in the markets, working against efficient production and product development, have to some extent offset clustering advantages.

In the following chapter, Van Dijk analyses the economic activities of poor households in Accra which enable them to cope with their poor conditions. He argues that networks are important for the poor during a period of structural adjustment in Ghana. Trade associations play an important role in a large number of trades. Finally, he concludes that the clustered firms are doing better than the ones dispersed in the neighbourhood.

The final part presents some examples of the relevance of networks and industrial districts in facilitating credit, technological change and small enterprises' internationalisation.

In Chapter 8, Bagachwa looks specifically at credit. He examines some of the mechanisms used by informal financial institutions in Tanzania to build trust among transacting parties. Informal financial institutions have developed a number of innovative informal arrangements through which externalities that are intrinsic in the highly imperfect residual market have been internalised. These include the use of a web of interpersonal relationships, market interlinkage, credit layering and specialised custom-tailored small-scale services in which formal financial institutions have a cost disadvantage.

Sverrisson looks in Chapter 9 at the importance of small- and medium-sized light engineering and metalworking enterprise networks for technological change in Arcra. The light engineering sector is a major provider of equipment and services to other sectors, but also depends on a range of middlemen for its inputs. Sverisson shows that co-operation among enterprises, besides a flexible approach to production and gradual mechanisation, are essential explanations of the viability of light engineering enterprises in an extremely hostile business environment.

In Chapter 10, Bagella and Pietrobelli investigate the hypothesis that the industrial districts' organisational form may enhance the internationalisation of small and medium enterprises, particularly in developing countries. The hypothesis of internationalisation of an industrial district is studied in a simple theoretical model with a leader firm. Some preliminary testings of the theoretical hypothesis are then carried out in some Latin American countries which have a perspective for co-operation with Italian industrial districts.

NOTES

1. Van Dijk and Secher Marcussen (eds.) [*1989*].
2. See Rasmussen *et al.* (eds.) [*1992*] and Pedersen *et al.* (eds.) [*1994*].
3. In November 1994 the EADI Working Group on Industrialisation organised a workshop on the theme 'Industrialisation, Organisation, Institutions and Innovations' in Vienna where a number of the contributions in this book were presented as papers and discussed. Support was received from the Austrian Department for Development Cooperation and the meeting was organised with the Vienna Institute for Development and Cooperation (VIDC), for which we would like to thank both the Department and the Institute. Carley Pennink did the language editing of the papers for publication.
4. External economies also refer to unpaid side-effects of or on consumption activities, but here the focus is on production externalities.
5. See, for instance, the co-operation between Italian shoe firms and the manufacturers of components or the producers of machine tools for the sector reported in the chapter by Rabellotti in this book (Chapter 3).

REFERENCES

Camagni, R. (1991): 'Local "Milieu": Uncertainty and Innovation Networks: Towards a New Dynamic Theory of Economic Space', in Camagni (ed.) [*1991: 121–44*].

Camagni, R. (ed.) (1991): *Innovation Networks: Spatial Perspectives*, London: Bellhaven-Pinter.

Dijk, M.P. van and H.S. Marcussen (eds.) (1989): *Industrialization in the Third World: The Need for Alternative Strategies*, London: Frank Cass.

Dijk, M.P. van (1994): 'The Interrelations between Industrial Districts and Technological Capabilities Development: Concepts and Issues', in UNCTAD [*1994: 3–51*].

Dijk, M.P. van (1995) 'Urban Environmental Issues in Asia and the Netherlands: The Potential of a Collective approach to industrial Districts,' Rotterdam: Erasmus University.

Ernste, H. (1992): 'Flexible Specialisation and Regional Policy,' Nijmegen: Workshop on Autonomy and Independent work.

Gambetta, D. (ed.) (1988): *Trust-making and Breaking Cooperative Relations*, Oxford: Basil Blackwell.

Holmstrom, M. (1994): 'A Cure for Loneliness? Networks, Trusts and Shared Services in Bangalore', Vienna, EADI Working Group on Industrialisation Workshop.

Marshall, A. (1890): *Principle of Economics* (8th Edition, 1986), London: Macmillan.

Pedersen, P., A. Sverisson, M.P. van Dijk (eds.) (1994): *Flexible Specialisation: The Dynamics of Small-Scale Industries in the South*, London: Intermediate Technology.

Platteau, J.P. (1994): 'Behind the Market Stage Where Real Societies Exist' (Parts I & II), *Journal of Development Studies*, Vol.30, No.3, April, pp.553–77; Vol.30, No.4, July, pp.753–817.

Rabellotti, R. (1995): 'External Economies and Cooperation in Industrial Districts: and Mexico', unpublished D. Phil. thesis, Institute of Development Studies, University of Sussex, Brighton.

Rasmussen, J., Schmitz, H. and M.P. van Dijk (eds.) (1992): 'Flexible Specialisation: A New View on Small Industry?', *IDSBulletin*, Vol.23, No.3, July, pp.1–68.

Sahlins, M. (1972): *Stone-Age-Economics*, Chicago, IL: Aldine.

Sandee, H. (1995): 'Innovation Adoption in Rural Industry: Technological Change in Roof Tile Clusters in Central Java, Indonesia', Ph. D. thesis, Free University, Amsterdam.

Schmitz, H. (1992): 'On the Clustering of Small Firms', *IDS Bulletin*, Vol.23, No.3, July, pp.64–8.

Stewart, F. and E. Ghani (1991): 'How Significant are Externalities for Development?', *World Development*, Vol.19, No.6, pp.569–94.

Sullivan, A.M. (1990): *Urban Economics*, Homewood, IL: Irwin.

UNCTAD (1994): *Technological Dynamism in Industrial Districts: An Alternative Approach to Industrialization in Developing Countries?* Geneva: UNCTAD.

Wilkinson, F. and J. You (1992): 'Competition and Cooperation: Towards an Understanding of Industrial Districts', *Working Paper*, No.22, Department of Applied Economics and Small Business Research Centre, University of Cambridge, June.

PART I

2

Clusters of Enterprises Within Systems of Production and Distribution: Collective Efficiency and Transaction Costs

POUL OVE PEDERSEN

I. INTRODUCTION

The concept of *collective efficiency in enterprise clusters* proposed by Schmitz [*1989*] and developed in the recent literature on flexible specialisation in developing countries [*Rasmussen et al., 1992; Pedersen et al., 1994*] is related to and partly takes the place of the older concept of *agglomeration economies.* Although both the empirical outlook and the theoretical basis of the two concepts are very different, we believe that a comparison between them may be fruitful to our understanding of collective efficiency.

While the term 'agglomeration economies' is used to describe external economies passively obtained by enterprises located close to each other, the term 'collective efficiency' describes advantages that enterprises may achieve through active collaboration. Whereas the concept of agglomeration economies is derived from static neoclassical equilibrium theory, in which individual enterprises relate to anonymous markets, the concept of collective efficiency stems partly from Schumpeterian dynamics, and partly from theories of economic restructuring, institutional economics, enterprise networks and flexible specialisation, which see individual enterprises as part of a specific interrelated system of production and distribution.

However, because of their strong focus on active collaboration among enterprises, many discussions on collective efficiency seem to concentrate only on the Schumpeterian background, overlooking a number of important, more structural processes in the production system, which may lead to collective efficiency in the enterprise cluster, but which are based on interdependency and mutual adaptation among enterprises both within and outside the cluster rather than on active collaboration.

In order to broaden our view of collective efficiency we focus here on the processes of vertical and horizontal specialisation and disagregation, both within and between sectors in the production and distribution system, which are the basis for small enterprises and their clusters, rather than on enterprise collaboration itself. In this way an enterprise cluster will be seen not as an isolated phenomenon, but as an element within the total production and distribution system. This will be done within a framework of institutional economics, where the enterprise cluster is seen as a loose organisation competing with other large and small enterprises, governmental and non-governmental organisations, households and other social organisations for resources and markets (sections II and III). Within this framework, the production system may be structured very differently in different economies and the role of small enterprises and their clusters will vary as well. To illustrate this we compare the structure of grain trade and milling in Tanzania, Zimbabwe and Uganda in section IV.

The collective efficiency achieved through clustering and the distribution of benefits depends on the structure of the cluster and its links with the rest of the economy. Different clusters comprise different combinations of vertically- and horizontally-specialised enterprises. In section V, on the basis of a discussion of two different types of clusters, namely the vertically-specialised industrial cluster and the horizontally-specialised market town, we present a typology of enterprise clusters. This typology is used to explain why some clusters seem to be more efficient than others, and why African clusters seem to demonstrate little efficiency [*Nadvi and Schmitz, 1994*]. Finally, in section VI, we discuss the limits of collective efficiency and of governmental policies to exploit them.

II. TRANSACTION COSTS AND UNDERSTANDING THE ENTERPRISE

Discussions of agglomeration economies in the traditional location theories, for example, Weber [*1929*] and Christaller [*1932*], were implicitly or explicitly based on an enterprise concept that saw the production enterprise as a black box into which production inputs were introduced at one end and the final product came out at the other end. The frame and content of the black box/enterprise were assumed to be fixed and not to be discussed.

When the processes of innovation diffusion through forward and backward linkages in the production system were introduced by Perroux [*1955*] and Hirschman [*1958*] in the 1950s, discussion of agglomeration economies in growth poles and production complexes became more dynamic. However, the discussions were still mostly framed in input–output relations between

12

homogeneous industrial sectors, and therefore implicitly based on a black box understanding of the enterprise.

It was only in the 1970s that diversity and structural change within industrial sectors came into focus, for instance, in the theory of industrial restructuring [*Massey and Meegan, 1979*]. With the introduction of new institutional economics [*Williamson, 1981; 1985, 1994*], theories of flexible specialisation [*Piore and Sabel, 1984; Storper and Walker, 1989*], informalisation [*Castells and Portes, 1989*] and enterprise networks [*Johanson and Matson, 1986*], the black box view of the enterprise was replaced by an understanding of the enterprise as a matter of enterprise strategy. The content of the enterprise is now no longer taken for granted, but has become a central research question.

This theoretical move has opened up a new understanding of economic externalities and agglomeration economies. However, it has happened at a time when policies based on growth pole theories have generally failed and transport and communication costs have dropped dramatically. At the same time, the process of externalisation of large enterprises has led to the dispersion of industrial functions and a rapidly increasing international division of labour rather than to new agglomerations. As a result, transport and communication costs, which have been the key variable in location theory and the understanding of agglomeration economies, were no longer seen as important. Industry has become footloose and its location determined by national and regional differences in government subsidies, wage levels and other production costs. In the new institutional economics, transport and communication costs are substituted by the broader concept of transaction costs. Transaction costs should logically include transport and communication costs as well as other costs of transactions. However, many recent authors who have attempted to apply the concept of transaction costs to economic and industrial development have narrowed it down to costs of corruption and the semi-legal misuse of political and bureaucratic powers to extract surplus [*North, 1989; Williamson, 1994*]. Similarly, in many discussions of the functioning of markets, distribution costs are completely left out and the market is reduced to a powergame only [*Gould and Von Oppen, 1994*]. Certainly power is important in explaining the structure of organisations and market, but power alone cannot explain the large diversity of economic and social organisations found in reality.

The dismissal of transport and communication costs as a factor of location (and thus of clustering) is something of a paradox, as it has occurred just as logistics are becoming increasingly important for large enterprises, and industries, especially in the industrialised countries, are lobbying heavily for improved transport and communications infrastructures. If transport and communication costs have become so unimportant, it is difficult to understand why industries should expend so much energy on logistics and lobbying for new

13

highways, tunnels and so on. The solution to this seeming paradox is that, although transport and communication costs per unit and kilometre have become much lower, the spread of production has so increased the amount to be transported that there are no indications that transport and communication costs as a percentage of total costs and of GNP have decreased. On the contrary, old transport costs have been increasingly substituted with the new concept of logistics costs, which include not only external transport costs, but also the costs of internal transport and storage. This is in logical accordance with the new understanding of the enterprise as an open system, whereby external transport is substituted, to a large extent, with internal transport and storage. Where external transport costs have traditionally constituted three to eight per cent of production costs, the logistics costs often make up more than a third of total costs, and therefore take on a new significance as a factor of location and clustering.

In addition, innovations and reduced costs of transportation and communication have not benefited all flows of goods, persons and information equally. In general, transport and communication innovations have especially benefited what one could call the large flows. For flows that are large, frequent, regular and standardised enough to warrant investment in specialised infrastructure and use of standardised containers, costs have often become very low and less dependent on distance. On the other hand, small irregular flows and unstandardised flows, in particular where goods and information have to be carried by persons, are still relatively expensive, although they may have become cheaper as well. This is also the case with flows in developing rural regions with little or no infrastructure. Thus, at the same time that improved transport and communication have been instrumental in the dispersal of many functions in the production and distribution system, the structure of transport and communication has also been decisive in determining which functions would or would not become footloose [*Pedersen, 1987*], and in the increased segmentation of markets [*Pedersen, 1991; 1992b*]. It has been an important factor, therefore, in determining the vertical and horizontal disagregations that have resulted from the current industrial restructuring.

Finally, although transaction costs other than narrow transport and communication costs are generally more important, they are to a large extent linked to transport and communication flows and caused mainly by bottlenecks, monopoly or poor quality in the transport and communication system. It is within such a new understanding of the enterprise as an open system, where activities may be externalised or internalised as a matter of strategy, and of the transport and communication system as a logistic system, where internal and external transport and communication costs may be substitutable, that collective efficiency in enterprise clusters take on a meaning different from that of agglomeration economies among neo-classic black box enterprises.

III. PROCESSES OF VERTICAL AND HORIZONTAL (DIS)INTEGRATION

In traditional economic theories, industrial sectors are implicitly or explicitly assumed to be homogeneous, consisting of similar enterprises producing the same goods with the same inputs and competing for the same markets. Inter-enterprise trade, therefore, only takes place between sectors, and production chains tend to be simple one-way flows, for instance, the flow of grain from the farmer to the miller, possibly to the bakery and then to the consumer.

In reality the picture is very different. Sectors are not homogeneous (even at very detailed levels of classification). They consist typically of a range of different enterprises varying in size and producing or distributing more or less specialised goods or services, often based on different sources of inputs, labour and capital and competing for different segments of the market. A large part of the inter-enterprise trade takes place within the sector, and production chains are complex, often with many parallel, though partly linked, flows. The production chain not only comprises producers but also traders, public and private services, subcontractors and suppliers/producers of investment goods. Many of these activities may belong formally to other sectors, but functionally they are an integrated part of the sector. Such an extended sector is sometimes called a 'fillière'.

In the grain sector, for instance, the farmer may sell the grain directly and unprocessed to the consumer, or the grain may be collected for depots or mills by traders or intermediaries ranging from small bicycle traders, larger truck traders and co-operatives to large, more or less monopolistic parastatal or private enterprises. It may be processed in small service mills or in large commercial mills, and it may be distributed to different food processing industries or through a range of different wholesale and retail channels from street vendors above small tuckshops to supermarket chains.

Large, intermediate-sized and small enterprises will operate typically at different segments of the market. The market segmentation may partly be determined by more or less effective government regulations. Such market regulations may grant, for instance, monopoly power over all or part of the market to large parastatal or private enterprises, or they may reserve certain products or functions for small enterprises, as has been the case in India. However, regulations may also be based on the preferential treatment of certain groups of enterprises with regard to taxation, allocation of scarce resources or foreign currency, or labour legislation. In addition, market segmentation will often be based on differences in product quality or in services related to transactions between enterprises and between enterprises and consumer, such as size of consignment, frequency of delivery, transport services and credit.

Large enterprises require large inputs, and these enterprises, operating at different levels of the vertical production chain, will often supply each other and be more or less formally integrated in order to secure stable deliveries. However, particularly at the end of production chains, large enterprises may rely on small horizontally disintegrated subcontractors, retailers or vendors.

Further, large enterprises are typically capital-intensive with large fixed costs. They require, therefore, stable deliveries and markets to operate efficiently, often having the economic, technological and political power to secure for themselves the most stable and secure parts of the market. As a result, small and medium-sized enterprises are often forced to operate in more unstable, peripheral markets. Here they will survive by (1) investing in flexible, multi-purpose machinery and employing relatively skilled labour to operate it, (2) using very little fixed capital and employing unskilled labour that can be hired and fired at short notice, or (3) operating on a very small and often variable scale, relying partly on other income sources from a broader household economy or wider social networks.

Such small enterprises may work as subcontractors to large enterprises, but may also deliver to other small enterprises or to the consumer market directly. They are also likely to be more vertically disintegrated than large enterprises, this vertical disintegration often being more pronounced in the collection and distribution system than in processing.

It is the development of such complex sectors or *filières*, comprising a mix of small and large enterprises linked to governmental and non-governmental organisations and social networks, that theories of institutional economics, enterprise networks, flexible specialisation, informalisation, economic restructuring and regulation try to assess in different ways and perspectives. Further, it is within such complex sectors that collective efficiency, through the clustering of small and medium-sized enterprises, must be understood as a strategy to improve the competitiveness of small enterprises *vis-à-vis* large enterprises and small isolated enterprises.

IV. THE STRUCTURE OF THE MAIZE TRADE AND MILLING INDUSTRIES

The structure of a whole sectoral system may vary considerably depending on government regulations, economies of scale in the sector, the distribution of power capital and incomes, the structure and development of the transport and communication system and a host of other factors. However, in general, scale economies in production themselves play a much smaller role than has traditionally been assumed, while government regulations, power relations and the structure of transport and distribution systems are more important factors. As an illustration of the very large differences often found between seemingly similar production systems, we shall look at the structure of the maize trade and milling industries in Tanzania, Zimbabwe and Uganda.

The milling industry in three African countries presented here is interesting because it so clearly illustrates how different national and local production environments result in very dissimilar industrial structures. In Zimbabwe, the highly centralised production system, until recently, made small-scale commercial milling almost impossible to operate; in Tanzania, on the other hand, small commercial mills have developed as a complement to large mills, while in Uganda, clusters of small mills have developed.

Tanzania

For Tanzania, Bagachwa [*1991; 1992*] finds that the milling industry is divided into a few large mills of varying size in the large towns and a large number of small service mills located in the rural areas, small towns and, increasingly, in the urban low income areas. The large commercial mills buy, process and pack maize meal primarily for the high and medium income urban population; the small service mills only process people's own maize for a fee and, therefore, only serve a local market. In a detailed analysis of the milling processes, Bagachwa found that there were no scale economies in the milling industry itself at the time of investigation (1982–83) – either within the group of commercial mills or between commercial and service mills. There is no justifications therefore, for favouring the large mills.

In his study, he does not include the collection and distribution costs incurred outside the mill gate. The reason for this is probably that the commercial mills have traditionally bought their grain from the grain parastatal at a fixed price. However, in reality, the collection and distribution costs of larger commercial mills are likely to be much higher than the costs for a small mill which only needs to collect grain from a much smaller hinterland. These costs are likely to be much more important for the final price than the milling costs. Thus, while Bagachwa finds that the value added in the milling industry is only two to three per cent, the price difference between what a farmer gets for his raw maize and what he will have to pay for the processed maize meal will easily be 50–100 per cent. There seems, in fact, to be considerable diseconomies of scale in the milling process.

Thus, there seems to be no justification for operating urban mills on a scale that requires them, on a regular basis, to collect grain from very large regions and distribute maize meal to distant smaller towns and rural areas. That such large mills are operating in Tanzania is due partly to the monopoly status granted to them through the regulations of the grain markets and pricing policies, and partly to the preferential treatment that the large industrial mills have been given in the government allocation of foreign currency and other scarce resources.

17

Zimbabwe

In Zimbabwe, the dominance of large commercial mills has been even more pronounced than in Tanzania and basically for the same reasons. The few attempts made during the 1980s to establish small or medium-sized commercial mills were not very successful [*Pedersen, 1992a; 1994*]. The main reason for this is probably that large and small commercial mills were forced to buy their grain from the Grain Marketing Board at the depot gate at a fixed price. This meant that the small mill in a small town was not able to benefit from its relatively low collection costs, while the high collection costs of the large mills were indirectly subsidised by the marketing board. In addition, the number of small service mills in the large towns was until recently very limited because private transport of whole grain outside the communal areas was prohibited, and the growth of maize in the urban areas effectively curbed.

In general, the high degree of centralisation in the Zimbabwean economy has meant that the access of small and medium-sized enterprises to financing, transport and wholesale markets, essential inputs to the milling business, has been very limited. This has made it virtually impossible for small mills to operate.

During the structural adjustment period and drought, the gradual liberalisation of the grain trade and the relaxing, from 1990, of permission to practice urban farming resulted in a very rapid growth in the number of small service mills in the large urban areas, and a rather dramatic reduction of the large mills' share of the market [*Rubey, 1993*].

At the same time, a number of medium-sized mills which operate both as service and commercial mills were established with technological support, in part, from two international NGOs [*Chipika, 1993*]. The main advantage of the mixed mills in their ability to operate as both service and commercial mills increased their flexibility towards changing market conditions and, thus, their capacity utilisation, but this ability fluctuated strongly during the early 1990s. This was due partly to urban food subsidies during the drought being paid through large millers only, and partly to these millers being rather successful – as distributers of groceries other than maize meal – in keeping small commercial millers out of the retailer's market through bonded sales. The small mixed mills operating most successfully as commercial mills were therefore those which had either their own distribution channels, or operated together with chicken and pig farms, which consumed a large part of the produce and made them less dependent on the local environment.

Although the liberalisation of the whole grain market has opened new opportunities for the small commercial mills, they are still restricted by very limited access to finance, transport and markets in the highly centralised Zimbabwean economy.

Uganda

In Uganda, small to medium-sized mixed mills play a much larger role than in both Tanzania and Zimbabwe. Uganda has a large-scale urban-based commercial milling sector which originally enjoyed a monopoly status. However, due to the general breakdown of the formal and parastatal sectors during the tumultuous years of the 1970s and 1980s, small-scale grain trading and milling have been permitted to a much larger extent in Uganda [*Nabuguzi, 1994*]. Iganga, a small market town of about 20,000 inhabitants in the maize-growing area of eastern Uganda, has nine small to medium-scale milling enterprises; small towns of similar size in Zimbabwe, at least until recently, have had none. The nine mills operate as mixed mills servicing local customers in the daytime and operating as commercial mills at night when the electricity supply is most stable. The mills pack maize meal in small paper packages for the focal retail market or for sale in Kampala, and in large bags for export, either to Kenya or through the World Food Programme. These are all located in the same street, taking advantage of joint access to customers, traders and transporters, and thus supported by a much more diverse and complex network of competing and collaborating small-scale grain traders and transporters than is found in Zimbabwe or Tanzania. Although the grain trade in Zimbabwe and Tanzania has been monopolised by parastatals and large, private truck traders, a large part of the grain in eastern Uganda is collected by much less capital-intensive bicycle traders and transporters.

The small and medium-sized millers, traders and transporters in Uganga make up what one could consider a Marshallian district in which the relative competitiveness of the millers is not a result of their own efficiency, but of the collective efficiency of millers, traders, transporters and financing. Similarly, the difficulties that the new small commercial millers in Zimbabwe experience are caused not primarily by their own inefficiency but a lack of a supporting network of small-scale financing, traders and transporters.

V. COLLECTIVE EFFICIENCY AND THE STRUCTURE OF CLUSTERS

Vertical and Horizontal Specialisation in Enterprise Clusters

Collective efficiency is based on the interdependency and co-operation between specialised, clustering enterprises or between the specialised enterprises of a cluster and their suppliers or customers outside it.

A cluster of enterprises may be based on vertically or horizontally specialised enterprises or a mixture of both. It may comprise a whole chain of vertical specialisations in a production and distribution chain from raw material to consumer, or it may be specialised in a single or a few links of the chain; it may also be horizontally broad comprising many different sectors or narrowly specialised in a single or a few sectors. The types of collective efficiencies achieved, and the distribution of the benefits resulting from these, depend on the structure of the cluster.

The recent literature on industrial clusters and collective efficiency has focused primarily on clusters based on vertical specialisation and collaboration, paying little attention to horizontal specialisation in clusters. The established literature on location theory and agglomeration economies [*Isard, 1956*] on the other hand, has been concerned both with clusters based on vertical specialisation and those based on horizontal specialisation. Clusters based on vertical specialisation are discussed in theories of localisation economies relating to specialised sector-specific industrial towns. Marshall's [*1892*] original work, which has recently given definition to the industrial cluster or Marshallian district [*Becattini, 1990*] is part of the tradition from which the present discussions of collective efficiency and industrial clusters have sprung. Clusters based on horizontal specialisation are discussed in the theories of central places and urban economies in which the clustering of activities in market towns is located.

In an attempt to incorporate further the subject of clustering based on horizontal specialisations into the present discussions on collective efficiency, we shall discuss in the following sections the role of collective efficiency and agglomeration economies in *sector-specific industrial clusters and market towns*. Sector-specific industrial clusters and market towns are used in this case as prototypes of enterprise clusters based on vertical and horizontal specialisations respectively.

The Sector-Specific Industrial Cluster or Marshallian District

Most discussions of collective efficiency have focused, in continuation of Hubert Schmitz's original work on the concept, on the benefits achieved by small, vertically disintegrated enterprises within the same broad sector and clustering in the same area. Such sector-specific industrial clusters have come to be known as Marshallian districts. The focus in the discussions of collective efficiency in industrial clusters has been on benefits derived from:

(1) collaboration between vertically specialised enterprises in the form of flows of goods, services and information between enterprises. Such vertical collaboration may take place between small enterprises or in subcontracting relations between small and large enterprises. The benefits of such a vertical collaboration within an industrial cluster include the ability to exploit scale economies beyond the size of the individual enterprises, the ability to specialise and diversify (thus attracting a wider range of customers), and the development of more rapid innovation diffusion through forward and backward linkages and labour mobility between the enterprises;

(2) horizontal collaboration between small enterprises in order to supply large orders. This comes in the form of the development of private and public services, joint labour markets and a market for second-hand capital equipment or in the form of more formal small enterprise-organisations with the purpose of lobbying for external/government resources and legal/political rights. These forms of horizontal collaboration are based on common interests and not on horizontal specialisation between enterprises. In fact, such horizontal specialisation is generally not perceived.

However, collective efficiency among small enterprises may also be achieved without active collaboration. In classical localisation theory, locational economies may be achieved by co-locating enterprises. This is done not because it increases their efficiency but because it reduces the customer's cost of reaching and searching in the market (it reduces their transaction costs). The co-located enterprise is therefore able to attract more customers than it would individually. On the other hand, Hotelling [*1929*] argues in his theory of imperfect competition that enterprises may be forced by competition to co-locate in order to retain their market share. He also argues that co-location does not increase the efficiency of the enterprises or their customers; in fact, it increases transport costs. However, even in Hotelling's case co-location would lead to reduced costs of market search for the customers. The difference in the argument on the classical localisation theory and Hotelling's theory can be interpreted as a trade-off between transport cost and search costs. However, the value of reduced search costs would be limited if there is no differentiation between the enterprises. The neo-classical assumption of homogeneous sectors in classical localisation theory is, therefore, self-contradictory, and horizontal specialisation or market segmentation will in fact often develop within such clusters.

The development of a full-blown, successful, innovative industrial cluster, exploiting the maximum of collective efficiencies and developing along what has been called the *high road* [*Sengenberger and Pyke, 1992*] probably requires that the cluster comprises and controls the whole, or at least a large part of the links in a vertical production chain. However, some industrial clusters, which have not been able to expand beyond a single or a few links in the production and distribution system, may develop along the *low road* or into clusters of simple subcontractors or petty commodity producers exploiting low wages and labour flexibility.

The Market Town

In Christaller's classical central place theory, traders or small-scale producers from different sectors co-locate in a market town in order to exploit agglomeration economies. These agglomeration economies are not occasions of increased efficiency on the part of the enterprises, but appear as reduced transport and search costs for the customers. Again this leads to enterprises as a group attracting more customers than they would have individually. In Lösch's [*1954*] work on central place theory, however, he argues that this larger flow of customers might make it possible for the enterprises to exploit larger economies of scale and agglomeration.

Such classical central places are characterised by the horizontal specialisation of enterprises among sectors. Individual sectors are assumed to be homogeneous and without overlap. All enterprises within a sector are therefore alike, and competition among them is pure price competition, in which there is no room for collaboration between enterprises within a sector. Supplies of goods and services for the enterprises in the market town are assumed unproblematically to be supplied from enterprises of higher order, larger towns via a perfectly competitive market. At the same time, the market town is assumed to have a spatial monopoly in its own hinterland. Thus the hierarchies of enterprises and urban centres are merged into one and the same.

However, these assumptions about homogeneous markets and strictly hierarchical supply systems are highly unrealistic. Enterprises from all levels of the urban and organisational hierarchy often compete for the same local market, and there is likely to be a considerable degree of market segmentation between both local and non-local suppliers [*Pedersen, 1991; 1992b*]. This market segmentation may, especially in the industrialised countries, be based on product differentiation and quality, but in developing regions it is more often based on the scarcity and availability of products and production inputs, on specialised sources of capital and labour, and on delivery services such as credit, size of consignment transport and close location. Such a market segmentation is a result of scarcity in the supply and distribution systems, and can be seen as an attempt to overcome such scarcities. Contrary to neoclassical economics, which sees such a segmentation as market imperfection and, therefore, a sign of inefficiency, we see it as an expression of collective efficiency. Such collective efficiency, based on marked segmentation, leads to a better utilisation of scarce resources from different sources than in both a monopolistic/parastatal collection and distribution system and a neo-classical competitive market. This is because both these markets depend on more standardised sources of production inputs, capital and labour and, therefore, are unable to utilise the diverse set of resources often existing in developing societies.

That enterprises operate in segmented markets does not mean that they do not compete. Enterprises may obtain a partial monopoly in their core market segment but compete over the borders of that segment. Segment borders may shift as a result of, for instance, innovation, increasing efficiency, changing input prices and government policies.

Such a horizontal specialisation and market segmentation within a sector is not based on direct collaboration among enterprises. Rather, it is based on a process of competition and mutual adaptation that may make horizontal collaboration more difficult. Many of the small industrial clusters found in Africa appear to have developed out of market towns rather than out of vertical sectoral disaggregation. They are often characterised by very limited vertical specialisation and diversification, and may develop into clusters of petty commodity producers rather than full-blown industrial clusters. This may be one reason for the limited success of many African enterprise clusters.

Typology of Enterprise Clusters

We shall conclude this section on collective efficiency by presenting a typology of enterprise clusters based on the discussion above (see Figure 1):

(1) The diversified industrial cluster is based on the vertical specialisation of individual enterprises and the vertical diversity of the cluster as a whole. The cluster is specialised in a broad, specific sector. However, within the sector neither individual enterprises nor cluster as a whole are narrowly, horizontally specialised. Thus, the cluster is able to shift between alternative local, national or international markets in competition with large enterprises. Many of the enterprises operate in markets with high transaction costs, but attempt to reduce costs by internalising a portion of them within the cluster. They react to instability on input and product markets through flexibility in individual production systems, exploiting each other's excess capacities and technological capabilities, and by collaborating on the development and acquisition of new resources and production capabilities. Collective efficiencies are derived from enterprise collaboration both within and outside the cluster.

(2) The subcontractor cluster is based on a narrow vertical and horizontal specialisation, both of individual enterprises and the cluster as a whole. Most of the enterprises will be dependent on and linked as subcontractors to one or a few large enterprises which may be located within or outside the cluster. By linking themselves as subcontractors to large enterprises, small enterprises with few resources of their own may improve their access to resources and markets. In developing rural regions with unstable markets, the recurrent cash flow problems caused by seasonal and climatic cycles in agriculture may be partly overcome, but at a cost of new instability caused by a lack of control over markets, prices and technological change. Collective efficiencies in such a cluster are not primarily based on collaboration between the small enterprises in the cluster, but on reduced transaction costs from dealing with a large enterprise, which may also appropriate most of the benefit. On the other hand, through collaboration, the subcontractor may be able to improve its competitive power both *vis-à-vis* alternative suppliers and in bargaining for better conditions with the large enterprise. Individual enterprises in a subcon-

FIGURE 1
TYPOLOGY OF SMALL ENTERPRISE CLUSTERS

1. Diversified Industrial cluster

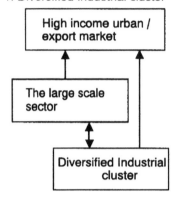

2. Subcontractor cluster

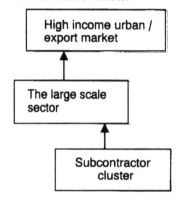

3. Market town or distribution cluster

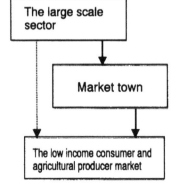

4. Petty commodity cluster

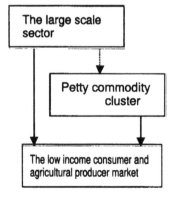

24

tractor cluster may attempt to reduce their dependency of the large enterprises by improving their technological and marketing capacity to reach alternative markets.

(3) The market town or distribution cluster: these enterprises are horizontally specialised between sectors and also, possibly, within sectors. The cluster as a whole is horizontally diversified between and, often, within sectors. There may be some vertical diversification in production, but the cluster is dominated by retailers and small producers supplying the local consumer or farm input market. Enterprises often depend on large non-local enterprises for their input and commodity supplies. They also often compete in direct distribution with large enterprises. Collective efficiencies achieved by clusters are not based on collaboration between the enterprises in the cluster, but on the reduced costs of transaction with customers (and, to a lesser extent, with suppliers), which increases the competitiveness of the market town *vis-à-vis* producers or retailers in the rural areas or in the larger towns. Such collective efficiencies may also be achieved through horizontal specialisation, market segmentation and the mutual adaptation of enterprises to each other.

This market segmentation may be based on product diversification in the use of different production inputs or in different delivery services (such as transport, location, credit and commodity availability). In developing rural regions with uncertain supplies, insufficient transport capacity and recurrent cash flow problems, such a horizontal diversification of the distribution system leads to improved capacity utilisation. In order to exploit the important social, political and economic contacts in a local market area, individual enterprises tend to expand through horizontal diversification within the market town rather than through vertical expansion into production and into non-local markets, which would imply high new transaction costs.

(4) The specialised petty commodity cluster: enterprises in such a cluster are specialised horizontally. Although most of the enterprises may be producers, they are also retailers producing directly for the local low income consumer market. Collective efficiencies achieved by clustering are due primarily to reduced transaction costs for customers, but some collaboration between enterprises may also take place. However, the petty commodity cluster typically operates with few resources and under very unstable conditions. It is often operated in tandem with the household economy, including peasant farming and other petty activities operated by the household. After a good harvest there may be capital to invest in a small business, but during the year there is likely to be a permanent lack of working capital and, sometimes, also of labour, because the available resources have to be used for consumption or in some other business. Enterprises, therefore, tend to be more closely linked to the household/agricultural economy and to wider social networks and

25

patron–client relations than to other enterprises in the cluster. These social networks may secure resources for the household and its businesses in times of pressing needs, but may also divert resources away from productive investments and make changes in the development strategy of the enterprise cluster difficult [*Hyden, 1983*].

The four types of clusters do not represent a development path from (4) to (1). It is possible that diversified industrial clusters on the high road to development may develop out of any of the three other types of clusters, but this certainly is not an automatic one-way route: first, because each type of cluster tends to develop social and economic support structures which may make the transition to a more attractive position difficult; and secondly, because each type of cluster may degenerate into a less attractive position as a result of internal or external pressures.

VI. LIMITS TO AND POLICIES FOR COLLECTIVE EFFICIENCY

The growth of small enterprise clusters and the exploitation of collective efficiency in small enterprise clusters require a growing market. Such growth in the market for the small enterprises may come from three different sources:

(1) a growth in the local market caused by increasing money incomes. Small enterprises may benefit from such a growth without increasing their own efficiency relative to the large-scale sector, because they often have a partial monopoly on the local market;

(2) the small enterprises may increase their share of the total local market in competition with the large scale sector. This requires that the small enterprises increase their collective efficiency relative to the large scale sector through vertical specialisation and collaboration, but especially through a horizontal specialisation and diversification;

(3) expansion into non-local/export markets: this requires that they increase their overall collective efficiency in absolute terms, primarily through vertical specialisation and collaboration.

Successful industrial clusters tend to expand in all three ways. Many African enterprise clusters, however, have grown along the first lines, or possibly the second only. Growth, therefore, has been limited.

Small enterprise clusters develop in competition with the large-scale sector for resources and markets. When the large-scale sector has obtained monopoly status the small-scale sector cannot develop. But where the large-scale sector is missing or very inefficient it may also be difficult for the small-scale sector to develop outside the local market. This is because the small enterprises often obtain access to non-local resources and markets via the large enterprises and their national and international networks, or because the large enterprises are often instrumental in the initial expansion of the moneterised economy in the rural areas.

In addition, small and large enterprises tend to supply partly different markets and use different resources and, therefore, often benefit from each other. Where the large-scale sector operates in a quasi-monopoly, it may be forced to carry out peripheral tasks which a large centralised organisation cannot do efficiently or may leave undone. On the other hand, when the large-scale sector collapses, small enterprises may operate in large markets which may well be profitable for them. However, they may not operate efficiently in these markets and competition may be limited so that prices rise.

Policies to develop enterprise clusters and collective efficiencies among small enterprises should 'seek' therefore to develop a balance between small and large enterprises by demonopolising large enterprises and developing the markets for small enterprises. Corresponding to the three sources of small enterprise market growth discussed above such policies should attempt to:

(1) increase the money incomes of the rural/low income population, for instance, by increasing agricultural productivity and prices;

(2) demonopolise the commercial industrial and financial sectors and support development of small and medium-sized enterprises. The primary goal of such a policy should not be to increase employment and incomes in the small enterprise sector, but to increase overall efficiency in the production and distribution system in order to lower prices and increase the buying power of low income people. Policies that aim directly at increased employment and income in the small enterprise sector are less likely to increase efficiency;

(3) expand production and distribution into export markets through foreign trade liberalisation. Such export orientation policies, however, tend to be in conflict with policies to raise low incomes, partly because they attempt to reduce wages, and partly because they tend to shift the focus of agricultural policies from food crops to export crops. Export orientation policies also will tend to support large enterprises and thus may be in conflict with policies to demonopolise. At the same time, import liberalisation leads to increased competition, which may hurt small-scale producers badly unless they are able to increase their efficiency. This may increase, on the other hand, the total buying power of low income consumers and, therefore, the market.

The policy elements presented here are very similar to those proposed by the current wave of structural adjustment programmes. However, in the structural adjustment programmes, the order of implementation has usually been the opposite, and policy conflicts have tended to be resolved in favour of product standardisation and export expansion, at the expense of income expansion and diversification of products and services for, primarily, the home market. These policies are detrimental not only to the development of small enterprises in general, but also to the creation of enterprises clusters which is based on horizontal and vertical diversification and segmentation of markets.

REFERENCES

Bagachwa, M.S.D. (1991): *Choice of Technology in Industry: The Economics of Grain Milling in Tanzania*. Ottawa: International Development Research Centre.

Bagachwa, M.S.D. (1992): 'Choice of Technology in Small and Large Firms: Grain Milling in Tanzania', *World Development*, Vol.20, No.1, pp. 97–107.

Baker, J. and P.O. Pedersen (eds.) (1992): *The Rural–Urban Interface in Africa: Expansion and Adaptation*, Uppsala: The Scandinavian Institute of African Studies.

Becattini, G. (1990): 'The Marshallian Industrial District as a Socio-economic Notion', in Pyke *et al. [1990]*.

Castells, M. and A. Portes (1989): 'The World Underneath: The Origins, Dynamics and Effects of the Informal Sector', in Portes *et al. [1989]*.

Chipika, S. (1993): *Report on Decentralized Agro-industry Seminar*, Harare: Intermediate Technology Development Group.

Christaller, W. (1932): *Die zentralen Orte in Süddeutschland: Eine ökonomisch-geographische Untersuchung über die Gesetzmäsigkeit der Verbreitung und Entwicklung der Siedlungen mit städtlichen Funktionen*. Jena: Gustav Fischer Verlag.

Gould, J. and A. von Oppen (1994): 'Of Rhetoric and Market: The Liberation of Food Trade in East Africa: Introduction: Representing the Market', *Sociologia Ruralis*, Vol.34, No.1, pp. 3–12.

Hirschman, A.O. (1958): *The Strategy of Economic development*. New Haven, CT: Yale University Press.

Hotelling, H. (1929): 'Stability in Competition', *Economic Journal*, Vol.39, pp. 41–57.

Hyden, G. (1983): *No Shortcut to Progress: African Development Management in Perspective*, London: Heinemann.

Isard, W. (1956): *Location and Space Economy*, Cambridge, MA: MIT Press.

Jayne, T.S. and L. Rubey (1993): 'Maize Milling, Market Reform and Urban Food Security: The Case of Zimbabwe', *World Development*, Vol.21, No.6, pp.975–88.

Johanson, J. and L.G. Matson (1986): 'Inter-organisational Relations in Industrial Systems – A Network Approach Compared with the Transaction Cost Approach', *International studies of management and organisation* Vol.40, No.2.

Lösch., A. (1954): *The Economies of Location*, New Haven, CT: Yale University Press.

Marshall, A. (1892): *Elements of Economies of Industry*. London: Macmillan (1964 edition).

Massey, D.B. and R.A. Meegan (1979): 'The Geography of Industrial Reorganisation: The Spatial Effects of Restructuring of the Electrical Engineering Sector Under the Industrial Reorganisation Corporation', *Progress and Planning*, Vol.10, pp.155–237.

Nadvi, K. and H. Schmitz (1994): *Industrial Clusters in Less Developed Countries: Review of Experience and Research Agenda*, Discussion Paper 339, IDS, University of Sussex, Brighton.

Nabuguzi, E. (1994): *Structural Adjustment and the Informal Economy in Uganda*, CDR Working Paper 94.4, Centre for Development Research, Copenhagen.

North, D.C. (1989): 'Institutions and Economic Growth: An Historical Introduction', *World Development*, Vol.17, No.9, pp.1319–32.

Pedersen, P.O. (1987): 'Impact of Advanced Technology in the Production Sector on Freight Transport and Communications', in P. Nijkamp and S. Reichman (eds.), *Transportation Planning in a Changing World*, Aldershot, UK: Gower in association with the European Science Foundation.

Pedersen, P.O. (1991): 'The Restructuring of Wholesale and Retail Trade in Zimbabwe's New

District service centres', *African Urban Quarterly*, Vol.6, Nos.3–4, pp.292–303.

Pedersen, P.O. (1992a): 'Agricultural Marketing and Processing in Small Towns in Zimbabwe – Gutu and Gokwe', in Baker and Pedersen (eds.) [*1992*].

Pedersen, P.O. (1992b): 'The Structure of Small Service Centres Under Conditions of Uncertain Supplies', *International Regional Science Review*. Vol.14, No.3, pp.307–16.

Pedersen, P.O. (1994): 'Structural Adjustment and the Structure of the Economy of Small Towns in Zimbabwe', in Pedersen *et al.* [*1994*].

Pedersen, P.O., A. Sverrisson and M.P. van Dijk (1994): *Flexible Specialization: The Dynamics of Small-Scale Industries in the South*, London: Intermediate Technology Publications.

Perroux, F. (1955): 'Note sur la Notion de Pôle de croissance', *Economie Appliquée*, Vol.8, pp.307–20.

Piore, M.J. and C.F. Sabel (1984): *The Second Industrial Divide*, New York: Basic Books.

Portes, A., M. Castells and L. Benton (1989): *The Informal Economy: Studies in Advanced and Less Advanced Countries*. Baltimore MD: Johns Hopkins.

Pyke, F., Becattini, G. and W. Sengenberger (1990): *Industrial Districts and Interfirm Co-operation in Italy*, Geneva: International Institute for Labour Studies.

Rasmussen, J., Schmitz, H. and M.P. van Dijk (eds.) (1992): 'Introduction: Exploring a New Approach to Small-Scale Industry,' *IDS Bulletin* (Flexible Specialisation: A New View of Small Industry?), Vol.23, No.3, pp.2–7.

Rubey, L. (1993): *Market Reform and the Development of Alternative Maize Marketing Channels*, Working Paper AEES/93, Department of Agricultural Economics and Extension, University of Zimbabwe, Harare.

Schmitz, H. (1989): *Flexible Specialisation: A New Paradigm of Small-Scale Industrialization*, IDS Discussion paper 26.1, University of Sussex, Brighton.

Sengenberger, W. and F. Pyke (1992): 'Industrial Districts and Local Economic Regeneration: Research and Policy Issues', in F. Pyke and W. Sengenberger (eds.), *Industrial Districts and Local Economic Regeneration*, Geneva: International Institute for Labour Studies.

Storper, M. and R. Walker (1989): *The Capitalist Imperative: Territory Technology and Industrial Growth*, New York: Basil Blackwell.

Williamson, O.E. (1981): 'The Economics of *Organis*ations: The Transaction Cost Approach', *Journal of Sociology*, Vol.87, No.3, pp.548–77.

Williamson, O.E. (1985): *The Economic Institutions of Capitalism: Firms, Markets, Relational Contracting*, New York: The Free Press.

Williamson, O.E. (1994): *Institutions and Economic Organisation: The Governance Perspective*, Paper prepared for the World Bank Annual Conference on Development Economics, Washington, DC, 28–29 April.

3

Footwear Industrial Districts in Italy and Mexico

ROBERTA RABELLOTTI

I. INTRODUCTION

In recent years industrial districts have generated a great deal of interest among development economists [*Schmitz, 1989*]. Traditionally, in less developed countries, small firms were seen as socially desirable, but their viability remained in doubt. Their role was to create jobs, to be a seed-bed for indigenous entrepreneurship, to make use predominantly of local resources, to create local markets for satisfying the basic needs of the poor, and to contribute to a more equitable distribution of income. Rarely, however, were small firms seen as able to become internationally competitive. The success of industrial districts in the West was thus taken as a sign that small firms could be economically viable and strongly contribute to the industrial growth of their country. The concept of the industrial district was then introduced in the study of industrial development in the Third World, both at the empirical and theoretical level [*Rasmussen et al., 1992*].

The aim of this chapter is to assess the usefulness of the so-called 'industrial district model' for analysing clusters of firms in less developed countries through a comparative study of two footwear clusters in Italy, the 'land' of districts, and two other clusters in a less developed country (LDC), Mexico. Through empirical research, I intend to investigate to what extent the core characteristics of the industrial district textbook model correspond to the realities studied, to classify the collective economic effects deriving from those characteristics and then compare the degree of collective efficiency of the different clusters.

In the next section, 'ideal-type' of industrial district and the concepts of external economies and co-operation effects are presented. Then, section III contains the results of the empirical investigation in Italy and Mexico on the

This chapter presents some of the results of the author's D.Phil thesis. During the work, she received constructive comments and suggestions from many people. She is particularly grateful for insightful suggestions from Roberto Camagni, Meine Pieter van Dijk, Giocchino Garfoli, John Humphrey and Hubert Schmitz.

linkages among the economic actors and section IV provides a classification and a comparison of the collective effects identified in the cases analysed. The implications of these findings are drawn out in the last section.

II. THE 'TEXTBOOK' MODEL

From the ideal type arising from the Italian experience, four key elements characterising industrial districts emerge:

(1) clusters of mainly small and medium-sized enterprises which are spatially concentrated and sectorally specialised;

(2) a strong, relatively homogeneous cultural and social background linking the economic agents and creating a common and widely accepted behavioral code, sometimes explicit but often implicit;

(3) an intense set of backward, forward, horizontal and labour linkages, based both on market and non-market exchange of goods, services, information and people; and

(4) a network of public and private local institutions supporting the economic agents in the clusters.

Widespread existence of external economies and co-operation effects, stemming from the above features and particularly from the last two elements, is commonly seen as the key stylised fact making small firms in the districts economically viable and internationally competitive, in other words, allowing the districts to reach a high degree of collective efficiency [*Schmitz, 1992, 1994*]. Schmitz defines collective efficiency as the sum of unplanned or incidental consequences and planned or consciously pursued effects. Taking the definition of collective efficiency a step further, further distinguish between static and dynamic external economies and between different co-operation effects [*Rabellotti, 1995a*]:

(1) external economies are the by-product of some activities undertaken within the districts. They tend to be characterised by non-rivalry and non-excludibility which can lead to under-investments in a market economy [*Cornes and Sandler, 1986*]. Moreover, external economies are part of a common pool from which every economic actor can freely draw. In industrial districts, a typical example can be the circulation of information about markets or technologies, freely available to every economic actor located in the district. Each can use the same information, adapting it to her or his potentially different needs. Other examples of external economies are the creation of a collective commercial image of the district and the diffusion of a professional and managerial culture;

(2) co-operation effects are the result of explicit and voluntary co-operative

behaviours which differ from external economies because of two important characteristics: excludibility and compensation. The existence of a mechanism for compensation accounts for the rational interest of economic actors to co-operate with each other, producing co-operation effects and increasing the collective efficiency of the system. In a long term perspective, compensation can assume various forms like monetary exchange, exchanges of information, technology, know-how or human capital, the build up of a reputation which can become useful in future interactions. Besides, the existence of a mechanism for compensation allows the introduction of excludibility in the exploitation of collective advantages deriving from co-operation effects. An example of the effects of co-operative behaviours in industrial districts is the explicit sharing of specific information within groups of firms linked by some form of formal or informal agreements. Other examples are projects on technology, marketing, training, design carried out jointly by the members of the entrepreneurial associations or by groups of firms which explicitly decide to co-operate.

Furthermore, external economies and co-operation effects can be static when they impact the level of productivity of the system, or dynamic when they impact the system's capability to grow and innovate.

In the rest of the chapter, I analyse the adequacy of the model of industrial organisation proposed in the literature on industrial districts by looking at four footwear clusters in Italy and Mexico. Given that the first key element of spatial concentration and sectoral specialisation is the initial condition explicitly satisfied by the selection of the case studies, our analysis investigates the existence, the level of intensity and the quality of backward, forward, horizontal, labour and institutional linkages as well as the economic collective effects which derive from them. Cultural and social background are not explicitly investigated in the empirical research, although they are implicitly considered through their interconnections with the economic and institutional aspects of the systems.

III. THE CASE STUDIES

Fieldwork was carried out in four clusters of footwear enterprises, two of them located in Italy (Brenta and Marche districts) and two in Mexico (Guadalajara and Leon). In these clusters a sample of firms was randomly chosen among the members of the local associations of footwear entrepreneurs.[1] The sample included 101 enterprises, 50 of them located in Italy (30 in Marche and 20 in Brenta) and 51 in Mexico (30 in Guadalajara and 21 in Leon). In order to take firms of different size into account, the sample is stratified by size, as can be seen in Table 1.

TABLE 1

THE SAMPLE, NUMBER OF FIRMS BY SIZE

No of firms	<50 employees	51–100 employees	>100 employees	Total firms
Italy	24	15	11	50
Mexico	17	14	20	51

Source: author's survey.

A closed questionnaire, which focused on investigating backward, forward, labour, horizontal and institutional linkages, was used in interviews in the sample firms. The information collected from the questionnaire was complemented with secondary data as well as open-ended interviews with Entrepreneurial Associations, sector experts, suppliers, buyers and representatives of institutions supporting the sector.

With regard to the first prerequisite, the existence of a critical mass of spatially concentrated and sectoral specialised enterprises, the four areas all satisfied this condition as it was a criterion for choosing the research areas:

(1) Marche there are 2,410 firms and in Brenta 680, out of a total 8,547 enterprises in the whole of Italy [*ANCI, 1994*]; and

(2) in Leon there are about 1,700 shoe enterprises and in Guadalajara about 1,200, out of a total of 4,500 firms in the whole of Mexico [*CANAICAL, 1993*].

The Italian Districts: Brenta and Marche

Before presenting the results of the inquiry in the two Italian districts, it is useful to introduce some essential background information about the Italian footwear sector.[2]

The recent history of the Italian footwear industry can be divided into two main periods, a first, long period of continuous expansion from the beginning of the 1960s until 1985 and a second, continuing period of crisis and restructuring of the sector which started in the second half of the 1980s. The outstanding growth of the Italian footwear industry has been export-led: at the beginning of the 1950s, exports represented a mere 3.7 per cent of the total production, in 1970, the proportion of exports increased to 63 per cent, in 1985, it was 83 per cent and in 1993, 84 per cent [*ANCI, 1994*].

More recently, during the 1980s, other European countries such as Spain and Portugal, some South-east Asian newly industrialising countries such as Taiwan and South Korea and some developing countries such as Brazil, India and China have become very competitive in the international market and greatly increased their export share. Notwithstanding its attempt to counter this increasing competition through a process of upgrading its exports, the Italian footwear sector has had to start to compete in a market where a large increase in the quantity of shoes supplied faces a stable demand. The

33

competition has become stronger because all the new producers could exploit a labour cost advantage with respect to Italy. The Italian footwear industry is therefore going through a very difficult time. After 30 years of continuous growth, it has to face increasing competition from countries with a clear advantage in terms of labour cost, both in the domestic market and in the international market.

(a) Backward Linkages

The existence of a very well-developed system of suppliers working for the footwear sector represents one of the main assets of the Italian shoe producers. It has allowed the sector to maintain some competitiveness in a market recently characterised by stagnant demand. The ability of suppliers to manufacture a wide variety of products with short delivery times allows the shoe producers to postpone to the last moment their purchases of inputs. This has several advantages. First of all, it reduces the stocks required for producing shoes; second, it leads to the progressive shortening of the period between order and delivery which characterises the sector and finally, it increases the capacity of shoe producers to diversify their products and to satisfy market demand.

This advanced system of production includes tanneries, producers of components and accessories, suppliers of machines and service firms. From the results of our interviews, as well as from other available studies [*Varaldo, 1988; Gaibisso, 1992*], it appears clearly that, in many cases, the collaboration between suppliers and shoe producers is facilitated by spatial proximity and by the existence of long-term relationships (often 15 to 20 years in length). These are crucial factors which allow continuous interaction, facilitate mutual understanding and provide important sources of learning for all actors.

Altogether, the relationships between shoe firms and their suppliers seem to be rather satisfactory. In fact 75 per cent of the sample firms have not encountered any particular problems and the remaining 25 per cent sometimes have to face some availability difficulties, namely delays in deliveries. The firms interviewed declare that when there are problems with the suppliers they normally try to solve them together. In most cases this works because, as seen before, they usually have well-established relationships which, due to physical proximity and the duration of the relationship, have often become friendships. Moreover, if something goes wrong in either direction, if, for example, the producer of components does not supply the quality required or the shoe producer does not pay for the orders, the information immediately circulates within the district. The consequence is a loss of reputation for the firm which has broken the agreement or ultimately the extreme sanction of exclusion from the community. This informal, but widely accepted, system of social and business rules contributes to creating a very efficient and co-operative system of production, able to satisfy a very diversified and volatile demand.

Wide circulation of information about products also takes place, because component manufacturers are the first to see the novelties and it is quite common for them to offer other firms models similar to what they are already making for one client. The diffusion of information helps smaller firms which do not have the capabilities to produce their own original sample collection. On the other hand, larger firms which may invest a lot of resources in the development of new products try to defend themselves from imitation by other firms in the area through the stability of the relationships with their suppliers, based on trust and long-standing collabouration. Naturally, the component suppliers have their own interests in maintaining stable and good relationships with their best clients and will therefore avoid making exact copies of the same products in the same season for other firms.

In the two areas analysed, Italian shoe producers may also count on the existence of a wide network of small subcontracting enterprises specialising in one or two phases of the production cycle. According to a survey [*Varaldo, 1988*], more than 80 per cent of the Italian footwear firms decentralise the production of bottoms to subcontractors, more than 70 per cent decentralise the phases of edging and sewing of uppers and more than 50 per cent externalise the cutting phase.

Results from the sample firms (Table 2) confirm Varaldo's study [*1988*] which reveals that the production of bottoms is the phase more frequently decentralised. This happens because the production of soles, insoles and heels is a separate phase from the rest of process, requiring the use of specialised machines, particular labour force skills, and larger scale economies than shoe production itself. The edging and sewing phases also tend to be decentralised to subcontractors because they are highly labour-intensive. However, in firms producing top quality products, these phases may be internalised to maintain greater control over the process. The cutting phase is important both with respect to the quality and cost of the final product, and this depends much on the ability of the labour force. For the production of sample sets every firm needs to have its own internal cutting department. This explains why cutting is somewhat less frequently decentralised than the production of bottoms. Finally, fitting and finishing are usually internalised because it is crucial to have a strict control on these final phases. Decentralisation to subcontractors is often adopted only in case of orders too large for the internal capacity of the firm.

According to the enterprises interviewed, the main reasons for decentralisation are the reduction of costs (according to 72 per cent of the firms), increased flexibility (54 per cent), the certitude of costs (28 per cent) can increased specialisation (26 per cent). The cost advantages of externally decentralising part of the production arise partly from greater tax evasion and higher exploitation of labour in small subcontracting enterprises. In addition, subcontracting enterprises, being more specialised, are able to better exploit the different economies of scale in the diverse phases of production, efficiently employing the production capacity available. The results are that they produce better products at lower costs, with a shorter lead-time.

TABLE 2

THE EXTENT OF EXTERNALISING PRODUCTION TASKS
(% OF SAMPLE FIRMS)

% of pairs externalized	None	<50%	51%–90%	>90%
Cutting	26	20	20	34
Sewing	6	16	20	58
Bottoms	10	10	2	78
Finishing	96	2	2	0

Source: author's survey.

Analysing the relationships among the shoe firms and the process-specialised firms (for example firms specialising in the sewing or cutting phases), they are mainly hierarchical and characterised by a strong dependence of the subcontracting firms on the shoe enterprises. Most of the subcontracting firms interviewed stressed that their activity depends heavily on the demand of shoe producers so that they move from periods of extra-work to periods in which they do not have enough work to occupy their workers. They are therefore obliged to demand extremely high flexibility from the workers. Often, they employ relatives or very young women who are normally paid on a piece-rate basis. Most of the subcontracting firms suffer from their dependence on shoe producers, particularly during periods of crisis, because their workload can be significantly reduced and it becomes difficult to make any organisational plans. They can only wait and hope to be given work by the shoe producers.

More rarely in these relationships, there are also aspects of co-operation. Some of the footwear enterprises interviewed stated that they often supply raw materials, workforce training, technological assistance and sometimes even credit to some of their subcontractors. They have stable relationships with their subcontractors in order to have more guarantees in terms of quality and service. From the interviews, it appears that this strategy is common mainly among firms which produce a medium-high or high quality products. In this case the stability of the subcontractor relationships is an essential condition for maintaining the required quality level.

(b) Forward Linkages

It Italian footwear industry led the international market until the mid-1980s and, for a long time, shoe manufacturers faced a market characterised by excess demand. Many of the entrepreneurs interviewed in Italy emphasised that until a few years ago, foreign buyers, mainly from Germany, used to go and visit their firms regularly and all they needed to do was to produce shoes. It was not necessary to make an effort to sell them. Therefore, traditionally the Italian shoe manufacturers did not care much about commercialisation and marketing. According to the Entrepreneurial Association [*ANCI, 1994*], most of the entrepreneurs still identify the quality of their product only from a purely manufacturing point of view, according to the quality of processing and raw materials. Rarely are they aware of the importance of other factors like the image of their products or their brand name.

In Italy, it has been argued that in the footwear districts, the efficient way of organising the production phase is not complemented by an equally efficient system of commercialisation [*Caibisso, 1992*]. Middlemen, who have been so important in other districts, specialised in different sectors, among which we can quote the famous case of Prato and its '*impannatori*', have had a very limited role in the footwear areas. Only recently in Brenta have some wholesalers begun to play an important role in organising the production of a number of small firms but they all come from outside the district. They are foreign or Italian wholesalers who take advantage of the production skills of some local firms unable to sell their own products on the market and are therefore obliged to become subcontractors. Among the firms interviewed, the few that sell their products to buyers stressed the risk of the dependence on a few or, more often, only one customer. Only one firm, interviewed in Brenta, was satisfied with this way of selling its products because it produces very high quality shoes for two, well known fashion houses and it believes that the quality of its products guarantees a high degree of bargaining power with customers, who have every interest in maintaining successful and stable relationships.

Commercialisation through non-exclusive agents took place in 76 per cent of the sample firms, through direct sales to customers in 22 per cent, through exclusive agents in 16 per cent, through trading companies or in shops owned by the same firm in eight per cent and, in the remaining eight per cent, through consortia with other firms. The relationship with non-exclusive agents often generates discontent among footwear firms because they do not control the activity of their agents and receive very little information about the market from them. Many of the enterprises interviewed realised they would need a more active commercial strategy to be successful in an increasingly competitive market. However, in marketing, economies of scale are important and very few of the Italian firms have the financial capacity to invest in advertising or market research, to set up their own shops or to employ exclusive agents.

A collective solution, rather diffused in the two area analysed, is the establishment of export consortia, set up for supporting the export activity of firms with an initial public financial contribution (see in the section on institutional linkages).

(c) Horizontal linkages

Evidence of formal agreements of co-operation is minimal. The only formal agreements among shoe firms found in the sample are agreements for commercial co-operation. Specifically, eight firms have created a trading company with some partners, in most cases aimed at entering new markets. The most common type of linkages among shoe firms are informal relationships. In the sample here, 42 per cent of the firms have frequent informal contacts with other firms in their area, 28 per cent have some contacts and the remaining 30 per cent very rarely have relationships. Considering size, small (42 per cent of the small firms in the sample) and medium firms (47 per cent) have more frequent informal contacts than large firms (27 per cent) (Table 3).

TABLE 3

INFORMAL CO-OPERATION BETWEEN SAMPLE FIRMS

Frequency of co-operation exchange	No of small firms	No of medium firms	No of large firms	% of total sample firms
Very frequent contacts	11	7	3	42
Some contacts	6	3	5	28
Very rare contacts	7	5	3	30

Source: author's survey

As regards the nature of these informal ties, the most important one is the meetings organised by the entrepreneurial associations (42 per cent of the sample), followed by spatial proximity (24 per cent). Moreover, 71 per cent of small firms, 60 per cent of medium and only 18 per cent of large enterprises believe that informal contacts are very important. This different approach of the different categories towards informal contacts may be interpreted as a tendency of small firms, who risk to loose, to rely on informal contacts are very important. This different approach of the different categories towards informal contacts may be interpreted as a tendency of small firms, who risk to loose, to rely on informal co-operation as a sort of solidarity network, allowing them to survive beyond market rules [*Rabellotti, 1995a*].

(d) Linkages with the Labour Market

The existence of a reservoir of skilled labour is always assumed to be one of the externalities of production organisation in highly specialised clusters of firms. The Italian industrial districts are described in the literature as areas where specialised jobs are taught to children by their parents and where skills are accumulated and transmitted from one generation to the other.

People and, therefore, know-how are circulated among firms through labour force mobility, which enhances local innovation capability. In other words, the innovation process, which usually takes place inside the firm, becomes a collective process in the industrial districts, based on common knowledge accumulated by people rather than firms. This mechanism was confirmed by the inquiry. The majority of the firms interviewed employ people who have already been trained in other firms, which are thus able to save on training costs.

Surprisingly enough a rather low availability of skilled labour was found in the Italian inquiry. Forty-six per cent of the sample firms believe availability to be low, 36 per cent good and 18 per cent very good (Table 4). According to the majority of the sample firms, the labour market has changed in the last ten years. A majority of the firms interviewed (55 per cent) stated that the availability of skilled labour was good during the period from 1980 to 1985, while in the second half of the 1980s, 70 per cent of the firms said it had dropped. According to the entrepreneurial associations and to a number of firms interviewed, improved welfare and better education, due to the expansion of the footwear sector in the areas, result in an increasing tendency for local young people, who are better educated than their parents, to abandon the sector if they can find an alternative, mainly non-manual jobs. The resulting interruption of the accumulation and transmission of skills from parents to children, from one generation to the other could, in the future, undermine the collective learning effect which has been so important in determining the competitiveness of the districts.

Concerning the availability of unskilled labour, it seems to be rather good according to the firms interviewed. 44 per cent said that availability is very good, according to another 44 per cent, it is rather good and in 12 per cent it is low (Table 4).

TABLE 4

AVAILABILITY OF WORKERS (%)

INFORMAL CO-OPERATION BETWEEN SAMPLE FIRMS

Availability of workers	Skilled workers	Unskilled workers
High availability	9	22
Average availability	18	22
Low availability	23	6

Source: author's survey.

In the two areas, the labour climate is also characterised by high flexibility of the labour force, in terms of the willingness to work extra-hours, week-ends and so on, and by generally good labour relationships. All but two of the firms interviewed declared that there is a high willingness among their staff to work extra hours when needed. This flexibility is crucial in an industry such as footwear where production is almost seasonal and the orders tend increasingly to arrive at the last moment. Finally, the existence of very friendly and easy relationships with the workforce is one of the main advantages of being located in the area, a fact stressed by a large majority of the entrepreneurs interviewed.

(e) Institutional linkages

The importance of institutional support in the growth process of Italian industrial districts has been much emphasised in the literature. This has fuelled the myth of an efficient local government able to intervene to support the needs of local industries, creating public or semi-public centres for real services, technological development, commercial promotion and so on [*Brusco, 1989; 1992*]. However, from a careful investigation of the available literature on industrial districts in Europe, Schmitz and Musyck [*1993*] conclude that the picture of institutional intervention is patchy and that there are few evaluations of the services supplied from the users' viewpoint.

From the investigation carried out in this study, it was clear that central government intervention was of limited importance. Only 20 per cent of the sample firms said they have received any financial incentives. Moreover, the majority of the firms complained about the enormous bureaucratic hurdles accessing incentive schemes which mainly consist of easy credit terms for small firms or enterprises with innovative projects.

Regarding local governments, they mainly contribute with financial support for some of the initiatives promoted in the two areas by the entrepreneurial associations. Both in Marche and Brenta, in fact, the main institutional actors are the local entrepreneurial associations which supply a number of services to the members and play an important role in promoting initiatives to support the sector. Among the sample firms, the most used services are tax counseling and the organisation of trade fairs.

In Brenta, the local association, Associazione Calzaturifici della Riviera della Brenta (ACRIB) was established by a few local entrepreneurs more than 30 years ago and, since then, it has supported several initiatives such as a large export consortium and a centre for technological assistance and training. The export consortium, named Consorzio Maestri Calzaturieri del Brenta, created in 1967 with initial public financing, manages collective advertising campaigns, assists firms in their export activities, and runs a data bank on 20,000 customers all over the world. Moreover, the consortium organises a collective exhibition in Dusseldorf twice a year and promotes research and market surveys. In 1986, with public money provided by a law aimed at supporting the crafts, ACRIB promoted a new initiative, the Consorzio Centro Veneto Calzaturiero. The main areas of intervention of this institution are technology assistance, quality control, environmental control and training.

Besides ACRIB, there is also a quite active association of artisan firms in

Brenta with more than 500 members in the footwear *filière* which supplies several services such as bookkeeping, labour and tax assistance and consultancy for facilitating access to credit.

In Marche, there are two entrepreneurial associations, in Fermo and in Macerata, which supply services like training, bookkeeping and fiscal and financial assistance to their members. In Fermo there are 650 members and in Macerata only 140, because the footwear area in this province is a smaller than in the area around Fermo. The two associations have recently launched a new initiative, a specialised center, Società per la Calzatura Marchigiana (SCAM) which supplies technological assistance, training, fashion information and promotional activities. The services are usually supplied at very low costs because they are partially financed by public grants (for example the training courses are financed through EC grants). An interesting project of the centre is a monthly trade fair where local producers exhibit and sell their products outside the traditional seasonal appointments of the main national and international trade fairs.

During the 1980s, thanks to an initial public grant, several export consortia were created in Marche to supply services such as translations, fax facilities and assistance with export procedures. Recently some of them have moved towards a more specialised variety of services such as market surveys and promotional activities in new markets (in particular, Japan, the Arab countries, Australia). Among the services supplied there is also access to international data banks about customers, inventories of unsold products and subcontracting opportunities.

In Marche there are also a few consortia to facilitate access to credit. One of them, promoted by the entrepreneurial association in Fermo, has 300-odd members and provides common guarantees, easy credit terms and access to long and medium-term credit.

In Marche and Brenta most of the firms prefer to deal with local banks because the employees often know them and this usually helps in obtaining credit. However, it must be said that easier access to credit in local banks, based on trust, friendship and high circulation of information, as opposed to national credit institutions, may become an important constraint when firms go through periods of crisis. Local banks immediately know about the difficulties and make access to credit even more difficult. This happened recently, according to a large portion of the firms interviewed in both Marche and Brenta, when the reaction of local banks to the difficulties in the footwear industry was to drastically reduce credit availability to shoe firms.

To conclude, the activities of Marche and Brenta entrepreneurial associations were, in general, assessed positively by the entrepreneurs interviewed, who also participate in them quite actively. However, the tradition of institutional intervention is more firmly established in Brenta than in Marche and this is confirmed by the well-organised activities supplied by the specialised centres. In Marche, according to many of the entrepreneurs interviewed, there is no tradition of collaboration and institutional intervention and this is confirmed by the only recent establishment of a service centre in an area of specialisation which is the most important in Italy. The need for greater institutional intervention is also confirmed by the general opinion among the entrepreneurs in Marche, who very often quote the Brenta case as a good example of how institutions can help the sector.

The Mexican Clusters: Guadaljara and Leon

Mexico was a protected market for a long time, having adopted an import-substitution strategy which was drastically abandoned in 1988 with the opening up of the economy to foreign competition. The acceleration of the opening up of the Mexican market to international competition, through the elimination of import licensing and tariff reduction, had a big impact on the footwear industry. The market was flooded with imports which increased from US$13.7 million in 1987 to US$148.2 million in 1991.

For many decades the domestic producers took advantage of a market in which there was excess demand. To make money in the sector was easy because every kind of product was sold, no matter what its quality, design and cost. Nowadays, international competition is becoming stronger and the Mexican footwear enterprises are starting to realise that they must increase their efficiency if they want to survive and grow [*Rabellotti, 1995b*].

(a) Backward Linkages

In Mexico the relationships between suppliers and shoe producers are less collaborative than in Italy, being based mainly on pure market mechanisms. Many sample firms complain about the low quality of components and raw materials, the scarce attention to fashion changes and the bad service provided by their input suppliers. In turn, suppliers do not accept responsibility for their low development and accuse shoe entrepreneurs of having always adopted a strategy more focused on price than quality. Suppliers complain of unstable demand, of small order sizes, of continuously changing products, and of delays in payments. Both the suppliers of components and the manufacturers blame each other and state that the main deficiencies exist in communication and collaboration among the two linked sectors.

However, with the opening of the market and the increase in shoe and component imports, the relationships between shoe producers and suppliers are improving and becoming more collaborative. The majority of the suppliers interviewed agreed that they now try to work closely with their customers in developing products and that they are also available to adapt products to the needs of the shoe producers. On the other hand, some of the footwear firms interviewed are now more satisfied with their relationships with suppliers and they are trying to set up stable linkages, building up an ability to cooperate in defining fashion trends and product characteristics.

To increase the stability of demand, some groups of shoe producers have tried to organise common purchases. Some wholesalers are also working in this direction, organising the purchases of components and raw materials for all their clients and therefore guaranteeing large and stable orders for the suppliers. Moreover, in both Leon and Guadalajara, the local credit unions of shoe entrepreneurs have recently launched a programme for pool purchasing. Their objective for the near future is to import components from abroad jointly.

Some efforts towards a more cooperative attitude between shoe producers and suppliers have also been undertaken by the Camara del Calzado, the footwear entrepreneurial association, and the association of suppliers in Leon, which have begun to organise meetings to discuss and jointly elaborate fashion trends. Together with the Camara del Calzado in Guadalajara, the two associations in Leon have also begun to work on the standardisation of the measurement system. The lack of a standard, commonly accepted measurement system is a major obstacle for the development of an efficient system of specialised firms. The case of lasts is representative of the situation. In Mexico every footwear firm requires its own models, based on a measurement system which is different for every firm.

Concerning subcontracting of phases of the production cycle, in Mexico, according to several recent studies [*Boston Consulting Group, 1988; CONCALZADO, 1991; Dominguez-Villalobos and Grossman, 1992*] and, according to the results of our own survey, the level of the division of labour is generally low (Table 5) and certainly much lower than in Italy (see Table 2). Mexican shoe firms generally only decentralise some phases of the production cycle when they receive orders too large for their internal capacity. About 50 per cent of the sample firms do not externalise any stage of the production process. This low level of the division of labour can be explained by two main factors:

(1) backward linked industries have remained at a low level of development with regard to design, fashion quality of components and service because the former protection of the domestic market has limited competition and, therefore, the incentive to innovate. We know from Adam Smith that division of labour is limited by the extent of the market and this seems to apply to our Mexican cases; and

(2) the sector lacks a standard technical language and a common, universally accepted, measurement system and this strongly increases the transaction costs and the costs of using the market.

The poor level of development and the difficulties of communication with backward-linked industries induce many shoe firms to internalise as many phases of the production cycle as possible in order to reduce their dependency on an unstable, low quality supply. Vertical integration means different phases of production are carried out inside the firm, with a lot of problems in the organisation of the production cycle, because the different phases are characterised by very different economies of scale, different degrees of labour intensity and different processing times. This production structure is even common among very small enterprises.

TABLE 5

THE EXTENT OF EXTERNALISING PRODUCTION TASKS (% OF SAMPLE FIRMS)

% of production externalized	None	<50%	51%–90%	>90%
Cutting	94	6	0	0
Sewing	80	20	0	0
Bottoms	59	4	4	33
Finishing	100	0	0	0

Source: author's survey.

Among the sample firms, decentralisation, even if it is not widely practised, shows a positive relation with profits. 47 per cent of the decentralising firms have obtained an average profit, 21 per cent a very good profit, while 24 per cent earned no profit or incurred a loss (the remaining eight per cent did not answer the question).

Among Mexican shoe firms, decentralisation seems, therefore, to have a positive effect on performance, flexibility and specialisation. These positive results, together with the diffused knowledge about the highly decentralised Italian production system, have recently induced a greater use of subcontracting among Mexican firms. This was confirmed by several sector experts interviewed in Guadalajara and Leon. There is an increasing number of firms which, after having interrupted their activity as shoe producers because they were hit by fierce competition, began to work as subcontractors specialised in the production of uppers. However, the subcontracting firms interviewed stated that they strongly depend upon and suffer from the still, very unstable flow of work from the shoe producers. According to them, this instability limits possibilities for the development of a well-organised and efficient system of process-specialised enterprises, as in the Italian districts.

To conclude, in the Mexican clusters relatively good local availability and high intensity of linkages between suppliers and manufacturers have been found. Besides, there is also a trend towards an increasing decentralisation of some phases of production which has shown a positive impact on performance and efficiency. However, to increase the degree of division of labour and the competitiveness of the industry, the two clusters need to become well-organised systems where shoe producers may rely on quality and prompt deliveries from subcontracting firms and their linkages with suppliers are not only based on a price factor, disregarding some important aspects such as fashion and design, material quality and delivery service. From this point of view, the Italian footwear districts may actually provide some interesting lessons.

(b) Forward Linkages

The Mexican footwear industry traditionally neglected commercialisation and marketing because the domestic market was closed to international competition for a long time and this allowed the domestic producers to produce shoes which were easily sold on the closed market, no matter what the quality, design, fashion content were. Generally speaking, therefore, the Mexican footwear firms suffer from problems similar to those of the Italian enterprises. They have limited control over their market and little knowledge of it, they depend on non-exclusive agents and they are not used to adopting active commercial strategy to sell their products on a competitive market. Among 63 per cent of the sample firms, the main factor of competition is price. Only 24 per cent of the firms interviewed believe that design is an important factor and 12 per cent that quality is important.

Considering marketing channels, 74 per cent of the sample firms sell part of their production through non-exclusive agents, 51 per cent through wholesalers, 16 per cent through trading companies or shops owned by the same firms and another 16 per cent directly to retailers.

One of the main consequences of a very fragmented distribution system dominated by independent retailers is the small size of orders. According to the Boston Consulting Group study [*1988*], the most common order size in the domestic market is around 300 pairs but shoe producers sometimes receive orders for very few pairs. The possibility of working on the basis of larger orders, therefore to be able to plan a production process on a longer term basis and to exploit the economies of scale deriving from specialisation in a few products, has pushed an increasing number of firms to sell to retail chains and supermarkets. Another important reason for this change, stressed by some of the firms interviewed, is related to better payment terms guaranteed by retail chains and supermarkets as compared with small family shops.

According to the firms interviewed which sell to retail chains, the relationships are definitely dependent because these chains generally adopt a strategy based on the search for the lowest possible price on the market. Many stories are told about some of these chains contacting some firms to buy their models and then commissioning other firms, on the illegal market, to manufacture the same products at a lower price. Some of these chains are also believed to be responsible for most of the illegal imports of very cheap synthetic or fabric shoes which have invaded the low-price market during the last few years.

However, a few firms interviewed told us that, although most of the retail chains still maintain a very traditional strategy of commercialisation based on price, some of them and particularly, supermarkets, are progressively increasing their attention to quality and some of the shoe producers, therefore, try to limit their dependency on them, increasing the stability of their relationship by supplying good service and a stable quality of products.

Recently, thanks to a few wholesalers, an interesting experiment was started aimed at developing a stable and constructive relationship. They adopted a new strategy aimed at selling a quality product and selected a group of shoe firms with which to collaborate. Technical staff employed by the wholesalers regularly call on the shoe enterprises, controlling quality and giving advice on technological and organisational matters. Moreover, the wholesalers organise a system of pool purchases of some key components or raw materials like leather in order to guarantee a stable quality level, better prices and good service. Among the firms interviewed, the ones linked to wholesalers through such a relationship were generally very satisfied, not only with the sales, but mainly with the complementary services they receive, like technological and organisational assistance. Many of them, due to collaboration with these wholesalers, have been able to introduce important improvements in the organisation of the production process and in the quality of their products. Naturally, they realise that depending on one main customer, who can always find another enterprise able to make the same product at a lower price, is very risky but most of the firms also realise that they do not have enough marketing and commercialisation skills to compete on the market on their own. Therefore, they try to build up a linkage with the wholesalers where both parties have an interest in collaborating, at least partially offsetting dependency.

(c) Horizontal Linkages

Co-operation among sample firms is more common in the two Mexican footwear clusters than in the than districts. The reasons for this interaction in 12 firms, are the exchange of technological information and sometimes of machines, subcontracting and farming out part of the production when there are excess orders in nine firms, and, in six cases the establishment of commercial agreements. In the majority of the firms interviewed the interactions take place among small groups of firms linked by family ties and/or long-standing friendships.

In Guadalajara, linkages among firms outside family groups have been favoured by an initiative promoted by the local *Camera del Calzado*, inspired by a UNIDO methodology initially aimed at favouring the growth of small rural enterprises to reduce emigration towards urban centers. The project consists of promoting the creation of *agrupamientos industriales*, initially based on a course for entrepreneurs who agreed to organise a visit to their own firms for other entrepreneurs in the group and to allow an outside expert (a business student in his or her final year) to make a diagnosis of their firms. In seven years seven groups, involving about 120 enterprises, began in this way. Afterwards some of these groups carried on with regular meetings to discuss problems related to technology, marketing, suppliers and so on and to exchange information about clients, machines, workers and orders.

Another interesting initiative has very recently been promoted at the national level for the creation of *empresas integradoras*. The program, which was inspired by the Ministry of Trade after a visit to the Italian industrial districts, aims at creating companies established by groups of firms for the joint sale of products, the purchase of inputs or any other common objective. The new companies enjoy financial and tax incentives and the program facilitates bureaucratic procedures. In the survey we found three projects for the creation of *empresas integradoras*. One is for the creation of a new common site for a group of seven enterprises linked by family ties. Another is a group of 15 very small firms in Leon (with fewer than seven employees in each firm), which after a successful experience of joint participation in the local trade fair, would like to create a trading company with a single brand name for all their products. Finally there is a group of five tanneries in Leon, which would like to create a company for joint purchase and sale, and the supply of common services like bookkeeping and training.

Apart from these initiatives aimed at favouring interactions among firms, informal relationships are frequent among 80 per cent of the enterprises interviewed and they are considered an important asset by almost all (Table 6). The role of the entrepreneurial associations seems to be very important in inducing informal contacts among firms because, according to 37 firms, events organised by the *Camara* are the most important opportunities for informal exchange with their colleagues. Family ties also play an important role in 17 firms and, finally, social events are important for 11 firms. Several forms of co-operation in many different aspects of a firm's life arise from these informal contacts. These include exchange of technological and market information, exchange of machinery and workers, sub-contracting of orders in case of excess demand, joint commercialisation, joint purchases of inputs, and joint recovery of credits.

Notwithstanding the fact that many informal linkages are occurring within the two districts analysed, 65 per cent of the interviewed firms expressed a desire for more formal agreements, in the sense of more stable relationships with other firms, organised and focused on specific objectives.

TABLE 6
INFORMAL CO-OPERATION BETWEEN SAMPLE FIRMS

Frequency of co-operation exchange	No of small firms	No of medium firms	No of large firms	% of total sample firms
Frequent contacts	14	11	16	80
Rare contacts	3	3	4	20

Source: author's survey.

(d) Linkages with the Labour Market

Analysing the characteristics of the labour market, the main problems emphasised by the sample firms were, in order of importance, the low availability of a skilled workforce and the high turnover of the labour force. According to 65 per cent of the sample firms (Table 7), skilled labour is a scarce resource and qualified workers demand relatively high salaries and good working conditions. This explains why small and medium firms, which usually can only afford to pay lower salaries and offer more unstable working conditions, because of the irregularity of orders, have more difficulty in hiring. Unskilled labour represents a less important problem (only four firms believe that there is locally a low availability) because there is a large reservoir of young people, mainly women, available for work.

TABLE 7
AVAILABILITY OF WORKERS

Availability of workers	Skilled workers	Unskilled workers
High availability	14	27
Average availability	4	20
Low availability	33	4

Source: author's survey.

According to most of the sample firms, the main problem with unskilled labour is the high turnover. Workers move away from the footwear sector as soon as they find a job in other, more remunerative sectors or, in the case of women, when they get married.

Training was also investigated. In most of the sample firms training takes place inside the same firm. External training is generally reserved for supervisors, technicians or designers. Less skilled workers like edgers are very rarely trained outside the firms. A problem emphasised by many firms is the risk of losing their workers sent to be trained outside because they find better paying jobs. Skilled workers are heavily sought after and frequently 'pirated' from one firm to the other. This is a very common problem among small-scale enterprises, which usually pay lower salaries than larger firms, a typical case of market failure which justifies some kind of extra-market intervention to make up for the firms' negative attitude about external training for their workers.

Finally, the rate of unionisation is very low both in Guadalajara and in Leon because the sector has grown in a family environment with entrepreneurs who, in most cases, started as manual workers in other firms and established relationships based on friendship and solidarity with their employers.

(e) Institutional Linkages

At the national level there are no specific policies addressing the footwear sector. Nevertheless, some of the sample firms which export part of their production have access to a scheme of financial incentives for exporting enterprises. Other firms have obtained easy credit terms from *National Financiera*, the Mexican bank for industrial development. A recent policy initiative which seems to have some potential for supporting the footwear industry is the programme to favour the creation of *empresas integradoras* described above.

At the local level, a number of important institutions have been identified both in Guadalajara and in Leon. Some are associations of firms, while others provide special services to the footwear industries. Entrepreneurial associations, *Camara del Calzado*, are the most important institutions supporting the footwear industry in Mexico. There are three local associations, in Guadalajara, Leon and Mexico City, and a national one aimed at coordinating the activities of the three local *Camaras*. The role of these associations, financed through membership fees and profits from the organisation of the trade fairs, is to supply services such as fiscal, legal and labour advice, managerial training, the organisation of trade fairs and lobbying activities at a political level. Entrepreneurial associations also exist for the tanning and component sectors.

In Leon there is also a centre for research and technological assistance, *Centro de Investigacion y Asistencia Tecnologica del Estado de Guanauajato* (CIATEG), created as an agency of the central government which can be considered an arm of the Mexican National Science and Technology Council. The centre was created with the objective of supplying technical and quality control services and specialised training to the footwear industry at the national level. In fact, it is mainly used by Leon's enterprises, leaving shoe firms in the rest of Mexico almost without any technological support.[3]

A similar institution in Guadalajara is the *Instituto Tecnologico del Calzado* (ITC), established in 1984 with the support of the local Camara and a grant from the World Bank and devoted to training and technological research. Its activities include a diversified program for training designers, skilled manual workers like edgers, and also managers and entrepreneurs.

In both Guadalajara and Leon there is a credit union with the power to borrow directly from *National Financiera*, which aims at obtaining credit for its members at more favourable conditions than the market rates. In Guadalajara the credit union is linked with the *Camara* and was promoted by an initiative of some entrepreneurs taking part in the *agrupamientos indus-triales*. Its activity has recently increased, thanks to the active participation of a number of small entrepreneurs who got involved in 1991 when the union was suffering a bad crisis due to the decrease in credit availability in the country. In Leon, the credit union was established fairly recently, in 1992, and does not have any linkage with the local *Camara*.

The existence of a relatively well-developed institutional support network for the footwear *filière* is a very important condition for the adoption of a growth strategy based on an approach at system level. Institutions like the *Camara del Calzado* can have a very relevant role in diffusing among entre-preneurs a systematic vision of their business, in other words, the idea that the survival and growth of their own firms strongly depends on the development of the whole system of shoe firms, suppliers, buyers, market agents, service firms and supporting institutions. Nevertheless, as in the Italian case, it is very difficult to evaluate the real role played by the existing institutions in the development process of the two clusters analysed.

IV. A COMPARISON OF COLLECTIVE EFFECTS

The aim of this section is to classify the collective effects of the linkages described above in terms of the concepts introduced: external economies and co-operation effects. In order to classify the collective effects that emerged from the linkages identified in the empirical investigation, a two-dimensional classification may be introduced. In Table 8 collective effects are mapped out on one side according to their incidence and excludibility, and on the other side according to their static or dynamic objectives.

Let us begin with external economies which derive from unplanned, incidental relationships among the economic actors who interact within the system. The most typical incidental relationships usually going on in every district and therefore also in the Italian and Mexican footwear clusters are the frequent social occasions, casual meetings in the streets, cafes clubs and busi-ness occasions, like meetings at entrepreneurial associations, at suppliers' facilities and so on. A flow of information about products, markets, fashion trends, bad and good customers, suppliers and process-specialised firms, tech-nology and so on is generated from these continuous interactions and freely circulates within the districts. This circulation of information generates both static and dynamic external economies.

With regard to static external economies, the free circulation of information may allow firms to be productive because they get access to information which they otherwise could not afford. This type of external economy is particularly significant for small firms which can rarely afford market studies, participation in foreign exhibitions, subscriptions to data banks, etc. The free availability of information also contributes to the birth and survival of small firms. This allows a continuous renewal of firms and recycling of the human and capital resources available in the districts. Nevertheless, it also permits the survival of some inefficient firms, which only have a very superficial market knowledge and which base their competitive edge on their ability to make shoes and take advantage of low-entry barriers. This category of firms can be defined as followers or, even free-riders of the district, because they usually tend to exploit resources created by other, more innovative firms. For instance, they imitate successful products at lower costs and lower quality can be said that these firms 'use' the district to compensate their structural and strategic short-comings. Furthermore, it should be added that, although during the period of excess demand they could easily find a market for their products both in Italy and in Mexico, nowadays they face increasing competition and are usually the first to suffer. So, for instance, in Italy many small firms unable to develop an independent product and marketing strategy become subcontractors for other enterprises, or even close down. In Mexico, the same phenomenon occurs, with an increasing number of firms closing down in the formal market to become informal activities, non-officially registered and therefore able to survive without paying taxes and salaries lower than the legal minimum wage. We can conclude that these external economies contribute to the collective efficiency of the systems analysed but firms which rely too much on such incidental effects have shown low performances.[4]

The free circulation of information can also have dynamic effects, generating a sort of demonstration effect on attitudes and motivations which may induce economic actors to introduce innovations in processes, products of forms of organisation and, thus, contributing to the growth of the system. This positive spontaneous effect of clustering is common in Brenta and Marche, in Guadalajara and Leon as well as in many other clusters of firms in industrialised and developing countries.

The local concentration of firms which produce or sell inputs, machinery and services or specialise in some phases of the production process at competitive prices, generates some important static external economies at a high level of specialisation. Every firm located within the district can, in fact, save on costs of production factors for several reasons. Prices are lower due to the high competition, transaction and transport costs are lower due to the spatial and cultural proximity and firms can maintain very little inventory, being able to buy what they need rapidly. Moreover, shoe firms can easily contract out some phases of the production process to highly specialised firms, which are able to exploit the different economies of scale which characterise the phases of the production cycle. These external economies definitely characterise the two Italian footwear districts and this represents one of the main competitive advantages which prompted the growth of the Italian footwear industry during the 1970s.

TABLE 8

COLLECTIVE EFFICIENCY: A CLASSIFICATION OF EFFECTS

		External economies	*Co-operative effects*
Static	Marche and Brenta	– high availability of free information; – high availability of inputs at competitive prices, at great speed, at low transaction costs; – high division of labour; – collective reputation;	– co-operation with process specialised firms; – co-operation in export consortia, in credit consortia, entrepreneurial associations, etc.;
	Guadalajara and Leon	– high availability of free information; – good availability of inputs at market conditions; – low division of labour; – collective reputation;	– co-operation in export consortia, in credit consortia, entrepreneurial associations, etc.; – co-operation in *agrupamientos* and *empresas integradoras*; – co-operation with buyers;
Dynamic	Marche and Brenta	– demonstration effects on attitudes and motivations; – high collective learning;	– strong co-opertion with suppliers of raw materials, components, machinery; – co-operation with process specialised firms; – rare co-operation in export consortia, credit consortia, entrepreneurial associations, etc.;
	Guadalajara and Leon	– demonstration effects on attitudes and motivations; – low collective learning;	– very little co-operation with suppliers of raw materials, components, machinery; – rare co-operation in export consortia, credit consortia,entrepreneurial associations, etc.; – rare co-operation in *agrupamientos industriales* and *empresas integradoras*; – co-operation with buyers

With regard to the Mexican clusters, the situation is different because the long closure of the domestic market has not encouraged the growth of a competitive industry of suppliers and process specialised firms. Mexican shoe producers in Guadalajara and Leon can therefore buy locally most of the inputs they need and may save on transportation costs, but the lack of competition has greatly reduced advantages in terms of price and service. Moreover as seen before, Mexican shoe firms are usually more vertically integrated and tend to contract out some phases of the production process only when they have excess orders, without any important gains in terms of specialisation. The low degree of division of labour is also partly due to the high transaction costs generated by the lack of a standardised measurement system. From the empirical investigation it appears that the advantages in terms of face-to face contacts, typical of clustering, are partially offset by the high transaction costs deriving from the lack of standardisation. This makes the relationships of shoe producers with suppliers of components and process specialised firms particularly difficult and costly and limits the gains from clustering in Mexico.

Another type of static external economies, typical of industrial districts, is the effect of commercial signalling, in other words the attraction of customers achieved by a large concentration of specialised producers. So, for instance, German buyers know very well that they can find high quality women's shoes in Brenta and they go there to buy. The same is true in Mexico. Guadalajara is the largest market in the country for women's shoes and Leon for men's and children's shoes. This enormously facilitates access to distant markets.

There is a negative side of these external economies too. The 'image' of the district is, in fact, usually rather homogeneous and therefore, for instance, shoe makers from Marche are known for producing a medium-low quality product. This 'image' may have a negative effect on firms trying to differentiate their production towards different segments of market.

Finally, the high local availability of skilled labour is a dynamic external economy of which the firms located in Marche and Brenta and, to some extent, the firms in Leon and Guadalajara take advantage. The accumulation of know-how in people moving from one firm to the other generates a process of collective learning which enhances the system's innovation capability. This typical characteristic of Italian industrial districts is less evident in the Mexican clusters where the availability of skilled labour is more limited. It must be added that some changes may soon also occur in the Italian districts with respect to collective learning as a consequence of the increasing tendency of well-educated young people to seek non-manual jobs, mainly in sectors other than the footwear industry.

Moving to co-operative effects, in Italy explicit co-operative linkages between the shoe producers and their suppliers of raw materials, components and technology have been frequently found in the empirical investigation. Shoe firms and their suppliers often work together to develop new products and the co-operation is based on the self-interest of both parties in maintaining a stable relationship. These co-operative linkages represent an important contribution to the system's capacity for innovation and growth and their effects' can be therefore defined as dynamic. Thanks to those linkages, shoe firms are able to supply a very diversified, quality product in a time-to-market which is shorter when compared with the shoe industry in many other countries.

The links between shoe producers and process-specialised firms are quite frequently characterised by a clear dependence of subcontractors on shoe enterprises which define the payment conditions and can choose another firm if they are not satisfied with the quality or the service. Nevertheless, in some cases there is also some form of co-operation because some shoe firms prefer having a stable relationship with their subcontractors and therefore try to solve incidental problems and supply the needed training and, sometimes even financial or technical help. Moreover, these linkage are facilitated by the low transaction costs within the districts due to the easy face-to-face contacts. The co-operative effects deriving from these linkages can be either static or dynamic.

In Mexico, similar co-operative linkages with process-specialised firms are very rare because shoe firms tend to be highly vertically integrated. Only a few firms have been recently pushed by increasing competition to move towards a higher division of labour and more co-operative linkages. But, this is still an *in fieri* tendency.

Also, the linkages with suppliers are less co-operative than in Italy and can be defined as market relationships, based on a price factor. This means that, thanks to clustering, the Mexican shoe producers can locally buy raw materials, components and machinery but, as opposed to the Italian districts, they rarely co-operate developing these inputs and must buy what is available on the market, at the market terms. The weakness of backward co-operative linkages can be explained by the long closure of the domestic market which has not favoured competition based on product quality, fashion contents and design, either in the shoe market or in the component and accessory market. Only with the recent change in trade policy, namely with the opening-up of the market, have some of the shoe firms and some of their suppliers begun to realise that they belong to a system in which the success of one firm strongly depends on its interactions with other firms. Therefore, relationships are becoming more co-operative and firms are trying to build stable linkages based on a mutual self-interest in improving quality and service.

In Italy, some co-operative linkages have been found among firms which belong to export consortia and in other commercial agreements. Linkages in export consortia may be defined as dynamic if they are aimed at discovering new markets, otherwise they are static. In Mexico, these type of consortia have not been found. Relationships within credit consortia, entrepreneurial associations and other service centers aimed at supporting the footwear industry can be also defined as co-operative linkages. They can be found both in the Italian districts and in the Mexican clusters. All these relationships are characterised by an explicit decision of a selected group of firms to co-operate in areas such as the joint sale of products, dealing with banks or utilising joint services supplied by entrepreneurial associations. Their effects are therefore static, apart from when they involve co-operation for carrying out some joint, innovative projects.

In Mexico, other forms of co-operative agreements are the *agrupamientos industriales* and the *empresas integradoras*. These are two experiences promoted precisely with the aim of favouring the development of co-operation among selected groups of firms. Their effect is more frequently static, as in co-operation between firms which exchange machinery, labour force or orders or buy inputs jointly. They became dynamic when, more rarely, they involve co-operation on innovative projects. Besides, we may add that these forms of co-operation can be also found among groups of firms linked by family ties.

Finally in Mexico, a few cases of linkages have been reported between shoe producers and buyers, based on cooperation to produce good quality products and, sometimes, to introduce innovations on products, processes and organisational forms. However, relationships based on a strong dependence from the shoe producers' viewpoint are also common because they often sell most of their production to only one customer. In Italy, with a few exceptions, buyers do not play a really significant role in commercialisation and tend to have a market relationship with their customers without intervening in the phase of product development and production.

The linkages with non-exclusive agents can also be defined as pure market relationships in both Italy and in Mexico. From the empirical investigation above, it appears, in fact, that the relationship with non-exclusive agents very rarely involve an exchange of information. In most cases they are instead pure market linkages in which agents sell the products of different firms, without a real contribution to the development of new products based on market needs. This represents an important limitation both for the Italian and the Mexican footwear industry which has developed very weak forward linkages with the market and is one of their biggest weak points in the commercial function.

In the Mexican case the reason for this weakness may be found again in the lack of competition, which has made it unnecessary to develop the marketing and commercial function for selling products in the closed market. The reason for the weakness of forward linkages in the Italian districts is more complicated. In this case the reason can be found in the capability of the Italian footwear firms, during the 1970s and the first half of the 1980s, to introduce their products on the international market without the need to develop a commercial and marketing function. Before the advent of the international competitors like Brazil, Spain or Portugal, Italian shoes were in fact bought for their quality and fashion content and for the service supplied in terms of speed, variety of products and flexibility. This characteristic of the market has favoured the development of districts that are highly developed on the production side but weak in commerical and marketing functions. Since the mid-1980s, the increasing competition in the international market, due to the 'arrival' of new products mainly from newly-industrialising countries, has generated some difficulties in the two footwear industrial districts analysed, as well as in many other Italian areas specialising in footwear. The number of firms has begun to decrease, the exports continuous growth has slowed and the domestic market has been invaded by imported shoes competing with the Italian products. As a result of these changes, the need for developing a marketing function has become clear to an increasing number of firms which have reacted to these changes in several ways, influencing the basic structure of the industrial districts [*Camagni and Rabellotti, 1995*].

Some conclusions about the degree of collective efficiency in the four cases analysed can be drawn from Table 8. These are in comparative districts in Italy and clusters in Mexico to assess the adherence of the realities analysed to the textbook model. Therefore, on the basis of the classification suggested, the main conclusions are the following:

(1) external economies emerge both in Italy and in Mexico. However, there are some main differences concerning the availability of inputs, the degree of labour division and the availability of skilled labour. In all these cases, the production of external economies is higher in the Italian districts than in the Mexican clusters;

(2) co-operative effects are definitely more common among the Italian firms than the Mexican ones. The main differences are in the relationships with suppliers and process-specialised firms which are based on co-operation in Italy and mostly on market rules in Mexico.

From what it has been said so far, we may conclude that the degree of collective efficiency to which external economies and co-operative effects contribute is higher in the Italian districts than in the Mexican clusters where firms can exploit fewer clustering advantages. Some further considerations about this conclusion are drawn in the final section.

V. THE REALITY COMPARED WITH THE 'TEXTBOOK' MODEL

From the results of the empirical investigations in the two Italian districts and in the two Mexican clusters we can derive an important confirmation about the importance of collective efficiency. The analysis of the collective effects deriving from the linkages among the economic actors within the Italian districts and the Mexican clusters has in fact confirmed the existence of a certain degree of collective efficiency.[5] Nevertheless, although collective efficiency matters both in Italy and Mexico, the empirical investigation has clearly highlighted some important differences concerning the intensity and quality of collective effects between the realities studied and the ideal-type of district.

The first important difference is the absence of well developed forward linkags in both Italy and in Mexico, compared with well developed backward linkages in the Italian districts. Moreover, in the Mexican clusters the intensity and the quality of the linkages with suppliers and with process-specialised firms is definitely lower than in Italy. Concerning external economies, they are important in the Italian districts and in the Mexican clusters, but some economies do not really favour the level of efficiency and the growth rate, but rather allow the survival of some of the firms. In Mexico, the low availability of skilled labour generates a weaker effect of collective learning than in Italy. The general conclusion which can be drawn is that different degrees of collective efficiency exist in the cases analysed. In Italy, collective efficiency is high but not as high as in the ideal-type. In Mexico it is even lower than in Italy.

The differences in the degree of collective efficiency between the Italian districts and the Mexican clusters may in part be explained by the existence of differences in external conditions. The most evident difference is trade policy. In Italy the existence of a competitive market has favoured the development of a highly efficient system of production, based on a high degree of division of labour among specialised enterprises and intense co-operative linkages with suppliers. In Mexico the long closure of the domestic market to international competition has induced the development of vertically integrated firms linked to their suppliers through pure market linkages. The important lesson which can be drawn, concerns the opportunity to carefully take into consideration differences in external conditions when the 'model' is used as a reference point for analyses in different contexts.

It must also be stressed that Mexican firms have recently tried to re-establish and improve their relationships with suppliers, in response to increasing competition, on a more collaborative basis. The same is true for forward linkages in Italy and in Mexico. A few firms are trying to develop a new marketing strategy and new links with the market to face their commercial weakness. A similar process of change in the quality of relationships was stressed in a study on the footwear industry in the Sinos Valley in Brazil [*Schmitz, 1993*].

This issue introduces the question of how the systems react to changes in external conditions and the possibility that differences between districts can be explained by the existence of different stages and paths in the development of clusters. The question of the innovative capacity of clusters to react to external changes transforming their internal organisation is central. The static 'industrial district' model does not take into account the possibility that an external radical change, like the change in the competitive position in the cases analysed, may represent a sign of rupture in the evolutionary path of the districts and may eventually result in a new organisational form, distinct from the original one, and possibly remote from the tradition and the archetype of the model.

In another paper [*Campagni and Rabellotti, 1995*], we tried to identify some typologies of changes and trajectories of evolution of the districts, based on the recent Italian footwear experience. The reaction of the Italian districts hit by increasing international competition to this radical change has not been homogeneous within the systems, but some leading firms have begun to face competition by developing aggressive marketing strategies, for which they have sought some complementary resources outside the districts. The impact of these new strategies on the structure of the districts is a tendency towards hierarchisation of the leading firms, which on one side organise the activities of a number of subcontracting firms within the districts and on the other interact strategically with other economic actors on the outside. To capture the realities of the Italian footwear districts it would be worthwhile to study how the structures of the systems evolve from one stage to the other, along their trajectory of development, as a reaction to external events. This involves explaining different ways the economic actors face change within the districts.

Similarly, in Mexico with the opening up of the market to international competition, a few leading firms have begun to change their relationships with suppliers and buyers, trying to set up cooperation linkages aimed at improving the product quality, fashion content, design and service. Some attempts to increase the division of labour among process-specialised firms have been also registered in the two clusters studied. Therefore, in the Mexican clusters as well, it is necessary to understand the evolution of the system, generated by a change in the trade policy, and led by the actions of some economic actors.

What is common among all the experiences analysed is the replacement of generic incidental relationships by strategic alliances with selected partners, aimed at providing specific complementary resources, in other words, an upgrading of linkages. The new partners tend to be located in the districts but some are outside because the districts have not sufficiently developed their commercial side. All of them continue to gain from the cluster's advantages but are also able to overcome the limitations of the districts, networking with the outside world.

To conclude, a more general indication for future research can be derived. The comparison of different clusters at a given point in time is an exercise which has severe limitations. A more fruitful exercise should appropriately compare trajectories of development, searching for common patterns in these trajectories. Are the trajectories of development of LDC clusters characterised by some common patterns? Do these patterns differ from those which characterise districts in developed countries? These are all questions for further research.

NOTES

1. The choice to include only members of the Associations is justified by the focus of our inquiry on the different forms of explicit and implicit co-operation among firms. We assume that firms taking part in the Associations are more likely than others to entertain relationships with other firms. Becoming a member of the Associations may in fact be interpreted as a sign of interest in getting in touch with other firms.
2. For a more detailed presentation of background information on the footwear Italian industry see Rabellotti [*1995b*].
3. There is recent project (1993) for the establishment, with the collaboration of the centre in Leon, of an institution like CIATEG in Guadalajara.
4. This is an important result of the correspondence analysis presented in Rabellotti [*1995a*].
5. This result is also confirmed by factor and correspondence analyses presented in Rabellotti [*1995a*].

REFERENCES

ANCI (1994) 'L'industria calzaturiera Italiana', Milan: ANCI, mimeo.
Boston Consulting Group (1988): 'Industria del Calzado', Mexico City, mimeo.
Brusco, S. (1989): 'A Policy for Industrial Districts', in Goodman E. and Bamford J. (eds.), *Small Firms and Industrial Districts in Italy*, London: Routledge, pp.259–69.
Brusco S. (1992): 'Small Firms and the Provision of Real Services', in F. Pyke and W. Sengenberger (eds.), *Industrial Districts and Local Economic Regeneration*, Geneva: International Institute for Labour Studies, pp.177–96.
Camagni R. and R. Rabellotti (1995): 'Alcune riflessioni sulla dinamica dei *milieux* calzaturieri in Italia', in Gorla G. and O.Vito Colonna (eds.), *Regioni e sviluppo: modelli, politiche e riforme*, Franco Angeli, Milan (presented in English at the V GREMI Meeting, Grenoble, 10–1-June 1994).
CANAICAL (1993): 'Perfil de la Industria del Calzado', Camaras de la Industria del Calzado, Mexico City, mimeo.
CONCALZADO (1991): 'Perfil de la Industriadel Calzado', *Calzavance*, Sept.
Cornes, R., and (1986): *The theory of Externalities, Public Goods and Club Goods*. Cambridge: Cambridge. University Press
Dominguez-Villalobos, L. and F. Grossman (1992): 'Employment and Income Effects of Structural and Technological Changes in Footwear Manufacturing in Mexico', *Workings Paper*, World Employment Programme Research, No.224, Geneva: International Labour Office.
Gaibisso, A.M. (ed.) (1992): *Struttura e competitività del settore calzaturiero in Italia*, Milan: Franco Angeli.
Rabellotti, R. (1995a): 'External Economies and Cooperation in Industrial Districts: A Comparison of Italy and Mexico', Institute of Development Studies, unpublished D.Phil. thesis, University of Sussex, Brighton.
Rabellotti R. (1995b): 'Is There an "Industrial District Model"? Footwear Districts in Italy and Mexico Compared', *World Development*, Vol.23, No.1, Jan. pp.29–2.
Rasmussen, J., Schmitz, H. and M.P. van Dijk (eds.) (1992): 'Flexible Specialisation: A New View on Small Industry?', *IDS Bulletin*, Vol.23, No.3, July, pp.64–8.
Schmitz, H. (1989): 'Flexible Specialisation – A New Paradigm of Small Scale Industrialisa-

tion?', *IDS Discussion* Paper, No.261 May Institute of Development Studies, University of Sussex, Brighton.

Schmitz, H. (1992): 'On the Clustering of Small Firms', *IDS Bulletin*, Vol.23, No.3, July. pp.64–8.

Schmitz H. (1993): 'Small Shoemakers and Fordist Giants: Tale of a Supercluster', *IDS Discussion Paper*, No.331, Sept., Institute of Development Studies, University of Sussex, Brighton.

Schmitz H. (1994): 'Collective Efficiency: Growth Path for Small-Scale Industry', Final Report to ODA, Feb., Brighton, mimeo.

Schmitz H. and B. Musyck (1993): 'Industrial Districts in Europe: Policy Lessons for Developing Countries?', *IDS Discussion Paper*, No.324, April, Institute of Development Studies, University of Sussex, Brighton.

Varaldo R., (ed.) (1988): *Il sistema delle imprese calzaturiere*, Florence: Giappichelli.

4

The Significance of Spatial Clustering: External Economies in the Peruvian Small-Scale Clothing Industry

EVERT-JAN VISSER

I. INTRODUCTION

The significance of spatial clustering for the performance of small industrial firms is subject to wide debate. A major theoretical argument relates to one feature of so-called industrial districts in industrialised countries. It stresses the potential for inter-firm division of labour and vertical specialisation of individual firms [*Sengenberger, et al., 1990; Nadvi and Schmitz, 1994*]. This enables firms to subcontract each others' services in order to lower costs, improve the quality of their products, and enhance their flexibility and innovativeness *vis-à-vis* volatile consumer markets. This argument will be reviewed and empirically tested in a case study of a spatial cluster of small clothing firms in Lima, Peru.

Firms located in the cluster perform better than those in other parts of the city. This is true for every size category. Moreover, larger firms within the cluster do not perform significantly better than small and micro firms, whereas in other parts of Lima, size does improve performance. These results suggest that external economies are important for firms in the cluster. However, the empirical evidence does not allow straight extensions of the industrial district model. Yet, the cluster subject to examination represents a 'hot' location in the Peruvian clothing industry. This chapter presents an alternative explanation for the relatively good sales performance of firms in the cluster area.

II. WHY CLUSTERING MATTERS: SOME THEORETICAL NOTES

The importance of processes of spatial clustering of small industrial firms should be stated in terms of their *competitiveness*. Competitiveness may be

The author is indebted to 103 clothing producers in Lima, who decided to trust him and provide him with the required information, as well as to Jan G. Lambooy, Bart Nooteboom, José I. Távara, Roger Teszler, and Indra Wahab, who all revised an earlier version of this chapter. Any errors and omissions are the author's.

defined as the capacity of a firm to survive, gain, maintain, and expand its market share on product markets which, in turn, depends on the price, the technical quality, and the 'market-fit'[1] of products on the one hand, and a firm's capacity to anticipate future developments in both markets, products and technologies on the other. A theoretical argument relating the widely observed phenomenon of spatial clustering of small firms in developing countries and their competitiveness thus entails the following elements:

(1) the productivity of inputs and services;
(2) the quality of materials and machines, as well as labour skills;
(3) the prices paid for inputs and services;
(4) technological upgrading;
(5) the adequate provision of information on consumer markets, products, inputs and technology; and
(6) cognitive capabilities.

We are concerned with *small-scale industrial enterprises* (SSIEs). They are characterised by a relatively small scale and limited scope, a relatively high degree of vertical specialisation and short-term experience, while their perception of the outside world tends to be dominated by one person, the owner-entrepreneur. Worded differently, SSIEs tend to face diseconomies of scale, scope, sequence, experience, as well as cognitive capability (Spulber [*1993*] and Nooteboom [*1993*]; see also Appendix 1). This is assumed to be detrimental to the competitiveness of SSIEs.

Two remarks can now be made. First, the above theoretical statement relates to a partial view of the firm; it only takes into account the internal resources at the disposal of a firm. Strategic responses and compensatory behaviour are not being considered. Second, the above view focuses on relatively isolated and dispersed firms. Given the extent to which these firms compensate for disadvantages through interaction with other agents (firms, traders, or other organisations), focusing minutely on an analysis of the performance of individual firms is less appropriate. Instead, when dealing with the relation between firm size and competitiveness, inter-firm linkages become a complementary unit of analysis [*Schmitz, 1990*].

For these reasons, current research on the performance of SSIEs in developing countries focuses on *the relation between the firm and its environment* [*Nadvi and Schmitz, 1994*]. In this area it is useful to distinguish between the functional, institutional, territorial and macro-economic dimensions of the environment of a firm. Asheim [*1994: 93*] mentions a functional and territorial dimension only. In view of current conceptual needs I prefer to also distinguish an institutional dimension. The macroeconomic dimension of the environment has also been added, as it influences the decisions of economic agents. Still, due to our focus on firm-level data, macroeconomics play a passive role. Finally, it must be noted that the territorial dimension is a non-exclusive category. It refers to local variations in the resources of a firm, the possibility to develop functional relations, and, above all, the institutional environment.

The term 'functional' refers to the transformation and transaction functions that agents fulfil with respect to physical attributes and property rights, of goods and services [*North and Wallis, 1994: 612*]. Hence, the functional environment of a firm relates to the extent to which the firm stands alone in the planning and realisation of its part in the process of value creation. The crucial feature of functional linkages is that the economic performance of one firm depends upon the activities of others. They thus become functionally interdependent. Examples are:

(1) a network of firms based upon vertical specialisation in one or a few steps in the transformation process and the mutual subcontracting of trans-formation services due to labour, capital, and knowledge intensity. Inter-firm division of labour is at stake here, augmenting the number of subsequent linkages between suppliers and users of intermediate inputs at the level of a certain branch of industry, involving vertical co-operation between users and producers of the intermediate goods;

(2) inter-industry linkages, with agents providing business services, equip-ment and components;

(3) horizontal co-operation between otherwise, competing firms involved in the transformation of products. This co-operation may remain either in this sphere (for example, joint subcontracting), or aim at up- or down-stream transaction relations with traders of final products and inputs (for example, joint purchasing or marketing of products); and

(4) upstream and downstream transactions with traders of final products and inputs, whereby producers may adjust their planning according to market information provided by the traders.

In the above settings, *transaction costs* are relevant, due to the incomplete information about present and future events and the subsequent uncertainty about the nature of goods and services. The concepts of 'adverse selection' and 'moral hazard' describe the associated risks. There is a need to formulate, update and modify verbal agreements or written contracts. Transaction costs are the costs of selecting and screening business partners, determining the contents of a functional relation, and 'writing, monitoring, and enforcing con-tracts, sequential bargaining over the distribution of benefit associated with sunk investments, and so on' [*Joskow, 1991: 118–19*].

Institutions are designed to reduce uncertainty and mitigate transaction costs.[2] They are defined by North as 'the humanly devised constraints that shape human interaction' [*1990: 3*]. The institutional environment consists of those devises that limit the risks of adverse selection and moral hazard, and hence facilitates the development of functional relations between agents. Subsequently, the territorial dimension of the environment of firms draws attention to the above elements at a specific location. Hence, the functional relations between agents and their institutional environment are considered in a certain region, city, neighbourhood, or other spatial entity, for example a spatial cluster of SSIEs. Location is characterised in terms of:

(1) the *density* of economic activity: the relative concentration of similar and/or dissimilar firms;

(2) the spatial *proximity* (or nearness) of actors; and

(3) its *history*, in a socio-cultural, institutional, infrastructural, and above all dynamic sense (for example, learning processes).

These factors mould territorially-specific conditions which add to macro-economic parameters in their quality of factors influencing the decisions and strategies of economic actors. This may result in local institutional change, which in turn, could mediate the development of new or different kinds of functional relations. In conclusion, not only the conduct of economic actors may be spatially differentiated, but also the degree of functional inter-dependence between agents.

An example clarifies these remarks. Marshall [*1964: 225*] argued that the historical presence of an industry in a neighbourhood enhances the quality of local entrepreneurship and labour skills. Furthermore, a relatively high density of similar activities in the area translates into a relatively large local demand for certain goods and services, increasing their supply. These two factors modify the local setting in which firms make decisions, for example whether to 'make or buy'. Firms may prefer to buy, considering the quality of local services, about which adequate information is available, for example in the form of favourable reputations of suppliers. In such an environment, the inter-firm division of labour progresses. This may result in personal trust being replaced by process-based trust, attracting new firms to outsource transformation functions. However, trust may more easily be built up in one place than in another, depending on local standards, norms, values, spatial proximity, and other factors. Therefore, the transaction costs related to maintaining interfirm linkages *vis-à-vis* internal labour relations will be spatially differentiated, resulting in different degrees of vertical specialisation.

The central argument in this section is that SSIEs compensate for dis-economies of scale, scope, sequence, experience and cognitive scope with flexibility in behaviour. SSIEs are sensitive to opportunities offered in their environment, and may develop functional relations of the earlier mentioned types, whereby the macroeconomic environment provides the incentives and limits are set by the availability of institutions to guide inter-firm linkages. SSIEs are able to enhance their competitiveness relatively more from *external economies*. This point is elaborated in the next section.

III. 'EXTERNAL ECONOMIES' IN ECONOMIC LITERATURE: A BRIEF REVIEW

The concept of external economies goes back to Marshall [*1920*], who defined it as cost savings due to the general development of an industry. Later attempts to define the concept led repeatedly to·controversy [*Mishan, 1971: 2, 4–6; Cornes and Sandler, 1986: 29*]. Therefore, the meaning we attribute to this concept should be clarified here. Our starting point is Scitovsky [*1954*], who discussed the existence of two concepts of external economies. The first is derived from the general equilibrium theory which deals with Pareto-optimality in competitive markets. The second appears in theories about industrialisation in developing countries.

In general equilibrium theory, the term 'externality' is used to describe the reaction of a firm's output or someone's consumption to the activities of other agents via the generation of effects that are *not* intermediated by the market [*Mishan, 1971*]. Only *direct* effects enter the concept, or 'real' effects in the sense that they have technological consequences. Hence, external effects influence the productivity of firms. They come free of charge and occur incidentally. Furthermore, they are unplanned, and apparently, have general consequences. They cannot be 'pecuniary' in the sense of inducing changes in profits, because that is not relevant to the issue of Pareto-efficiency. All that matters is the difference between social and private costs.

In theories about industrialisation in developing countries, on the other hand, external economies are 'invoked whenever the profits of one producer are affected by the actions of other producers', either through direct *or* through indirect relations [*Scitovsky, 1954: 146*]. External economies that are due to interdependence through the market mechanism are said to be 'pecuniary'. Consequently, they are more prevalent than 'real' effects. This explains why, according to Scitovsky, 'one gains the impression from the literature on under-developed countries that the entrepreneur creates external economies and dis-economies with his every move' [*ibid.*].

Marshallian external economies are direct and indirect with respect to market-intermediation. On one hand, they are direct, for example in case of a local milieu enhancing the quality of human resources. As Marshall put it: 'great are the advantages which people following the same skilled trade get from near neighbourhood to one another. The mysteries of trade become no mysteries: but are as it were in the air, and children learn many of them unconsciously' [*Marshall, 1964: 225*]. So, tradition and near neighbourhood enhance the quality of human resources. The quality of business and of productive services may similarly be improved.

The effects that Marshall described for the generation and diffusion of innovations may also be indirect. In a spatial cluster, 'good work is rightly appreciated, inventions and improvements in machinery, in processes and the general organisation of the business have their merits promptly discussed: if one man starts a new idea, it is taken up by others and combined with suggestions of their own: and thus it becomes a source of further new ideas' [*ibid.*]. If communication takes place verbally, the advice is either sold, and thus a market relation is reached, or advice may be transferred without a charge in a setting of reciprocal relations. Both imply indirect effects. Note, however, that the exchange of information may also take place through one-sided observation by one individual. Then, direct effects are at stake, since no relation carries the influence.

Another example of indirect effects is the enhanced supply of specialised services. The argument is as follows. Spatial clustering of similar firms implies a local concentration of the demand for specific services, thus provoking specialisation in the provision of the latter, based upon internal economies of scale and scope in production and marketing [*ibid.: 220–21*]. Thus, increasing the density of economic activity at a certain location enhances a downward shift of the supply of goods and services as a consequence of the sum of market transactions at the meso-level. An individual firm then benefits from the locally improved supply conditions.

Suppose, however, that vertical specialisation is on its way, and firms subcontract productive services to one another. The emerging inter-firm linkages may then either be coordinated by the price mechanism (in which case market transactions occur) or by trust[3] (in the setting of co-operative relations; Knorringa [*1994*]. The latter type of relation serves as a platform to induce, purposefully, additional external effects. In such a context the indirect, external effects may become strategic, planned and specific in the sense of accruing to some trading parties.

In conclusion, Marshallian external economies are partly direct and partly indirect. In fact, this distinction becomes blurred on the one hand and is limited on the other, as 'indirect' relations traditionally refer to price-regulated transactions between firms, excluding the possibility of coordination based upon trust. Moreover, there is no unambiguous relation with the distinctions between strategic and incidental, planned and unplanned, and specific and general effects. Marshallian external effects often are positive in nature, whereas they seem to be both 'real' and 'pecuniary'.[4] In so far as indirect effects emerge in non-market relations, they are specific to some economic actors, for example, firms involved in a vertically disintegrated production system, or in diagonal relations with agents supplying business services.

For these reasons, I adopt a definition of external economies that incorporates both direct and indirect effects. Moreover, the process of value creation is considered along the production chain, while the point of view of the individual firm is adopted. An external effect may then be defined as a change in the cost–benefit relation of activities of producers and traders, due to the activities of other producers and traders. External effects occur (or are purposefully generated) in a setting of functional relations between economic actors. Therefore, institutions matter in so far as they are related to and lower transaction costs associated with inter-firm linkages. So, external economies encompass not only the costs of the transformation of inputs, but also transaction costs.

Through time, institutional developments may facilitate new ways of production and exchange. So, while in a *static* perspective external effects boil down to changes in the multiple aspects of the cost–benefit relation (the productivity, price, and quality of the factors of production, the costs of organising and transacting, as well as the quality and market-fit of the final product), from a *dynamic* point of view, they relate to improved innovative capabilities of economic actors. The latter induce changes in one or more of the above elements of the cost–benefit relation.

Examples of static external economies are lower costs per unit of product, improved quality of (intermediate) inputs, shorter delivery times (or the time needed to launch new products), and enhanced availability of technical, product or market information. Examples of dynamic external effects are the development of labour skills, increasing knowledge about markets and technology, and technological progress (through specialisation on one hand, and cross-firm learning[5] on the other hand). Evidently, these effects do not occur simultaneously and only to some extent, depending on the maturity and nature of interfirm linkages.

IV. THE TERRITORIAL DIMENSION OF THE ENVIRONMENT OF FIRMS

In the above perspective on economic life, functional linkages between economic actors involve transaction costs, which are to be mitigated by institutions. Transaction costs arise in market transactions as well as in relational contracting [*Williamson, 1985*]. In this context the territorial dimension of the environment of firms is closely related to:

(1) the search for, and matching of products (in the setting of a spot market); and

(2) the screening, selection, and monitoring of business partners, as well as enforcement of contracts (in the setting of relational contracting).

The costs of search and matching refer to the costs of using the market [*Coase, 1991: 22*]. They are relevant under market conditions, and involve transportation costs (for example, time loss and financial expenses), as well as the costs of gathering information. In general, a producer first needs information about consumer preferences in product markets and the specific demands of market channels in order to derive the required product characteristics. Then, information is needed about the types, the availability and the quality of inputs, production techniques, equipment, components, and productive and/or business services (in so far as they are used).

An increasing density of similar economic activities clearly reduces the above two types of transportation costs described above. Correspondent cost savings do not only accrue to producers, but also to the traders of inputs, equipment and output (wholesalers as well as retailers); to firms supplying business services to producers; as well as to the final consumers (in so far as these purchase products directly from producers in a cluster).

Furthermore, spatial proximity facilitates the gathering of information. Personal contacts are likely to be more frequent due to the stochastic nature of 'density'. Besides, local norms and values may stimulate the circulation of more delicate information, resulting in the diffusion of information without any transaction taking place. In so far as information flows about markets, products, and inputs are territorially constrained and result in more complete information at relatively low costs, the capacity to compete in product markets will clearly be enhanced.

In the second setting in which transaction costs arise, namely in relational contracting, the activities of search and matching, in fact, applies to people, and hence we refer to screening, selection, monitoring and enforcement costs.[6] These in turn imply, again, transportation costs, but information costs become especially important. Nearness helps to reduce pecuniary transportation costs and time losses, and, potentially, information costs. In so far as the latter costs are locally constrained, the demand for functional relations may rise, which, in turn, enhances the potential to reap external economies.

For the latter effect to become relevant, nearness would have to enhance reputation-effects. In this regard, Dei Ottati [*1994*] argues that investments in reputation are facilitated in environments where repeated transactions occur with the same agents. The agent's behaviour may be observed and default can be punished. These conditions are better met in a spatial cluster of similar firms, where agents do not only abide permanently, but also have face-to-face contacts. Then, the need for information may also diminish, as this is inversely related to trust. At first, trust may be specific to a certain trading party, but after a while a good reputation is established among other people in the neighbourhood, and even more so in a context of spatial clustering where the above conditions are met. Of course, there have to be incentives for trust-building. This depends upon the strategies of firms to enhance competitiveness, and on their subsequent decisions on whether to internalise ('make') or externalise ('buy') one or more phases of production. Macroeconomic conditions play an important part in this respect.

In conclusion, the first role of the territorial dimension of the environment is the reduction of uncertainty and transaction costs. In this respect, territorial issues complement or strengthen the institutional environment. Note that uncertainty plays its part in price-coordinated market transactions as well as in backward and forward linkages of a co-operative nature, both at the level of the transformation process in a specific industry and beyond, in upstream and downstream relations. The territorial environment of firms thus may alter the demand for goods, services, and specific types of eternal linkages.

Other conditions however, for example those related to the macro-economic dimension of the environment, determine the extent to which this potential is exploited. For instance, protectionist policies help firms to maintain market shares and to raise profits, providing minimal incentives to achieve the same objectives through functional relations with specialised sub-contractors.

The second role of the territorial environment is supply-related. This is connected with the Marshallian argument that the local concentration of similar firms, with their combined demand for various goods and services, enables some firms to exploit economies of scale and scope, both in the production and in marketing. Hence, the supply of these goods and services will be enhanced.[7] Additionally, in combination with more complete information on the demand side and fierce horizontal competition on the supply side, a downward movement of prices may be induced locally.

Finally, in so far as the above territorially-constrained external economies mutually interact for a wide range of agents operating at subsequent levels of the value chain, a specific site may become highly commercial ('hot'). This is all the more true with respect to SSIEs, whose transactions are (increasingly) small in scale, varied in content, and changing in time,[8] which raises even more the unitary costs of transacting goods and services.

The above theoretical framework for dealing with the significance of a process of spatial clustering of small firms offers various advantages. It shows that, in principle, the generation of external economies is relevant for *all* SSIEs, not only for those operating in spatial clusters. The distinction between the functional, institutional and territorial dimensions of the environment facilitates a comparison between firms maintaining functional relations outside the sphere of spatial proximity and those operating in a cluster.

Next, this framework clearly identifies one source of external economies, namely the territorial conditions related to the location of a firm. We differentiate between a high density of similar or dissimilar activities, provoking a local concentration of the demand for different products (for example, final products, enhancing the importance of the reputation of a location to the outside world); spatial proximity between economic actors; and a territorially specific history that brings along specific institutions, such as established personal reputations, information flows, quality standards and so on. These territorial conditions reinforce the generation of external economies through supply and demand effects.[9] Put differently, external economies may be territorially constrained and enhance, only locally, the competitiveness of SSIEs.

V. EMPIRICAL EVIDENCE OF THE EFFECTS OF CLUSTERING

In this section, the performance of clothing firms that are spatially clustered in a neighbourhood close to the centre of Lima will be compared to the performance of firms operating elsewhere in the city (the control group). The question to be answered is: to which extent a possible difference in gross sales can be explained by territorially bound external economies? Another question may also be raised: to what extent do 'transportation and information costs constrain the geographical availability of external economies' [*Phelps, 1992: 43–4*]? Special attention will be paid to the incidence and deepness of vertical division of labour between firms, to the importance of subcontracting at subsequent steps in the production process (and corresponding transfers of resources of several types), and to the extent to which forms of *horizontal co-operation* have developed between otherwise competing firms, as these are crucial features of the so-called 'industrial districts' of SSIEs in industrialised countries.

Small-scale clothing in Lima is concentrated in a neighbourhood locally known as 'Gamarra', named after the street where, until two decades ago, people used to live a quiet life. Today, however, the area is flooded with clothing producers, traders of inputs, equipment and final products, and even local consumers. They take the trouble of climbing the stairs to the tenth floor of one of the 133 buildings which has been constructed in this highly commercial area of Lima.[10] Indicative of the area's attractiveness to traders and producers is the fact that, in August of 1994, the ground floor of the latest building was sold at $4,000 to 5,000 per square metre.

The clothing cluster consists of, approximately, 60 blocks [*Ponce, 1994: 5*]. However, only about 35 of these are effectively used by producers and traders. The cluster seems to be expanding steadily, through street vendors invading formerly quiet parts of the area. According to one estimate, the cluster lodges some 6,800 businesses, among which 50 are medium scale and 1,950 are micro and small clothing firms, about 4,100 trading firms selling inputs or final products, 300 are (street) restaurants, and 150 are trading companies selling equipment and accessories [*Ponce, 1994*].

In February 1994, a survey was carried out to assess some basic characteristics of the clothing firms in the cluster and to consider these characteristics in a comparative perspective. The sample frame comprised clothing firms with less than 100 workers in the metropole of Lima, and which had once registered at the Ministry of Industry. The sample frame was subdivided by district.[11] As the clothing cluster is located in the 'La Victoria'-district, this area was immediately selected for further study. With respect to the relatively dispersed firms, a distinction was made between high-income and low-income areas. For practical reasons, two-stage sampling was used to select three areas from the low-income group.[12] The total size of the sample was 130 firms, the overall response rate being 79 per cent. In the following analysis of the data, the results of the survey of the cluster in its strict sense (see the definition above) have been separated from those for the rest of 'La Victoria'. In fact, the former category contains 24 cases, while the latter category comprises 17 cases. The last mentioned category has been labelled 'La Victoria (OG)' (acronym for La Victoria, *O*utside *G*amarra).

First, firms in the cluster are *large* in terms of the number of workers, compared to clothing firms elsewhere in Lima, except for those operating in high-income areas (see Table 1).

TABLE 1

SIZE OF FIRMS BY STRATUM (IN TERMS OF THE NUMBER OF WORKERS, INCLUDING THE ENTREPRENEUR)

stratum	mean	S.D.	F-test	Prob. value
High-income areas	16.2	23.9	2.67	0.052
Gamarra	10.4	16.4		
La Victoria (OG)	5.8	5.2		
Low-income areas	6.2	4.4		

Source: survey February/March 1994.

Note: standard deviations are large, especially for the high-income group and the Gamarra-cluster. This indicates that differentiation of firms within the different strata is important and should be dealt with. In high-income areas, five firms employed more than 20 workers in 1993, whereas in the cluster two firms employed more than 20 people.

Second, firms in the cluster typically have two establishments: a workshop and a sales outlet (in a building or out on the street). While they are thus typically integrated into the wholesaling and retailing of their products, the opposite is true for their colleagues in other parts of the city of Lima, who occasionally have their own sales outlet.[13]

Third, average monthly sales per worker in 1993 were significantly higher for firms in the cluster (Table 2). This indicator of the performance of firms is influenced by two factors: production volumes and sales prices. If the relatively high gross sales of firms in the cluster area are the result of a relatively large production volume, there are still two possible explanations:

(a) these firms achieve a relatively high level of productivity; and/or
(b) working days in these firms are longer; and/or
(c) production is being subcontracted.[14]

Obviously, the first option would fuel speculations about the relevance of internal economies of scale (through specialisation of labour and/or indivisibilities of certain investments) and/or external economies of experience. A better sales record may also be due to a price effect, hence another three factors may play a part:

(d) the quality of goods produced in Gamarra may be relatively high compared to similar products made in for example low-income areas;
(e) the downward pressures on turnover are lower because there is less need to offer discounts, due to the concentrated demand for garments in the cluster area; and
(f) standard profit margins are higher.

TABLE 2

AVERAGE MONTHLY SALES PER WORKER IN 1993, BY STRATUM
(IN US-DOLLARS)

stratum	mean	S.D.	F-test	Prob-value
High-income areas	510	354	5.94	0.0009
Gamarra	1,148	852		
La Victoria (OG)	380	346		
Low-income areas	660	777		

Source: survey February/March 1994.
Note: the data refer to gross sales, including sales of products that have been partly made by subcontracted firms. Second, the data have been adjusted for the length of the working day. This has been done only to some extent however. If one, a few, or all people work part of what an entrepreneur considers to be a working day, a correction has been applied. However, the perception of the length of a working day may differ across the strata, generating an additional difference in total labour time among the groups. This has not been captured yet.

The question is *which* of the above factors do contribute to an explanation of the good sales record of firms in the cluster area. As SSIEs normally do not keep books, the collection of data on costs, working hours and hence productivity is difficult. Non-sampling measurement errors are reported to be high, due to recall and other problems [*Liedholm, 1992*]. Second, more detailed data on the marketing process (the number of items sold, sale prices per type and size of product, and discounts) have not been collected, due to the above reasons, and because of the time intensiveness of finding answers to the relevant questions.

Note, however, that firms in the cluster typically assume the functions of transforming inputs and transacting output, not only in wholesaling and retailing, but also in sales to final consumers. This explains part of the size difference between firms in the cluster and those located elsewhere. Hence, a relatively large firm size in Gamarra does not automatically imply a relatively large scale of production and consequent scale-effects (based upon specialisation and/or indivisibilities of investment.[15] On the other hand, internal economies of scale may also be due to product specialisation. The finding that 65 per cent of the firms in the cluster specialise in one product suggests that they may be in a better position to refine the division of labour *within* the firm and pick the fruits of consequent specialisation of workers, especially economies of scale.

A second way to enhance the productivity per worker is through experience. The data indicate that 62 per cent of firms in Gamarra started before 1985, against 46 per cent for the sample as a whole. While this may generate internal effects of experience, the fact that an industry has a long history at a particular location may generate effects of experience that are external to a firm. Such effects are territorially defined and positively affect the quality of labour and entrepreneurship, hence possibly raising productivity [*Marshall, 1964*].[16]

With respect to the other elements which may contribute to an explanation of the good sales record of firms in the cluster area, short remarks are made here. First, part of the working day effect has been taken into account. Second, information about the quality of products sold in Gamarra or the relevance of discounts is missing. Furthermore, margins are not likely to be larger in the Gamarra cluster as its reputation is based exactly upon low sale prices. Finally, outcontracting and subcontracting cannot explain the gross-sales differential because these practices are rather less common in the cluster (see below).

In conclusion, the relatively good sales record of firms in the cluster seems to be sustained by a higher productivity, (perhaps) a longer working day, and better quality. However, the driving force is external to firms, and relates, for example, to the good trade connections with several regional markets. These external effects of the cluster are territorially specific. Note also that the total effect is considerable for SSIEs. It is equal to the multiplication of the relatively high number of workers with a relatively high value of gross sales per worker.

In the light of the above evidence on the good performance of firms in the cluster, two possible explanations will be dealt with below. The generation of external economies may take place either at the level of the clothing industry (in the transformation process; the following three sections), and/or in upstream and downstream relations (in the transacting process, involving traders of inputs, equipment, and final products, as well as other agents; later sections).

Vertical Inter-firm Linkages at the Level of the Clothing Branch of Industry

Functional linkages between clothing firms may be established in two directions: vertically and horizontally. Data are provided on the degree of vertical division of labour between firms, on entrepreneurial motivations to specialise and subsequently subcontract certain steps in production, and on the corresponding type of transfer of resources (financial, technical, human, physical). Furthermore, the information about concrete forms of horizontal inter-firm co-operation will be discussed briefly.

The development of functional linkages in whatever direction may occur in two different situations: an industrial network which is not spatially bound; and a network of firms that are located in a spatial cluster. The data reveal that vertical division of labour is relatively *under*developed in the cluster. The level (or deepness) of labour division is measured here in terms of the number of phases in the production process that are actually subcontracted by clothing firms (see Table 3). The number of functions which a firm is unable to realise is also considered (see Table 4).

Firms that do not subcontract at all, take care of all steps in the production process (all operations). They are therefore vertically integrated. These firms represent 25 per cent of the sample, and about 20 per cent of the firms in the cluster. This is due to the relatively high proportion of firms in the latter stratum claiming to subcontract *one* operation: 38 per cent (which is the modal value for the cluster). However, as far as the cluster is concerned, the tendency at this point to subcontract weakens. On the other hand, firms in other parts of Lima more often subcontract a relatively large number of operations (see Table 3, the lower parts of the columns).

These data are confirmed by data on the number of operations a firm is *not able* to perform. Clustered firms typically report one function in this respect. On the one hand, they seem to be more aware of an operation they cannot perform (see the first row of Table 4), while on the other hand, only 25 per cent of the firms in the cluster area report being unable to perform *more than one* operation (against 38 per cent of the sample). The latter fact suggests that these firms are relatively well equipped.

These results are *not* consistent with earlier conjectures about the degree of vertical specialisation and the relevance of subcontracting in the Gamarra cluster. The level (deepness) and wide dissemination of this phenomenon has been emphasised [*Villarán, 1993: 178; Ponce, 1994; Nadvi and Schmitz, 1994: 17*]. Of course, the discrepancy may relate to the sample frame we used, which excludes young micro firms that have not yet been registered. These micro firms may be the ones that rely more heavily on external productive services, for example to overcome problems concerning the indivisibility of investments and/or a lack of technical and market knowledge. It may be that the conduct of these micro firms has influenced the conclusions of other authors. A second reason may be that the firms in the cluster render productive services to clothing firms elsewhere in the city. This would explain the numerous signs announcing such services.

TABLE 3

THE SUBCONTRACTING BY CLOTHING FIRMS OF SPECIFIC STEPS IN
THE PRODUCTION PROCESS PER GROUP (IN PER CENT OF COLUMN-TOTALS)

No.	Sample	High-income areas	La Victoria(OG)	Gamarra	Low-income areas
0	25	27	28	21	26
1	22	17	17	38	19
2	20	13	17	21	29
3	14	13	17	8	16
4	6	7	5	8	3
5	6	10	5	4	3
6	4	7	11		0
7	2	3			3
ALL	1	3			
	100%	100%	100%	100%	100%

Source: survey February/March 1994.
Note: the figures have been rounded up (which is the reason why the sum of two columns is not equal to a 100 per cent).

TABLE 4

STAGES IN PRODUCTION THAT CANNOT BE PERFORMED BY THE FIRMS THEM-
SELVES PER GROUP (IN PER CENT OF COLUMN-TOTALS)

No.	Sample	High-income areas	La Victoria(OG)	Gamarra	Low-income areas
0	37	47	39	29	33
1	25	13	6	46	33
2	19	23	17	17	19
3	12	7	17	8	16
4	3	0	17		
5	2	3	6		
6	1	3			
7	1	3			
	100%	100%	100%	100%	100%

Source: survey February/March 1994.
Note: the figures have been rounded up (which is the reason why the sum of three columns is not equal to a 100 per cent).

Anyway, the degree of vertical specialisation and the role of subcontracting in the cluster have been overestimated. The present survey data facilitate a comparison between firms operating in the cluster and those located elsewhere, and justify the conclusion that the spatial clustering of small scale clothing firms has so far not been accompanied by an intensive and extensive vertical division of labour between firms. Subcontracting and specialisation do not seem to be considered as a strategy to enhance competitiveness. This has also been observed by Rabellotti in small-scale footwear production in Mexico [*1994: 9*].

There is more to this. Relatively dispersed firms in high-income areas *consistently* subcontract more activities than the ones they cannot perform in house. This is indicative of a relatively strong tendency towards the development of functional linkages in these areas. One entrepreneur even decided to outsource all productive activities, and to dedicate himself to the coordination of service firms and the subsequent distribution and marketing of final goods. There are several reasons why this would happen in high-income areas more than elsewhere. A first reason could be the type of products made and the market segments served (which seem to be more complicated and more demanding, respectively), while a second reason relates to the need of 'focal' firms to realise production in the shortest time possible. Service firms that are relatively dispersed tend to be more loyal in this respect, due to a shortage of alternative work opportunities (lack of orders, working capital and so on).

Clothing firms in high-income areas may derive more income from selling services to other clothing producers than do clustered firms. However, one should not exaggerate this point. Only two firms in the sample named the sale of services as their main source of income (one of these two is located in a high-income area). A minority of firms (12 per cent) stated that they *supplement* their income in this way. So, for the sample of small-scale clothing in Lima as a whole, full specialisation in a particular phase of production and the provision of services seems to be an exception rather than the rule.

So far no distinction has been made between the *types* of subcontracted operations. Table 5 gives information in this respect. Preparatory operations, such as cutting, are normally realised under the control of the entrepreneur. This stems from risks of an inefficient use of raw materials, lack of technical standards among subcontractors (affecting the quality of the final product), and/or robbery of cloth. None of the firms in the cluster subcontracts a preparatory operation.[17] Firms who do so are mainly located in the low-income stratum.

Concerning assembly activities, 37 per cent of the sample subcontract one or more operations. This figure is much higher in high-income areas (53 per cent) and relatively low in the cluster, where the score is 29 per cent only.[18] Some finishing activities, such as printing, computerised embroidery, washing/dyeing, and buttonholing/fixing are usually subcontracted. Firms in the cluster take the lead. A relatively high proportion of firms subcontracts one finishing activity (42 per cent, compared to 28 per cent for the sample as a whole), and the lowest share of firms indicated never to subcontract such an operation. So, subcontracting by clothing firms in the cluster often involves a finishing operation. Specialisation is relevant at this level of the value chain.

The question is whether these data are indicative of a territorially-enhanced demand for this type of productive services, or whether other variables play a role too. The fact that 65 per cent of the firms in the cluster are product specialised, often in T-shirts or sweaters, may, because of consumer preferences, be increasing the demand for finishing services. Internalisation of the above finishing activities is not attractive for several reasons. First, the demand is diversified and volatile for printing, washing, dyeing and embroidery services. Hence, their production needs to be flexible. Furthermore, the activities are technologically 'strange'[19] and space-intensive (particularly in case of printing and washing and dyeing, which is a problem where rents are high and physical infrastructure fixed). They require substantial amounts of financial capital (this applies above all to washing/dyeing and computerised embroidery, but also to the operations of placing buttons and making buttonholes). For the above reasons, specialisation leads to economies of scale, experience and scope, and is, therefore, attractive.

TABLE 5

IMPORTANCE OF SUBCONTRACTING PER TYPE OF OPERATION AND IMPACT OF SPATIAL CLUSTERING

# of operations	Preparatory		Assembly		Finishing	
	Sample	Cluster	Sample	Cluster	Sample	Cluster
None	90%	100%	63%	71%	37%	29%
One	9%		13%	13%	28%	42%
Two	1%		14%	13%	23%	21%
Three			6%	4%	8%	8%
Four			4%		2%	
Five					2%	
	100%	100%	100%	100%	100%	100%

Source: survey February/March 1994.

No data are available on the supply of finishing services in the cluster as compared with other locations. It is reasonable to assume, however, that the demand for finishing services in the cluster is relatively high as a result of territorial influences. Proximity, as well as the local concentration of demand and information flows about supplies, results in these services being easy to find, in adequate supply, and reasonably priced. This is due to competition, to the fact that prospective clients can easily make price and product comparisons. But above all, this is the result of internal economies for the specialist in the production and marketing of services. Furthermore, the quality of these services may be enhanced through intergenerational learning as well as through information and reputation effects, the latter offering opportunities for enforcement of contracts.

Other evidence of the possible effects of spatial clustering for the supply of and demand for specialised services is the relative prevalence of 'pure' entrepreneurial activity[20] in the cluster. Firms in Gamarra may be better able to coordinate such a business effort. Although they seem to be more animated in this respect than their colleagues in low-income areas, the survey data also show that firms in high-income areas are even *more* active. Assuming, by following the above arguments, that supply constraints may be overcome in the cluster, it seems that the demand for 'pure' entrepreneurial business lags behind (see Table 6).

TABLE 6

PURE ENTREPRENEURIAL ACTIVITY BY GROUP (IN PER CENT OF
GROUP-TOTALS)

	High-income	Gamarra	Low-income	La Victoria/OG
sometimes operates that way	20%	17%	10%	12%
often operates that way	7%	0%	0%	6%
always operates that way	3%	0%	0%	0%

Source: survey February/March 1994.
Note: sometimes = less than 33% is produced in a pure entrepreneurial way; often = more than 33%, but not always; always = 100% of production is realised by full outsourcing of activities.

The provision of business support services may also be subject to territorial influences. Again, the survey data are restricted to the *use* of such services by clothing SSIEs. Firms in the cluster contract maintenance, repair and book-keeping services (including legal advice). None makes use of services related to marketing and new technologies, while training is also notably absent. No clustering effect is observed in the demand for novel services in diagonal relations.

Finally, the external effects of subcontracting linkages have to be assessed. The potential to lower costs, improve quality, cut lead times, and/or generate dynamic effects can be deduced from the *motives* inducing producers to sub-contract. 'Cost reduction' is never mentioned on its own, although it is some-times (in 14 per cent of the cases) mentioned in combination with other motives, such as inadequate technology, insufficient capacity, and/or short delivery times. 'Quality improvement' is also not mentioned on its own. These data confirm the conclusion that subcontracting in small scale clothing in Lima does not appear to be a strategy to reduce costs and/or to enhance quality.[21] Only a few firms form an exception to this rule, but these firms operate in high-income areas and not in the cluster.

Another indicator of the importance of subcontracting due to dexterity and quality is the eagerness of entrepreneurs to use their knowledge about the capabilities and talents of their ex-workers starting up their own clothing busi-ness. Firms in the cluster more often benefit from this by maintaining relations with their ex-workers, even though they are selective in this respect (compared to entrepreneurs elsewhere).[22]

78

Cross-firm transfers of resources accompanying subcontracting linkages are also relevant in the light of the generation of external economies. These transfers seem to be relatively rich when preparatory and making-up activities are subcontracted. In these instances, almost 20 per cent of the firms in the sample provide their subcontractors with three different types of resources: technical assistance, advance payments, and inputs (besides mere instruction), whereas at least 49 per cent provide a subcontractor with one or two of the above resources. However, there seems to be no clustering effect.[23]

Horizontal Linkages at the Level of the Clothing Branch of Industry

External economies may also become relevant in horizontal interfirm linkages characterised by a curious blend of competition and co-operation [*Pyke, 1992: 4*]. Collaboration may be more or less comprehensive in nature, directed towards the settlement of one, a few, or many jointly perceived financial, technical and/or economic problems, and, therefore, often implies a temporal state of affairs.

The available evidence indicates that horizontal co-operation is relatively less frequent among firms in the cluster. Only one firm in Gamarra and nine firms elsewhere report to participating in a group of clothing entrepreneurs to solve one or more problems. The group in the cluster aims at improving the terms of transactions (price, quality, credit) in *upstream* transactions through the joint procurement of cloth inputs. Groups elsewhere in the city mainly emerged in high-income areas. These groups are often oriented to improving the terms of *downstream* linkages through joint marketing of their products.

Of course, horizontal co-operation may also involve just two firms, for example when one contracts another to fulfil an order within a specific time-limit (capacity contracting). Of all firms in the sample, 24 per cent sometimes or frequently do so (Table 7). For firms in the cluster, the figure falls to 12 per cent. Firms in low-income and high-income areas, on the other hand, are particularly active in this regard. So, firms in the cluster appear to be relatively self-sufficient. The same applies to other forms of horizontal co-operation involving two partners.[24]

TABLE 7

CAPACITY CONTRACTING BY DISTRICT (% OF SUBTOTAL OF COLUMN)

Sample frequency	*High-Income Areas*	*La Victoria (OG)*	*Gamarra -cluster*	*Low-Income Areas*
never 76%	73%	76%	88%	68%
sometimes 20%	20%	24%	12%	26%
frequently 4%	7%			6%

Source: survey February/March 1994
Note: sometimes = in less than one third of total production; frequently = in more than a third of total production

79

The Effects of Spatial Clustering at the Level of the Clothing Process:
A Summary

The above evidence can be summarised as follows. Vertical division of labour between firms in the cluster appears to be just starting. It is more common in high- and low-income areas. In the cluster, a firm typically subcontracts *one* phase of the production process, often a finishing activity. In fact, subcontracting is widespread and vertical specialisation is common at this level of the production process. In the industry as a whole, however, subcontracting does not seem to be perceived as a strategy to enhance competitiveness, but mainly as a way to resolve bottlenecks in production capacity (quantity, quality, and type of machines). This also explains why the subcontracting of assembly activities is less common in the cluster, where firms seem to be relatively well-equipped.[25]

Something similar can be said about horizontal co-operation. It does happen, people do co-operate, but no clustering effect could be observed. Firms in the Gamarra-neighbourhood seem again to be relatively self-contained. The general conclusion is that the territorial dimension of the environment of firms does not specially influence the development and nature of vertical and horizontal linkages among clothing firms in the cluster.

The working hypothesis following from this is that external economies at the level of the clothing process are not likely to explain the relatively good sales records of firms in the cluster. The development of the cluster neither appears to be supported by a deep inter-firm division of labour[26] nor by strategies at the level of the firm aiming at such a division. The potential to lower the associated transaction costs is not tapped to the full extent. This makes the Gamarra case peculiar with reference to the industrial district model [*Rabellotti, 1994: 2*].

In the following sections, therefore, the advantages of spatial clustering will be considered for (the transactions and linkages between) agents operating at subsequent levels of the value chain: suppliers of cloth and other inputs, clothing producers, as well as traders of final goods.

Vertical Inter-firm Linkages Along the Value Chain

A clothing producer needs, above all, adequate cloth inputs in order to compete in consumer markets.[27] To find the right type of cloth and other inputs and services, time and money have to be spent. These costs have been labelled search and matching costs, which involve the transportation of persons and goods on the one hand, and the collection of information on the other.

The positive effects of spatial clustering on the magnitude of the above *costs* have been addressed theoretically above. However, costs are only part of the story. Information advantages due to spatial clustering also affect qualitative aspects of forward and backward transactions, for example consumer preferences in a distant market and the design of cloth inputs, respectively. Information improves the market-fit of products and may increase the speed of adjustment in production (models, designs, quantity and quality). With latest fashion developments on display in the territorial environment of firms, show-ing the details of new products, firms can be stimulated to compete (through imitation and/or inspiration).

Second, an important consequence of more effective and efficient search and matching has been highlighted. Clothing firms in the cluster may be better able to reduce *input* prices. The proximity of similar firms and their suppliers enhances the sharing, among the former, of information about prices, quality and market-fit of inputs, thus stimulating competition between the latter. Input prices are locally reduced, due to more complete information among buyers and the competition between sellers.

This effect is likely to be passed on in the forward trades of clothing firms. Spatial concentration of clothing producers and their clients (wholesalers, retailers and final consumers) enhances information-sharing between those who are not direct competitors, and hence stimulates price competition among clothing producers making similar products. In such an environment, a price set too high will immediately result in lower sales, so profit margins will be tight for firms in the cluster. The cost advantages in backward transactions are transferred to the clients, who get their merchandise at the lowest possible price.

Third, the downward pressure on the prices of inputs and final goods due to savings on transaction cost may be reinforced at various levels of the value chain by economies of scale and of scope in production, distribution and marketing of products. Here the point of view of trading agents is important. They are interested in various features of the territorial environment: the degree of local concentration of the demand, the reputation of the cluster with outside clients at subsequent levels of the value chain, and local insights into personal reputations.[28]

The two former factors produce effects of scale and scope. For instance, the problem of indivisibility of investment in the sales infrastructure is tempered when the scale of business increases. The same applies to additional costs of labour. Furthermore, a location with a favourable reputation, for example a cluster, allows for reductions in absolute terms of the costs of advertising and other marketing efforts. Local information flows and reputation effects may also play a part in this respect.

Fourth, history repeats itself along the value chain. The above scale effects are not only relevant for firms trading inputs and machinery, but also for agents trading final goods, such as forwardly integrated clothing firms, whole-salers (as far as they sell their merchandise in the cluster) and retailers. Scope effects only apply to the additional labour costs of clothing firms, whose shop assistants may perform finishing activities in lean times. Both size effects become more important when a cluster enjoys a better reputation at different levels of the value chain. In principle, clothing producers from all over Lima may be attracted to purchase inputs and services. Traders from all over the country and even from export markets may come over to obtain merchandise. Final consumers in Lima are become interested, especially in the context of rural–urban migration, stagflation, and sharply decreasing purchasing power (as was the case during the booming years of the cluster, 1982–92). The over- all result is a locally-enhanced supply of sharply priced inputs, machinery, specialised productive services, professional business services and final goods.

In short, the crucial argument in this section concerns, first, the *interaction* between savings on transaction costs for one trading party and cost savings of transformation and transactions for the other party: second, the *accumulation* of these advantages for agents along the value chain; and, third, possible *iterations* of this cost-saving process over time. The following sections deal with survey data supporting one or more of these points.

Empirical Evidence Regarding Backward Linkages

A first eye-catching detail is the appearance of an unique type of supplier in the cluster, the licensed distributor of large cloth firms. This is indicative of economies of scale in the marketing of inputs (clothes, sewing cotton, elastics, zip-fasteners and so on). Other suppliers, such as wholesalers, retailers, and street sellers, apparently perceive the same advantage, considering the total of 4,100 trade firms which in part are suppliers of input [*Ponce, 1994*].

At least two-thirds of the firms in the sample report that their main cloth supplier is located in the cluster. Hence, the demand for clothes in the cluster not only comes from clothing producers in the cluster, but also from those operating elsewhere in Lima. Two elements of the territorial environment are relevant from a trader's point of view: the local concentration of the demand, and the favourable reputation of the cluster as a whole. The fact that clothing producers from all over Lima travel more than two hours to purchase inputs in Gamarra suggests that they too enjoy the advantages of low input prices or assortment, in addition to the lower costs of search and matching. Interactive cost savings seem to be relevant at this level of the value chain.

An equally, if not more important, observation is that for their cloth inputs, clothing firms in the cluster rely, above all, upon *market transactions* in their neighbourhood, supplanting backward linkages of a more co-operative kind with textiles producers outside the area. Apparently pleased by the presence of a licensed distributor, none of the firms purchase directly from large cloth plants, though this is more common among firms in the high-income areas (whose score is 38 per cent in this respect).

Furthermore, backward contracting of yarn spinning, weaving and dyeing services is an attractive way to obtain cloth inputs at low prices, to improve quality, and to enhance the market-fit and exclusiveness of design. Again, however, firms in high-income areas score higher than those in the cluster (20 versus 12.5 per cent respectively). Still, the score of the cluster is high compared to low-income areas, where only one of the 31 interviewed firm owners indicated having obtained cloth inputs through backward contracting.

On the whole, firms in Gamarra rely, above all, on traders of inputs: wholesalers, licensed distributors, and retailers (for small, sudden needs). Articles can usually be obtained at relatively low costs due to information and competition effects, and they may fit well into common fashion trends. However, the cloth products obtained are not exclusive (available to all competitors), while opportunities are not created to improve their quality or to introduce novel designs. Firms in the cluster are apparently *not less* dependent on market supplies than their colleagues elsewhere, while their colleagues in high-income areas are.

Empirical Evidence Regarding Forward Linkages

Regarding forward linkages, the evidence of the degree of forward integration of firms in the cluster should first be mentioned. About 75 per cent of the firms own one or more shops or at least a booth. By contrast, the figure drops to 28 per cent for firms elsewhere in Lima. Apparently, the local concentration of demand and the cluster's reputation in the outside world facilitate economies of scale and of scope in the distribution and marketing of final goods. In so far as the reputation of Gamarra is stated in terms of easy access to a wide assortment and sufficient quantities of cheap and qualitatively acceptable products, the advantage is interactive, and traders of final goods save on costs of search and matching. Here, proximity and local information play an important part.

The above economies in the distribution and marketing of products are expressed in the relatively large proportion of firms in the cluster producing stock instead of specific orders. The figures are 75 per cent for the Gamarra neighbourhood, 60 per cent for firms operating in low-income areas, and 50 per cent in the high-income sample. The data also show that firms in the cluster are well connected to different geographical markets, suggesting adequate access to the products by traders. Clothing products made in Gamarra are sold at every imaginable location in Lima, the Peruvian highlands and province,[29] and in neighbouring countries in the Andes (mostly informal exports). The data finally indicate that firms in the cluster often serve the most demanding market channels in Lima: boutiques. This suggests that the advantages of clustered firms are not limited to costs, but also extend to other components of competitiveness: the quality, design and novelty of products.

The Effects of Spatial Clustering Beyond the Clothing Process

What follows are the last sources of evidence sustaining our proposition of interactive, accumulating and iterative costs savings. First, we return to the observation that firms in the cluster achieve high gross sales per worker, both in relative and absolute terms. This is not likely to be due to a standard feature of 'industrial districts': vertical specialisation, inter-firm division of labour, mutual subcontracting, and the prevalence of external economies at the level of the transformation process. A crucial, second observation is, however, the finding that firms in *every size category* achieve relatively high sales per worker. Micro firms in the cluster do better than micro firms elsewhere; the smallest small/scale firms also sell more in Gamarra than do homologous firms in other neighbourhoods of Lima; and so on (see Table 8).

Third, in the context of spatial clustering, performance is only weakly correlated with the size of a firm (the low correlation-coefficient of 0.12 is not significant). Firms at the bottom of the small-scale category (five to nine workers) show better results than micro firms, but that is it; the trend does not persist. The differences between the means of the subgroups are not significant (F-test = 0.25, with a P-value of 86 per cent). On the other hand, elsewhere in Lima, and especially in low-income areas, 'big *is* better': the sales performance of firms does improve with size.

TABLE 8

AVERAGE MONTHLY GROSS SALES PER WORKER BY FIRM-SIZE AND
LOCATION (in 1993, and in US dollars)

	micro	*small scale*			*medium*	*F-test (P-value)*	*Corr. (P-value) sales/size*
	1–4	*5–9*	*10–14*	*15–19*	*20–100*		
High-income areas	414 (243) 9 obs	301 (171) 7 obs	705 (560) 5 obs	970 (180) 2 obs	596 (322) 5 obs	2.54 (0.07) 30 obs	0.18 (0.19) 28 obs
Gamarra	949 (930) 6 obs	1286 (961) 12 obs	935 (473) 3 obs	– 0 obs	1229 (641) 2 obs	0.25 (0.86) 24 obs	0.12 (0.30) 23 obs
Low-income areas	359 (231) 14 obs	658 (657) 11 obs	679 (1011) 3 obs	1877 (1922) 2 obs	– 1 obs	4.45 (0.01) 31 obs	0.64 (0.00) 31 obs
La Victoria (OG)	210 (190) 9 Obs	473 (314) 6 obs	– 1 obs	– 0 obs	– 1 obs	6.29 (0.01) 18 obs	0.40 (0.06) 17 obs
Sample as a whole	430 (462) 38 obs	767 (766) 36 obs	804 (612) 12 obs	1424 (1232) 4 obs	925 (710) 9 obs	3.19 (0.02) 99 obs	0.14 (0.08) 99 obs

Source: survey February/March 1994.
Note: – implies the cell is either empty or it contains just one observation. Standard deviations are given between the brackets: they are high in most cases (> 33% of the mean), but not too high to draw conclusions in the text.

The above data suggest that, in the cluster, location effects overrule size effects. This can be explained by pointing at territory-specific external effects, which are, above all, generated *beyond* the level of the clothing branch of industry. For a clothing firm, the effects boil down to cost savings in:

(a) search and matching of inputs (especially clothes and labour), and productive and business services;
(b) the purchase of inputs; and
(c) the distribution and marketing of products.

These effects are due to spatial proximity, local availability of business information, and a relatively high density of similar activities (or, a concentration of demand). Small firms in the cluster diminish diseconomies of scale and of scope in the marketing of their products through the combination with finishing activities. Superior information about diverse consumer markets in the Andes region encourages producers to improve the market-fit of products and enhances the degree of product differentiation, thus mitigating the importance of scale economies in production.

Of course, all firms may enjoy these advantages, also large firms, but they are most important for micro firms. First, transactions in micro firms are relatively small in scale, varied in content, and maybe even changing more rapidly through time, elevating unitary transaction costs. Second, micro firms have limited resources, hence they face the greatest diseconomies of scale, scope, sequence, experience, and cognitive scope (see Appendix 1).

A few remarks about the profitability of clothing firms in the cluster are in order. First, these firms may well achieve relatively high gross sales per worker, but the question as to the extent to which this is due to price or volume effects remains open. Price effects are unlikely as the reputation of the Gamarra cluster is based upon its low prices. Unsold stocks may be less of a problem (due to the local concentration of demand on the one hand, and a relatively good quality and/or market-fit of products on the other), but competition is still tough enough to ensure the lowest possible sale prices. There are indications that productivity is somewhat higher in the cluster: this would be due to Marshallian external effects of experience. Yet, the larger production volume in the cluster may also be achieved through longer working days. On the whole, however, the rate of return does not seem to be higher in the cluster: garment-making in Gamarra does not seem to be more profitable than elsewhere in the city of Lima. One may raise net income though, through the production of larger quantities and subsequently higher sales.

Second, data on production costs would indicate the extent to which, presumably, high rents in the cluster on the one hand, and the passing on of cost advantages (to traders of final goods) on the other, push down profits. However, these data are not yet available. Third, the fact that clothing producers are forwardly integrated should be subject to discussion. This integration is the result of territorially defined economies of scale and of scope in the distribution and marketing of products. Although the firms involved are small-sized with limited resources (finance, time, cognition), these firms take charge of two entirely different activities: production and marketing. This probably leads to improvisations and inefficiencies in both activities, at least in the long run, and more so if foreign competition increases. Thus, the opportunity costs of forward integration may become high over time (see Appendix 1).

A Few Remarks on the Role of Institutions and Macroeconomic Conditions

One question has not yet been dealt with. *Why* did spatial clustering stimulate neither vertical specialisation and the division of labour between firms, nor horizontal co-operation? North [*1990: 34*] argues that 'non-specialisation is a form of insurance when the costs and uncertainties of transacting are high. The greater the specialisation and the number and variability of valuable attributes, the more weight must be put on reliable institutions that allow individuals to engage in complex contracting with a minimum of uncertainty about whether the terms of the contract can be realised.' Non-specialisation keeps transaction costs low, but at the cost of high transformation costs. Third-party enforcement may help, for example, to introduce standard technical norms for the measurement of attributes of clothing services: but this seems to be lacking in Gamarra. Apparently, the territorial environment of firms cannot replace formal institutions in moderating these problems.

In addition, macroeconomic conditions play a role in providing incentives to specialisation. In Peru, however, protectionist industrial policies over three decades have resulted in limited domestic competition and few incentives for innovations. This situation lasted until 1990 and was especially relevant for established large-scale industry. Small firms, especially those operating in the cluster, were able to outcompete established industry without having to resort to interfirm division of labour. Tax evasion and territorially defined cost advantages sufficed to beat large-scale competitors. Small-scale industry in Gamarra inherited a small domestic market, however, the majority of which is poor. Many people were impoverished by the soaring inflation in the end of the 1980s. Small and poor markets are not likely to promote interfirm division of labour.

The above remarks draw attention to the solitary development of the Gamarra cluster. Formal institutions are scarce. Until 1994, there was no specific confederation of small-scale clothing producers in Gamarra, while their membership in a general association (APIC) is very small. Only street vendors are organised, since they face external pressures from the local government as well as from the forwardly integrated clothing firms. They also need clear rules and procedures to solve internal conflicts. There is no sign of any government support to the cluster. The only central government office the entrepreneurs are familiar with is the SUNAT, whose inspectors repeatedly organised raids to collect taxes (especially in 1991 and 1992). The local government also collects taxes and distributes licenses, but does not provide adequate services (cleaning, electricity, town and environmental planning, traffic control).

The macroeconomic setting seems to have two faces. Rural-urban migration, an employment crisis in the second half of the 1980s, falling incomes due to hyperinflation during 1988–89, rural poverty throughout the decades, as well as a historical pattern of industrial concentration (which also affects the availability of industrial inputs in rural areas and intermediate cities) provided for a dramatic economic situation, but at the same time constituted an adequate setting in which migrant clothing producers in the cluster could create an alternative to a pattern of socio-economic exclusion. They did so by relying on territorial advantages, albeit in a passive way.

VI. CONCLUSIONS

In the case of the Peruvian clothing industry, spatial clustering does indeed enhance the competitiveness of the SSIEs. The sales performance of clothing firms is spatially differentiated in favour of those operating in the cluster. The available evidence suggests that territorially constrained external economies are relevant in at least two aspects of competitiveness: the unitary costs of inputs and services as well as the costs of business information (about consumer markets, products, inputs and technology). Products made in the cluster are relatively cheap and fit well with consumer preferences in the variegated markets in the Andes region.

The likelihood of other plausible effects, for example, on the productivity of firms or dynamic capabilities could not be assessed, due to data limitations. With respect to the marketing of products, however, we found that firms in the cluster enjoy economies of scale and of scope, due to the local concentration of demand for apparel from all over the Andes region. For this reason, these firms often integrate forward and sell their products to both wholesalers and retailers, as well as to final consumers.

A major finding is that the functional interrelations of clothing firms is only, to some limited extent, due to a vertical division of labour at the level of production, while horizontal co-operation between otherwise competing producers is even less of a factor contributing to this. In fact, spatial clustering has not yet facilitated such relations at the level of production. On the other hand, upstream and downstream linkages with traders seem to be more important for generating external economies and for explaining the relatively good sales performance of firms in the cluster. The cost-saving process was found to be two-sided and cumulative, that is to say, accruing to down-stream agents .

One final remark is in order. The above argument still concerns only the short-term effects of spatial clustering, with a focus on costs. Dynamic effects on the quality and market-fit of products, on the improvement of production techniques, labour and management skills, as well as on the external organisation of firms, tend to be overlooked. More comprehensive *learning* effects should be taken into consideration in order to fully explain the development of the cluster. Such dynamic effects are important in the Peruvian setting of rural–urban migration[30], in areas with poor education and a scarcity of specialised training institutes, particularly in the rural areas where most entrepreneurs come from.[31] Not only migration and urbanisation, but also spatial clustering of similar firms mitigates these problems for the groups that lag behind in society. In this sense, the cluster may function as an incubator of entrepreneurship.

NOTES

1. Market-fit is defined as the correlation between traits of products and consumer preferences.
2. Implicitly a static approach is adopted. North and Wallis [*1994: 610*] argue that 'institutions are chosen to minimise the sum of transformation and transaction costs, given the level of output'. Technical change (in one sector) may lower transaction costs (in other sectors), while institutional change may increase transaction costs if at the same time transformation costs decline even more. In a dynamic perspective, institutional change may be an independent source of growth.
3. Trust in turn depends on mutual personal knowledge, past business experience, reputation, and the social embeddedness of transactions.
4. The difference between 'real' (technological) and 'pecuniary' effects is not straightforward; the former often translate into the latter [*Lambooy, 1972*].
5. This concept is taken from Nooteboom [*1992*], who emphasises firm-size effects on the capacity to assimilate external information, anticipate, learn, and innovate. The development and maintenance of inter-firm relations is a strategic necessity for SSIEs in order to overcome the tacitness of knowledge and cognitive limitations due to the perception, interpretation and evaluation 'on the basis of categories that condition knowledge in the double sense of enabling and limiting it' [*Nooteboom, 1993: 286–7*] and the dominant role of the owner-entrepreneur in SSIEs.
6. Enforcement is involved because transactions involve time, and hence the behavioural risk of default becomes relevant.
7. There may be a multiplier effect here; enhanced supply of one service can augment access to other goods or services. For instance, an agent specialising in legal and administrative assistance to firms in a cluster on their way to obtain bank credit, helps to improve the SSIEs' access to formal financial services.
8. In this respect the role of product markets is emphasised. Markets are said to become more diversified and complex and to change over time. This undermines economies of scale and of scope, and puts a premium on the production of small batches, flexibility and innovativeness.
9. The relation between territorial features and dynamic external economies is not a straight-forward one. Asheim [*1994: 95–6*] refers to improvements in local skills and innovative capabilities, while the latter would be 'conditioned by spatial proximity and cultural homo-geneity', the presence of trust and a certain 'industrial atmosphere'. However, Nooteboom

[*1992*] argues that innovation is dependent on the quality of inter-firm interaction with respect to the extent that perspectives are fruitfully crossed and investments are made in common language. In my opinion, Nooteboom rightly emphasises cultural heterogeneity as a necessity to cross perspectives and invest in common language. This makes the relation between spatial clustering on the one hand, and specialisation and innovation on the other, less direct and unambiguous.

10. Preliminary case-study information reveals that (at least) some of these buildings have been constructed by groups of migrant entrepreneurs, integrating people coming from a particular region in Peru. After land had been acquired, construction is self-financed (using own funds, family and migrant labour), while group coherence is maintained through common norms and values, strong and 'democratic' leadership, and clear enforcement rules (interview, 20 October 1994).

11. Note that the term 'district' refers here to a certain neighbourhood in the city of Lima that has been delegated local functions (such as environmental planning, maintenance of infrastructure, distribution of licenses) and rights (for example, the collection of local taxes). It is an administrative unit, and thus bears no relation with the 'industrial district'-concept [*Rabellotti, 1994*]. I will nevertheless use the term 'area' in the text to avoid confusion.

12. The sample is thus not representative, firstly because the sample frame contains registered firms only, and secondly due to the purposeful selection of certain areas, which creates a bias towards more viable SSIEs. Hence, the results of the survey are not representative for the clothing branch in Lima, nor has this ever been the objective of the research. In fact, our goal is rather to identify small-scale enterprises with growth potential, the hypothesis being that spatial clustering may help in this respect [*Schmitz, 1990*].

13. The percentage shares of firm-owners indicating not to have a sales outlet is 77 and 78 per cent, respectively.

14. Suppose firm A outcontracts or subcontracts part of the production of a specific order to firm B, while including it in its gross sales. This would raise the gross sales per worker ratio for firm A while lowering it in case of firm B. So, in the evaluation of cross-section data on gross sales per worker, the relative importance of outcontracting and subcontracting by firms in the cluster should be taken into account.

15. Furthermore, a second survey among 20 clothing firms in the cluster and 19 in a low-income area (carried out in October 1994), did not confirm the size-difference to be large and very significant. The average size of firms in Gamarra was found to be 7.75 (SD 5.73) while in the low-income neighbourhood it was 5.1 (SD 3.9). The F-test is significant (2.7) but with a P-value of 11 per cent.

16. Through time, the Marshallian argument applies to intergenerational learning and a local improvement of the quality of two human production factors: entrepreneurship and labour.

17. This is in line with other case studies, for example, on small-scale footwear in Trujillo, Peru [*Távara, 1994: 102*], and a cluster of small cotton knitwear producers in India (Cawthorne, in Nadvi and Schmitz, [*1994: 16*]).

18. The average number of subcontracted making-up operations is highest in high income areas (1.2; SD 1.35) and lowest in Gamarra (0.5; SD 0.88). The F-test on the difference between the strata is acceptable (2.34; P-value 0.08). This variable may well be correlated with the type of product and market segments attended.

19. The concept of 'technological strangeness' was introduced by Hirschman [*1968*] to discuss the factors which limit the development of 'linkages' in a process of import substitution. In the present discussion 'strangeness' refers to the fact that the technology associated with clothing (a mechanical process) has little to do with the technology of finishing processes, which is of a chemical nature (like washing, dyeing, and printing).

20. This concept is derived from Dei Ottati [*1994*]. The pure entrepreneur separates the marketing and productive functions, takes care of the former and subcontracts all production phases. This is a conscious strategy directed towards specialisation, to be differentiated from *ad hoc* solutions, for example, when a client needs products that lie outside the competence of a producer but the latter still decides to take care of the order.

21. This conclusion is preliminary as it depends upon one-shot survey data, which are furthermore one-sided (that is, focusing on one side of the relation). Besides, motives to outsource

an activity have not been recorded separately, per type. Ongoing research is designed to shed light on these issues, but results are not yet available.

22. In 57 per cent of the clustered firms one or several workers left to set up their own clothing business. In about half of these cases the mother firm develops a relation with the new born (for productive and/or commercial purposes). Entrepreneurs in Gamarra appear to be more selective in the sense that they do so with a relatively low number of ex-workers.

23. Two remarks are in order. First, the effects of these transfers cannot be quantified, we only know they occur. Secondly, the absolute number of cases are low, so the percentage shares should be interpreted with care.

24. Fourteen per cent of the sample firms participated once, or a few times, in a joint purchase of cloth inputs. In just two cases a trend towards specialisation and a separation of the marketing function was reported, both in high-income areas.

25. Relevant data have been gathered to sustain this point, but the results are not yet available.

26. The question is here: why did clustering not stimulate the development of such functional interfirm relations at the level of the clothing branch in the case under review? This question relates to the overall macroeconomic context: the protectionist policies during the 1960s, the 1970s and the second half of the 1980s, which remains outside the realm of the present endeavour.

27. In this sense the clothing-industry is considered to be highly supplier-dependent.

28. In so far as these transactions are coordinated by trust, personal knowledge, or social embeddedness (instead of prices), behavioural risks may also be better manageable in a spatial cluster, due to more complete information, face-to-face contacts and local reputations. For instance, cloth traders may be better able to screen a client to determine whether or not to sell on credit, translating into a more important role of unconditioned supplier credit in the cluster.

29. Which is not so evident as it seems, taking into account the rough Peruvian landscape and variable weather circumstances, a poorly maintained road and telecommunication infrastructure. These factors render geographical distances importance.

30. The urban population is estimated to have risen from 46 per cent in 1960 to 71 per cent in 1992, while the population of Lima-Callao would have increased to 7.4 million, which is a 57 per cent increase compared to 1980 [*Economic Intelligence Unit, 1993: 8*].

31. 75 per cent of the entrepreneurs in the Gamarra cluster are migrants originating from the highlands and the provinces, mainly Puno, Huancavelica, La Libertad, Cajamarca, Huanuco and Cusco. Only 25 per cent was born in Lima.

REFERENCES

Asheim, B. (1994): *Inter-Firm Linkages and Endogeneous Technological Capability Building*, Geneva: UNCTAD, pp. 91–142.

Coase, R. (1991): 'The Nature of the Firm', in O. Williamson and S.G. Winter (eds): *The Nature of the Firm*, Oxford: Oxford University Press, pp.34–47.

Cornes, R. and T. Sandler (1986): *The Theory of Externalities, Public Goods, and Club Goods*, Cambridge: Cambridge University Press.

Dei Ottati, G. (1994): 'Trust, Interlinking of Transactions and Credit in Industrial Districts', *Cambridge Journal of Economics*, Vol.18, No.6, pp.529–46.

Economic Intelligence Unit (1993): *Country Profile: Peru 1993/94*.

Hirschman, A. (1968): 'La Economía Política de la Industrialización a través de la Sustitución de Importaciones en América Latina', *El Trimestre Económico*, No.140.

Jameson, K.P. (1979): 'Designed to Fail: Twenty-five Years of Industrial Decentralization Policy in Peru', *The Journal of Developing Areas*, Vol.14, pp.55–70.

Joskow, P.L. (1991): 'Asset Specificity and the Structure of Vertical Relationships: Empirical Evidence', in O. Williamson and S.G. Winter (eds): *The Nature of the Firm*, Oxford: Oxford University Press, pp.117–37.

Knorringa, P. (1994): 'Lack of Interaction in the Agra Footwear Cluster', in P.O. Pedersen, A.

Spatial Clustering: The Peruvian Clothing Industry

Sverisson and M.P. van Dijk (eds): *Flexible Specialization: The Dynamics of Small-Scale Industries in the South*, London: Intermediate Technology.

Lambooy, J.G. (1972): *Externe Effekten en de Ontwikkeling van het Stedelijk Woon- en Leefmilieu*, Assen: Van Gorcum.

Liedholm, C. (1992): *Data Collection Strategies for Small Scale Industry Surveys*, East Lansing, MI: Michigan State University.

Marshall, A. (1964): *Principles of Economics*, London: Macmillan, 8th edition.

Mishan, E.J. (1971): 'The Postwar Literature on Externalities: An Interpretative Essay', *The Journal of Economic Literature*, Vol.9, No.1, pp.1–28.

Nadvi, K. and H. Schmitz (1994): *Industrial Clusters in Less Developed Countries: Review of Experiences and Research Agenda*, Discussion Paper of the Institute of Development Studies, University of Sussex, Brighton.

Nooteboom, B. (1992): 'Towards a Dynamic Theory of Transactions', *The Journal of Evolutionary Economics*, Vol.2, pp.281–99.

Nooteboom, B. (1993): 'Firm Size Effects on Transaction Costs', *Small Business Economics*, Vol.5, pp.283–95.

North, D.C. and J.J. Wallis (1994): 'Integrating Institutional Change and Technical Change in Economic History: A Transaction Cost Approach', *Journal of Institutional and Theoretical Economics*, Vol.150, No.4, pp.609–24.

Phelps, N.A. (1992): 'External Economies, Agglomeration and Flexible Accumulation', *Transactions of the Institute of British Geographers*, No.17, pp.35–46.

Ponce, R. (1994): *Caen las Murallas: Génesis, Estructura, y Perspectiva del Conglomerado Comercial y Manufacturero de Gamarra*, Lima: Friedrich Ebert Foundation (in press).

Pyke, F. (1992): *Industrial Development through Small-Firm Cooperation: Theory and Practice*, Geneva: International Labour Organisation.

Rabellotti, R. (1994): 'Is There an "Industrial District Model?" Footwear Districts in Italy and Mexico Compared', *World Development*, Vol.23, No.1, pp.1–13.

Scitovsky, T. (1954): 'Two Concepts of External Economies', *Journal of Political Economy*, pp.143–51.

Schmitz, H. (1990): *Flexible Specialisation in Third World Industry: Prospects and Research Requirements*, Geneva: International Institute for Labour Studies.

Sengenberger, W. et al. (eds, 1990): *The Re-emergence of Small Enterprises: Industrial Restructuring in Industrialised Countries*, Geneva: IILS.

Spulber, D.F. (1993): Economic Analysis and Management Strategy: A Survey, *The Journal of Economics and Management Strategy*, Vol.1, No.3, pp.535–74.

Távara, J.I. (1994): *Cooperando para Competir: Redes de Producción en la Pequeña Industria Peruana*, Lima: Consorcio de Investigación Económica/DESCO.

Villarán, F. (1993): 'Small-scale Industry Efficiency Groups in Perú', in B. Späth (ed.), *Small Firms and Development in Latin America: The role of the Institutional Environment, Human Resources and Industrial Relations*, Geneva: IILS, pp.158–94.

Williamson, O. (1985): *The Economic Institutions of Capitalism*, New York: Free Press.

APPENDIX 1

FIRM-SIZE EFFECTS AND THE COMPETITIVENESS OF SSIES: BEHAVIOURAL RESPONSES TO DISADVANTAGES IN RESOURCES

factors determining efficiency & competitiveness	sources of firm size-effects	effects (dis/economies)	small business (number of workers)	behavioral responses (fields of application between brackets)
TRANSFORMATION & TRANSACTING	joint inputs in subsequent production stages	SEQUENCE --->	highly correlated w/ short vertical extent (disadvantage)	joint action & joint venture (inputs, finance, and infrastructure)
VARIABLE COSTS: inputs, distribution, marketing, finance	specialisation (increase in productivity); laws of physics & mathematics (costs increase less than proportionally with capacity)	SCALE --->	highly correlated w/ small scale (disadvantage)	inter-firm division of labour (inputs, marketing, finance & support); joint action (distribution & marketing); agglomeration (distribution)
	indivisibilities (threshold costs)			
(SEMI-) FIXED COSTS: infrastructure, space, staff support, management	complementarity (materials, time, risks, brands); interaction (inseparability of resources)	SCOPE --->	highly correlated w/ limited scope (disadvantage)	joint action (infrastructure, distribution, and support services); agglomeration (infrastructure, distribution, support services, and marketing through local reputation)
	expertise (elimination of redundancies); reputation (lower perceived risks)	EXPERIENCE --->	correlated with relatively short experience (disadvantage)	joint action or agglomeration (inputs, among others)
TRANSACTION COSTS: search, screening or selection, negotiation, contracting, monitoring or coordination, enforcement	indivisibilities (threshold costs); bounded rationality (contingencies, adverse selection and moral hazard); opportunism (risk-spreading, vulnerability to opportunism, temptation to 'hit and run'; risk of default); asset-specificity, frequency & uncertainty: P,M	SCALE, SCOPE & EXPERIENCE --->	less width (scale), depth (education) & variety in collection of info: BA ↑; less products, partners & markets + lower sales: OPP ↑	contracting of professional services within a personal network; agglomeration to lower search and monitoring costs (partners); information-sharing in networks; sunk costs (one-sided solution); trade associations and other institutions promoting business rules and norms 'social embeddedness'; interlinked credit arrangements
ANTICIPATION: R&D + training, external information, opportunity cost	learning through categories (enabling & limiting); path & context dependent; tacitness of knowledge (unawareness)	COGNITIVE SCOPE --->	lower level of education/stubbornness; short distance between markets and strategic decisions	inter-firm division of labour as a way to stimulate 'economies of cognitive scope'; information-sharing in personal networks; agglomeration: secrets of industry are in the air vs. the danger of cogn. narrowness

Note: The building blocks of this diagram are the different types of firm-size effects, which have been derived from Nooteboom [1993] and Spulber [1993]. The last column was added and additional specifications were made (for example, the issues of transaction costs and the need to anticipate) for present purposes.

PART II

5

Opportunities for Women in Ouagadougou's Informal Sector: An Analysis Based on the Flexible Specialisation Concept

HANNEKE DIJKMAN and MEINE PIETER VAN DIJK

I. INTRODUCTION

Much informal sector research focuses on identifying the constraints for micro and small enterprises. In this chapter, we want to point to opportunities as well, in particular for female entrepreneurs. In Burkina Faso, economic liberalisations were announced right after the death of president Sankara in 1987. The new government started negotiations with the Bretton Woods institutions in 1988 and the first adjustment program covered the period from 1990 to 1993. When negotiations concerning structural adjustment started with the World Bank and the International Monetary Fund (IMF) many people in the capital Ouagadougou, anticipated difficult times. Almost half of the 350 micro and small enterprises interviewed in 1991 started up during two years previous, allowing the owners to make a living in some way. In some neighbourhoods, 50 per cent of the entrepreneurs were women.[1]

The three major actors in the adjustment process were the new government, the Bretton Woods institutions, which helped to design the adjustment programme, and the small entrepreneurs. We will argue that a major role in the ensuing economic upturn was played by small entrepreneurs, and particularly, female entrepreneurs, who managed to find money to start small businesses in a time of recession with very little support. They saw new opportunities. We

-----

This chapter is based on a study for the World Bank; it does not, however, necessarily reflect the Bank's point of view. H. Dijkman worked at the University of Ouagadougou for the University of Groningen, at the time of the research.

intend to analyse these developments with the help of the flexible specialisation concept [*Rasmussen et al. (eds.), 1992*]. The concept helps to point to the most important elements of the dynamics of small enterprises: their specialisation and flexibility. We use the flexible specialisation concept as a heuristic device.

II. FLEXIBLE SPECIALISATION DEFINED

Van Dijk [*1992*] defines flexible specialisation as a higher order concept, which points to six important, and often interrelated, characteristics of the dynamic small enterprise sector:

(1) an innovative mentality on the part of the entrepreneur;

(2) the technology used by personnel trained on the job, which often has a multi-purpose character;

(3) inter-firm co-operation often in the form of subcontracting;

(4) clustering of micro and small enterprises (cluster as a geographical grouping);

(5) networking of micro and small entrepreneurs (networking defined as the set of relations in which an entrepreneur operates); and

(6) specialisation and proven flexibility.

The result of the interplay of these characteristics is often a collective efficiency for the units working in the cluster [*Schmitz, 1992*]. We will discuss these characteristics in turn, after a section describing the research design. Some examples of the opportunities women in the informal sector will be given. We also discuss diversification strategies in some detail, since such strategies seem to be the contrary of specialisation. At the end of this chapter some conclusions about opportunities for female entrepreneurs and the usefulness of the flexible specialisation concept will be drawn.

III. METHODOLOGY

This research was a follow-up to a survey of the informal sector survey carried out in Ouagadougou in 1976. In the previous survey 300 small entrepreneurs were interviewed, 40 of which were women.[2] For the follow-up study, we decided to assess the role of female entrepreneurs more specifically and interviewed as many male as female entrepreneurs. A sample of 350 small entrepreneurs was interviewed in April 1991. The sample was stratified according to sex (50/50), location (spread evenly over the city) and type of activity (18 different types). The type of activities selected included, in addition to those types studied previously (for comparative purposes), a number of activities which are typical of female informal sector activities. Some new and, potentially promising, activities were also included in the sample. The female entrepreneurs in our sample were active in specific activities. They show different economic characteristics than male entrepreneurs and can be described as a different group in terms of social variables [*Dijkman and Van Dijk, 1993*].

Flexible specialisation strategies have enabled small entrepreneurs in different countries to survive, and have allowed their entreprises to become more competitive than larger enterprises.[3] The concept of flexible specialisation includes certain characteristics, such as, entrepreneurs with an innovative mentality, which are difficult to study in a survey. To make up for this problem, we checked each enterprise in the sample for market innovation (types of clients, where the client comes from). We noted down instances of subcontracting (entrepreneurs selling to other enterprises), co-operation between enterprises and different modes of organisations (whether they worked alone or with others), links with other sectors (inputs from the informal or the formal sector), the use of skilled manpower and diversification strategies (the opposite of specialisation). We determined whether enterprises are part of a cluster and whether the entrepreneur functions in a network. In total, 16 indicators were defined to operationalise flexible specialisation in this study. The entrepreneurs were scored on all these variables.[4]

The enterprises in our survey showed a limited number of the flexible specialisation characteristics. Few enterprise scored positively on half of the indicators mentioned. Those who scored positively on five or more variables were considered to be flexibly specialised entrepreneurs. 80 male- and 43 female-headed enterprises were labelled as such. Female-headed enterprises scored less well than male-headed enterprises. However, enterprises with flexible specialisation characteristics (called flexibly specialised firms) performed better than other enterprises.

A clear relation exists between the score on flexible specialisation and the level of sales, income, expenditures and investment. The differences are all statistically significant for both genders. Male-run flexibly specialised enterprises performed better than male, non-flexibly specialised enterprises. The same applies for female-headed flexibly specialised and non-flexibly specialised enterprises, although the differences were less pronounced and the differences in income were not statistically significant.[5] Whether flexibly specialised enterprises were male- or female-headed did not influence the average higher sales, incomes, expenditures and investments, however.

95

IV. TECHNOLOGY AND AN INNOVATIVE MENTALITY

Competition is fierce in Ouagadougou. Consequently, some entrepreneurs have tried new ways to access clients, either by looking actively for clients, or by moving (part of) their enterprises to a more favourable spot. Entrepreneurs have tried to make their products more attractive, either by improving the quality of the product, by improving the way in which the product is presented, by offering clients credit or by adding something special to the product.

Some entrepreneurs have tried to attract clients by selling their goods on credit. This often leads to non-payment of loans by clients and therefore, lower benefits. Music also attracts clients. One female hairdresser uses a tape recorder to amuse her clients. One of her colleagues considers her tape recorder as part of the shop. A man who sells bread and coffee bought a tape recorder to attract clients; batteries costs him 400 FCFA each week.[6]

Of the 350 entrepreneurs interviewed few entrepreneurs specialise. One example of specialisation is a motorcycle repairman who repairs only rear view mirrors. Entrepreneurs in upholstery discovered a market in the upholstery of car seats. One entrepreneur apprenticed in both sectors: for the first four years, in the upholstery of home furniture, then, four years in upholstery of car interiors. He now employs four apprentices. A female hairdresser provides her clients with the option to subscribe. The clients have their hair curled about four times a week.

A man who repairs all kind of electrical appliances (refrigerators, air conditioners, typewriters) finds most of his clients in modern private enterprises and actually travels to them. Unlike most of their colleagues, two young female weavers sell their fabrics at the central market (le grand marché) of Ouagadougou. This way, they manage to sell five fabrics a week. A blacksmith making brass art statues does not only sell at his workplace, but also has a stall at the central market. To keep his clients, he has business cards, reminding them of where he is located. One female owns six sewing machines and participates in fashion parades to show her products. A male entrepreneur, who processes aluminium, selected a particular spot close to other related enterprises. He actually sells most of his products to traders, also visiting the location.

Examples of entrepreneurs with innovative mentalities can be given. Process innovation is defined here as changing the production of a product, by enhancing the efficiency or the effectiveness of the production process. Several female entrepreneurs hire kiosks from the Chamber of Commerce so that they can better protect their fruits and vegetables against sun, rain, wind and theft. Beer brewers build improved stoves (foyers améliorés) to reduce the wood needed to prepare beer. A particularly active man, presently working as a civil servant, was the first in Ouagadougou to start making spare parts for motorcycles. He has trained a lot of apprentices since. These spare parts are now produced in considerable quantities in Ouagadougou.

Other examples can be given of process innovation, though in some cases the term is not completely appropriate. However, what term do you apply to the behaviour of a 35-year-old electric repairer, who because he has no soldering iron, warms a piece of iron and applies it to a piece of solder. Also, somewhere in between market innovation and process innovation is the young woman who sells snacks. Unlike most women, she does not stay in one place to sell them, or walk with a small box on her head, but uses a cart with two tyres to transport her merchandise, selling while travelling. Another young woman does the same with meals of beans and millet. A male entrepreneur, who has a kiosk from which he sells small meals and drinks, uses a system of fiches (plaquettes), which clients get before they are served.

V. INTER-FIRM CO-OPERATION

Etrepreneurs in Ouagadougou are very creative in co-operation. We distinguished five forms of co-operation. First, entrepreneurs in one activity work together to limit competition or to reduce costs. Secondly, entrepreneurs in different, but complementary activities work together to be more attractive to clients. Thirdly, entrepreneurs make use of other enterprises to obtain equipment and/or training and gradually develop their own business. Fourthly, people simply become co-entrepreneurs and finally, entrepreneurs let their workshop to another entrepreneur, or they open a branch office.

Entrepreneurs with the Same Activity Joining Together

To reduce costs or to limit competition, some entrepreneurs in the same activity work together. For instance, electrical repairmen regularly provide spare parts to each other from broken down equipment. Women brewing beer in some neighbourhoods have agreed to take turns brewing, so that they do not have to face competition. A similar arrangement seems to have been made by Ghanaian mobile tailors. One of these men explained that they came to Ouagadougou as a group of ten. Collectively, they rented sewing machines. They have divided the city into areas and walk through their chosen neighbourhoods with their machine on their heads.

Another example is a woman who sells fruits and vegetables. She often buys in bulk with other women; they divide the products and sell independently. Some young, handicapped women rent a space together for weaving cloth. They received a training at a centre for handicapped people and decided afterwards to stay together. They do, however, work individually. One woman, who grills groundnuts and makes groundnut oil, shares her equipment with several other women. The two machines (8,500 FCFA each) are used to grill the groundnuts and are owned by a group of nine women.

Co-operation between Complementary Activities

Entrepreneurs in different but complementary activities can work together to make their business more attractive for customers. This can either be done by a sharing arrangement, or by some form of subcontracting. For instance, one carpenter decided to associate with an entrepreneur in upholstery. A car repairman has established his workplace near the small workshops of electrical repairmen to whom he entrusts certain jobs. The same man asked a welder and a sheet metal worker to install themselves at the same location. The three types of enterprises remain independent but work together.

Similar arrangements were made by two brothers: one of them fixes lorry engines, the other has a welding shop. The enterprises are separate but, as the first brother said: 'we complement each other in our work' (nous nous complétons dans le travail). A female hairdresser gets her supplies from a cousin who travels from Abidjan to Ouagadougou. This cousin used to be the owner of the hairdresser's shop but sold it to the entrepreneur interviewed.

A man, collecting and transporting sand, has a cart in which he transports the sand to his brother who makes bricks. In the beer business it is quite common that brewers sell their beer to an intermediary. It can be sold on credit: the beer is delivered one day and, the next day, the brewer brings new beer and collects the money due the day before. Alternatively, the intermediary visits the brewer at the end of the day to pay for the beer that she delivered in the morning.

In another case, three brothers work together. The first buys cooking equipment for the second, his younger brother, who serves breakfasts. The third brother also prepares and sells salads at the same location. Some entrepreneurs locate complementary activities in one place increasing sales for all. One brewer sells beer alongside a woman (another wife of her husband) who sells rice. The two work together. One woman who sells rice asked another woman who sells 'bassi' (a product made of millet or red sorghum) and yoghurt to join her at the same spot.

Using Other Enterprises for Equipment and/or Training

Entrepreneurs have proved to be very good in creating an enterprise out of virtually nothing. Through other people, they are able to acquire skills, equipment, or a workplace and to develop their enterprise gradually. A female weaver worked with her mother, who does the same work. Now she is married and rents the loom from her mother for 1,450 FCFA per week. One starting entrepreneur, looking for a location, built a workplace on somebody else's plot. They agreed that he would be exempt from rent payments until the cumulative value of the rent equaled the total cost of construction.

A female tailor started with a rented sewing machine (1,500 FCFA per week). In a few years, she was able to buy two sewing machines. Similarly, a man making bricks rented his tools, but has gradually been able to buy his own. A young man transporting and selling water (using a cart, two barrels and a donkey) sometimes rents an extra cart and employs a boy in order to make extra profits. One of his colleagues uses two barrels which he pulls himself. One barrel is his, the other one is rented. In the long water lines, he aligns one barrel under the tap, while he leaves to sell the contents of other one. The owner of the second barrel is paid at the end of the day by delivering two full barrels of water.

A male metal furniture maker works under the name of another entrepreneur, to avoid taxes. The other entrepreneur pays the professional tax, but has a deal with the taxman (ils se sont arrangés). A female seller of fruits sells fruits for herself and on behalf of a supplier for whom she earns a fee.

Being Co-Entrepreneurs

Only six cases were found in which entrepreneurs worked together with somebody else, apparently sharing management and profits. Often, these were two wives of the same husband. The following example was found in which two 'co-wives' worked together. Their mutual husband provided a shed. The co-wives could either work together full-time, or take turns working at home and working for their enterprise. Men sometimes do the same. For instance, one male construction worker (able to build, as he states from basement to roof), is sometimes assisted by his older brother (two associated construction workers). A female tailor works with her brother.

Renting out the Workshop or Opening a Branch Office

A male tailor worked in Ivory Coast but returned because he preferred his own country. He left behind a workshop in Abidjan with an electric sewing machine, which is now rented to a tailor who sends him regular instalments on the profits made. A female entrepreneur sells meals and has two sisters working as family labour. She recently installed one sister at another spot, because she is insecure about right at her present location.

VI. CLUSTERING

Both modern and traditional forms of clustering and networks exist in Ouagadougou. Entrepreneurs take advantage of those forms which are beneficial to them. Different forms of networks distinguished are large, formal groups; small informal groups such as the Rotating Savings and Credit

Associations (RoSCA's or tontines in Burkina Faso) and small groups of mutual supporting entrepreneurs, based on family, tribe or regional relations. Traditional clusters can be clusters of entrepreneurs belonging to one tribal group or clusters of enterprises closely located on their own initiative and benefiting from being together. Industrial estates, handicraft zones and municipal markets are considered modern clusters. Family networks will be treated in the next section.

A large number of Burkinabè entrepreneurs are reluctant to work in groups. When asked if they would like to co-operate, almost a third answered that people were not to be trusted (les gens ne sont pas honnêtes). Others refused to co-operate unless they were forced to (à moins que l'état me l'oblige!), or stated that it is difficult to work with other women (les femmes sont difficiles à comprendre). A young man who transports water literally said that other people are not to be trusted (les gens sont des faux types). Another male entrepreneur sighed: 'can we work in a co-operative, given the mentality of the people'? (on se demande si l'on pourra travailler en coopérative à cause de la mentalité des gens).

Others are willing to work in a co-operative. Half of the entrepreneurs responded positively to this question, while about a sixth formulated some conditions. One tailor was very much interested in co-operation. He had previously been a representative for other tailors, when they were asked by the authorities to co-operate. By doing so, the tailors accessed new markets, for instance, for school uniforms. Similarly, a female tailor joined such a co-operative. A male art painter was a member of two associations: the 'association des artistes plasticiens du Burkina' and the 'association internationale des arts plastiques'.

Women often form tontines or use their networks to generate money. For instance, a beer brewer participates in a tontine of ten women. Each contributes 3,000 FCFA per month. Each month the total amount collected is given to one of the members. Another woman sells a local soft drink called bisap and runs a tontine of 12 women. Each pays 5,000 FCFA per month. A woman selling fruits and vegetables participates in a tontine of 12 women each of which puts aside 200 FCFA per day.

Sometimes the fact that other enterprises are located nearby becomes a decisive factor for an entrepreneur who wishes to locate his/her enterprise in a specific spot. For instance, an entrepreneur who sells corrugated iron chose a place near where where a metal worker and a welder were already working. Caste or tribe can also influence the choice of a location. A Nigerian male hairdresser chose, to settle in a particular place, where other Yorubas live.

VII. NETWORKS OF FAMILY AND FRIENDS

The subject of networks of family and friends was investigated in a number of different ways. Family and friends can be very helpful to entrepreneurs by providing them labour, work space or capital. Relatives can provide cheap family labour, and a workshop, a plot or shed can be provided at a reduced price. Finally, family or friends can provide the capital for initial or additional investments.

Almost two-thirds of the entrepreneurs make use of help from their family or friends. One-fifth even use the help in more than one way. Women, more often than men, use their connections (72 versus 54 per cent, respectively).

In some activities entrepreneurs make more use of aid from family and friends than in other activities. This occurs in edible products (in 19 out of 25 cases), metal working (in 13 out of 22) and electric repair (nine out of 17). These data are probably an underestimation, since other relations between the enterprise and the family (the use of family for channelling output or receiving training) were not recorded systematically.

Entrepreneurs can receive informal education through their family or friends, or they can be dependant on them for the purchase of inputs or the sales of outputs. Some entrepreneurs indicated that they lack these relations and, therefore, have problems in developing their enterprises. One entrepreneur reported having good relations with someone in the government through whom he received large government orders.

Household expenditures also interact with running the business. Entrepreneurs can provide their family or friends with money or gifts, but can also receive help from them. For instance, a woman selling meals gives money to a family member who lives in a village and to others who live in Ouagadougou. A female tailor specified that she spends about 20,000 FCFA per year for her mother and 5,000 FCFA for her father.

Assistance can also be given the other way around. For instance, a male bicycle repairman cum farmer and his wife, who sells vegetables, cannot earn enough to support themselves and their five children. Often, they receive assistance from friends and family. A female entrepreneur whose husband is ill is sometimes supported by her son, who is a carpenter. Male entrepreneurs are also supported by their wife/wives and other relatives so they can satisfy the basic household needs. For instance, a male entrepreneur who makes metal furniture is unable to provide sufficient food for his eight children. His wife sells peanut butter and his daughter also works, to support the family.

101

VIII. SKILLED MANPOWER

Entrepreneurs get their education in various ways. They sometimes go to other countries to learn new skills. A male metal furniture maker went to Ivory Coast to learn how to assure water tightness and air tightness, allowing him to make tanks. Examples of informal sector entrepreneurs who employ skilled labour are scarce. Skills are important, however. A male bricklayer, for example, says he works with precision to gain the trust of his clients and to get good references from them. Many skilled people start their own businesses and train the apprentices or labourers themselves.

One electric repairman employs an apprentice plus, very unusual in the informal sector, a secretary who writes the bills and makes cost estimates. He also uses his own skills in a somewhat different way than most electric repairmen. He buys old radios or television sets, repairs them and sells them again. To acquire the skills needed to do this, it was necessary for him to go to Ivory Coast. He also regularly seeks advice from a friend from Guinea. Not surprisingly, he is not afraid of competition 'if you know your work' (quand on fait bien son travail, on ne craint rien des autres, c'est quand on n'est pas sûr que le problème se pose).

IX. FLEXIBILITY

Numerous examples can be given of entrepreneurs making use of the changed economic and policy environment to start or expand their businesses. For instance, they may change to another activity or establish relations with the formal sector. Female entrepreneurs, especially change frequently from one activity to another. It is often not clear why they do this. This remains an interesting area for further research. For instance, a woman of 30 years of age, sold fruits and vegetables for two years, but previous to that she sold other small meals or snacks, which she still sells, 'dégué' (mealy products) for two years, 'attiéké' for three years and fish for one year. If she would get a loan of 300,000 FCFA, she could find a girl from her village to take care of the enterprise. She would travel to Cotonou or Lomé to trade cloths (pagnes), jewellery and shoes.

After selling vegetables for 15 years, one woman changed 13 years ago to selling fruits, probably because profits are now higher in this sector. When the former president of Burkina Faso forced people to wear locally woven cloths, many weavers benefited from the extra demand. A woman who inherited the weaving profession from her parents replaced her traditional loom with a modern, less tiring one. Most women in fruit sales make use of the possibility to buy fruit from a fruit production project in Bazega. One of them stated that she would add tinned fruit juice to her stock, if she would get a credit. In

Ouagadougou, theft and robbery is quite frequent. To avoid theft of her stock, a female seller of fruits employed a guard for 5,000 FCFA per month.

To obtain a location to sell fruits near a governmental building, several women helped to clean the surroundings of the building. They reached an agreement with the government employees and now have a free spot for their activity. There are also entrepreneurs who have established links between informal and modern sector enterprises. This is typical for repair and services firms, but the men who sell breakfasts (bread with butter, coffee, tea) also try to cater to employees from the formal sector. In addition to this, they buy bread on credit from a baker and are paid a certain commission on the number of loafs of bread sold. One man serving breakfasts even obtained his small store from a modern flour mill.

X. DIVERSIFICATION: EXPANDING THE ACTIVITY

An approach often used by the entrepreneurs interviewed to expand their business is through diversifying production. This is the opposite of specialisation. They can add related products, complementary products, more expensive products and so on. They can either offer several products at the same time, or sell them at different moments. Other forms of diversification treated below, include vertical integration and entrepreneurs who also work as farmers or as employees for other enterprises.

Young men who repair (motor)cycles also trade in spare parts. Clients can buy the parts directly or provide money for the repairman to acquire the parts. Electronic repairmen can also diversify. Instead of only repairing radios and tape recorders, one repairman has expanded to video recorders and television sets. Others also repair fans, freezers, refrigerators and air conditioners. One also raises sheep, chicken and ducks.

Of the men who run coffee and tea tables, some began by selling cigarettes and sweats. A starting entrepreneur can buy one package of cigarettes and sell the cigarettes one by one, thus acquiring a small benefit. A male tailor started sewing shorts for tailors on the market. Now he sews both for men and women in his own workshop. He disposes of two sewing machines and one embroidery machine.

One shoe repairman would like to expand his enterprise. If he could get a start making shoes. One of his colleagues has the same desire. For women, the same desire to diversify holds. For instance, a woman started selling groundnuts and gradually expanded the business by adding eggs, fruits and vegetables and so on. A female tailor diversified selling embroidery products. Some female beer sellers also sold cigarettes, meat sauce, charcoal and drinks.

Some female entrepreneurs have two activities, sometimes spread over the day. One woman interviewed sells doughnuts in the afternoon, and fruits in the morning. A female tailor also sells jewellery. She plans to start a tailoring training centre for girls.

Other Types of Diversification

Vertical integration is defined here as starting additional activities which provide inputs for, or use outputs of, the initial activity. Vertical integration is not very typical among small Ouagadougou. One way entrepreneurs try to increase their income is by executing different activities, or by working at the same time in the formal sector.

A woman brewing beer buys wood in considerable quantities, and, therefore cheaply. She uses it for the production of beer, but also transforms it into charcoal, woman selling fruits and vegetables not only buys for herself, but also for others, her business from retail to wholesale. Finally, a woman cultivates beans in the rainy season, and prepares and sells them in the dry season.

Other examples of diversification are a female tailor who, simultaneously, takes care of some children to gain some additional money. A man serving breakfasts also is trained and works as a carpenter. A male entrepreneur who is a traditional weaver also works as a guard. During the day he weaves, at night he guards a house. A woman whose husband died two years ago and who used to earn a small income knitting, has added preparing and selling a drink with cereals (bouillie de millet) to her activities since the death of her husband. According to her, the two activities combine very well. Another woman combines knitting with selling fruits.

Some entrepreneurs work for themselves as well as providing daily labour for others. One entrepreneur in the construction sector is regularly contracted to build houses, but when he is out of work, he seeks employment with a big entrepreneur for 1,000 FCFA per day. Something similar is done by a female hairdresser. Although she has her own workshop, she often goes into town to assist friends who are also hairdressers. A male metal furniture-maker has his own enterprise. However, when he has no orders, he goes to family members who are painters and works with them. Or he works building metal sheds.

Diversification: Being an Entrepreneur and a Farmer

Informal sector entrepreneurs also work as farmers in the rainy season to obtain food or inputs for their household or main activity. Sometimes women are sent by their husbands to the rural areas during the rainy season. Some of the entrepreneurs interviewed presented themselves as informal sector entrepreneurs who farm during the rainy season. For instance, a 43-year-old woman has for seven years woven cloth during the dry season, and worked the land during the rainy season.

A woman who makes doughnuts says she farms to cultivate the inputs for her dry season activity. A 49-year-old farmer with a family of 22 started making bricks this year after the rainy season. Due to the drought his harvest was too small. Other farmers have adopted the same approach, although one has found that it is difficult to make good bricks and that sales are low during the rainy season. A female entrepreneur with no economic activities admitted that her husband sends her to the fields in the rainy season. She is not the only one who is forced by her husband to do so (pendant l'hivernage, mon mari m'oblige à aller en brousse).

XI. RECOMMENDATIONS

Economic growth has been very important for the reduction of poverty in a large number of countries. This also applies for Burkina Faso, where the agricultural and industrial potential needs to be fully developed. The government should formulate and implement the macroeconomic policies necessary to create conditions for economic growth. A more positive attitude should also be taken to the economic activities of women and an attempt should be made to stimulate the necessary increase in the productivity of these activities. Appropriate macroeconomic policies will help the development of micro and small enterprises. Technology policies could be directed towards developing products and to improving the production methods of these entrepreneurs. Physical planning policies can help to make available land and the appropriate infrastructure.

At present, many rules and regulations make the life of small entrepreneurs complicated and selective deregulation may stimulate the development of this sector. Similarly, a large number of taxes need to be paid and it is not always clear to the entrepreneurs how much and which taxes need to be paid for which purpose. The government could clarify the system and redesign it in such a way that small enterprises are not driven into illegality because of the large number of taxes and a lack of clarity about them. Education and training need to be geared more to the market, in this case the needs of small entrepreneurs.

A whole range of projects and policies directed at small enterprises, in general, and at the economic activities of women, in particular, can contribute to a labour intensive development of these economic activities. Often, the private sector will have to be stimulated to start these activities, to provide access to small entrepreneurs and to subcontract to them. The following includes:

(a) the development of associations of small entrepreneurs. In many branches there are already associations and some of them work very well. They should function as a platform for discussion, exchange of new ideas and experiences, and should be the interlocutor for negotiations with government. Giving small entrepreneurs the opportunity to communicate will also help them to build up the networks they need to expand their businesses. Female entrepreneurs often participate and sometimes play a key role in these organisations;

(b) local and municipal governments should reserve space and provide infrastructure for micro and small enterprises;

(c) the tax system needs to be clarified and the government should communicate with entrepreneurs about how they will benefit from the payment of these taxes;

(d) subcontracting and other relations between micro, small, medium and large enterprises need to be developed;

(e) technology development and innovation diffusion need to be stimulated. Female entrepreneurs need special attention. Multi-purpose equipment can help them to become more innovative;

(f) the development of clusters of economic activities should be stimulated, including the physical grouping of enterprises of different sizes;

(g) aid should be given to female entrepreneurs to gain access to credit, training and marketing channels. Private banks and training institutes should be stimulated to become involved in this important market;

(h) innovation diffusion centres can play an important role in the development of small and micro enterprises. To assure a maximum use of these centres, also by female entrepreneurs, a business and technology support system needs to be put in place [*Pedersen et al. (eds) 1994*];

(i) entrepreneurship development programmes can be useful, particularly for female entrepreneurs and enterprises, which are blocked at a certain level and find it difficult to make the next step;

(j) clusters, networks and different forms of co-operation should be used to bring in new ideas in this dynamic sector;

(k) access to credit and government orders should be facilitated for entrepreneurs who cooperate and for those who participate in clusters and networks;

(l) barriers to entry should be diminished through deregulation and by facilitating administrative procedures. Information and assistance should be given to entrepreneurs on how to deal with existing formal requirements;

(m) specialisation should be stimulated through training entrepreneurs in changing designs, products, production methods and marketing channels.

XII. CONCLUSIONS

The concept of flexible specialisation provides a new analytical framework to look at the dynamics of small enterprises. With such a different framework one discovers different aspects of the reality of small enterprises than the classical small enterprise studies. We found a very dynamic sector with skilled, creative and innovative entrepreneurs trying to develop their business. Particularly women use their networks and benefit from clusters and mutual co-operation. Creating the conditions for this kind of development is a challenge for many Third world countries.

The urban informal sector has shown an enormous dynamics. Women have a large number of opportunities in the informal sector. The list of recommendations provided shows a role for all the actors mentioned at the beginning of the chapter. The World Bank helped to create the proper macroeconomic context, by helping to change the economic policy context after adjustment. Entrepreneurs reacted in large numbers, by starting massively at their own account. They use their skills, tools and location to improve and expand their businesses. The authorities should now give these (female) entrepreneurs more opportunities by removing as many constraints as possible.

Specialisation is important for small enterpreneurs. The flexible specialisation concept helped to bring out a number of factors which explain the dynamics of the urban informal sector in an African context. Moving to other locations is an important part of the dynamics of small enterprises and can be encouraged by the urban authorities. Flexibility is also an asset which needs to be promoted. Entrepreneurs will find an optimum between specialisation and diversification by moving from niche markets to broader markets and back.

NOTES

1. In three neighbourhoods all economic activities were counted, to get an impression the population of small enterprises in Ouagadougou and to allow a comparison with an earlier census in two of the neighbourhoods.
2. 26 weavers, six potters, six female traders, one women active in the construction sector and one involved in straw weaving. The 1976 research is summarised in Van Dijk [*1986*].
3. See cases studies in Rasmussen *et al.* (eds.) [*1992*].
4. Some indicators were related to the experience of the entrepreneur outside their enterprise (having received some kind of training in that way), to employing personnel (and paying salaries), to working together with someone, to mobility (having moved their enterprise), motivation for organisation (yes or no), sales to other than households and level of technology.
5. Lack of statistical significance for income may be related to the problem of getting a reliable income estimate, which is particularly difficult in the case of male entrepreneurs.
6. 100 FCFA equalled two French francs, while five French francs were roughly equal to one US$ at the time of the fieldwork.

REFERENCES

Carrizo, A. (1986): *Urbanisation, secteur informel et emploi: Les micro-entreprises à Ouagadougou: analyse et stratégie de développement*, Geneva: ILO.

Dennis, C. (1991): 'The Limits to Women's Independent Careers: Gender in the Formal and Informal Sectors in Nigeria', in Elson [*1991*].

Dijkman, H. and M.P. van Dijk (1993): 'Women in the informal sector of Ouagadougou', *Development Policy Review*, Vol.11, No.3, 1993, pp.273–89.

Dijk, M.P. van (1986): *Burkina Faso: Le secteur informel de Ouagadougou*, Paris: L'Harmattan.

Dijk, M.P. van (1992): 'How Relevant is Flexible Specialisation in Burkina Faso's Informal Sector and the Formal Manufacturing Sector?', in Rasmussen *et al.* (eds.) [*1992: 45–51*].

Elson, D. (1991): *Male Bias in the Development Process*. Manchester: Manchester University Press.

INSD (1989): *Recensement général de la population: Analyse des résultats définitifs*, Ouagadougou.

Lougué, M. (1990): *Les statistiques, la femme et le secteur informel au Burkina Faso: analyse des données statistiques sur les activités des femmes dans le secteur non structuré*, PNUD/INSTRAW, Projet RAF/87/042.

Lubell, H. (1991): *The Informal Sector in the 1980s and 1990s*, Paris: Development Centre OECD.

ONPE (1987): *Enquête sur le secteur informel 1987*, Ouagadougou: Office National de la Promotion de l'Emploi.

Pedersen, P.O., A. Sverrisson and M.P. van Dijk (eds.) (1994): *Flexible Specialization: The Dynamics of Small-Scale industries in the South*, London: Intermediate Technology.

Plan directeur (1990): *Plan directeur pour la promotion de l'artisanat au Burkina Faso*, Ouagadougou.

Rasmussen, J., Schmitz, H. and M.P. van Dijk (eds.) (1992): 'Flexible Specialisation: A New View on Small Industry?' *IDS Bulletin*, Vol.23, No.3, July.

Schmitz, H. (1992). 'On the Clustering of Firms' in Rasmussen *et al.* (eds.) [*1992: 64–9*].

6

Industrial District or Garment Ghetto?
Nairobi's Mini-Manufacturers

DOROTHY McCORMICK

I. INTRODUCTION

Clusters of small firms performing similar activities are a common sight in the urban areas of developing countries. Metal workers, mechanics, and second-hand clothing vendors gather in sectorally-specific, geographically-bound agglomerations. Recent research on Marshallian industrial districts suggests that such clusters could play a vital role in industrialisation.

Garment manufacturers located in two large Nairobi markets are an example of such clustering of small firms. The individual businesses resemble one another enough in their relations with supply, labour, and product markets to constitute a unique firm-type within the garment industry which we call the 'mini-manufacturer'. The clusters exhibit some features of successful industrial districts elsewhere, but differ in important respects. The markets could be embryonic industrial districts which, if properly nurtured, would bring about a new form of industrial development in Kenya. Alternatively, they may simply be ghettos where marginal businesses congregate because they have no other place to go.

This chapter examines the present situation of the garment markets and assesses their potential for contributing to Kenya's industrialisation. It has six sections. Section II and III give the theoretical and methodological under-pinnings of the research. Section IV describes Nairobi's garment industry. Section V, the heart of the analysis, compares observed characteristics of Nairobi's garment markets with features of the typical industrial cluster in a developing country. The final section summarises the findings, outlines needs

McCormick was the principal researcher in all three phases of the research. She worked alone in the first phase; Mary Njeri Kinyanjui and Grace Ongile collaborated in the second and third phases. They gratefully acknowledge the financial support that made the research possible: Social Science Research Council (USA) for the first phase, Centre for Development Research (Denmark) for the second phase, and the International Centre for Economic Growth (USA) for the third phase. They are also grateful to the business owners who responded to their many questions over the last five years.

for further research, and discusses interventions aimed at strengthening the garment markets.

II. THE BENEFITS OF CLUSTERING

Theory and empirical evidence suggest that clustering offers economic benefits for participating businesses and fosters overall industrial growth. The theory has its roots in Marshall's observations on the textile and metal working regions of England, Germany, and France during the latter half of the nineteenth century [*Marshall, 1890; 1919*]. Marshall believed that the clustering of small firms of a particular industrial activity offered the possibility of interfirm division of labour which, in turn, enabled the industry to operate more efficiently. Marshall also thought that a common set of cultural and social values could reinforce the specialised knowledge that developed within the cluster. He noted that skills and information were 'in the air' in industrial districts where they helped to form a business culture that fosters entrepreneurship and technical innovation.

Industrial districts have recently returned to prominence partly because of the success of regional, small firm industrial clusters in various parts of Europe [*Piore and Sabel, 1984; Storper and Walker, 1989; Pyke and Sengenberger, 1992*] and partly as a result of a more general interest in network models of social organisation [*Mitchell, 1969; Williamson, 1975, 1980; Thompson et al., 1991*]. The European success stories have prompted researchers to examine the relevance of the model for industry in developing countries [*Schmitz, 1992; 1993; Rasmussen, 1992; Sverrisson, 1993; Schmitz and Musyck, 1993; Nadvi and Schmitz, 1994; Pedersen, 1995*].

Industrial districts are geographic concentrations of firms involved in similar productive activities. Pyke *et al.* [*1990*] define them as 'productive systems characterised by a large number of firms that are involved at various stages and in various ways in the production of a homogeneous product'. They observe that a significant feature of industrial districts is the high proportion of small and very small firms. A supportive structure of values, social practices, and institutions is also essential to Marshall's concept of an industrial district [*Storper, 1990; Asheim, 1992; Sverrisson, 1992*]. Brusco [*1990: 1*] captures both aspects of the industrial district when he defines an industrial district as 'a set of companies located in a relatively small geographical area [that] . . . work, either directly or indirectly, for the same end market'; and then goes on to assert 'that they share a series of values and knowledge so important that they define a cultural environment; and that they are linked to one another by very specific relations in a complex mix of competition and cooperation'.

In advanced economies, where industrial districts play an important role in the restructuring of an existing industrial base, observers have identified two avenues from the old structure to the new [*Storper and Walker, 1989; Pyke and Sengenberger, 1992*]. Firms on the 'high road' invest in multipurpose machinery and employ skilled labour, in order to stabilise their production by shifting output between different markets. Other firms take the 'low road', where they achieve flexibility by minimising their investments in machinery, and relying on unskilled labour that can be hired and fired at short notice.

In probably the most comprehensive review of the literature on clustering in developing countries to date, Nadvi and Schmitz [*1994*] compare small firm clusters in Latin America, Asia, and Africa with the experiences of European industrial districts. Based on this analysis they contend that the high-road/low-road distinction fails to capture what has occurred in clusters in developing countries [*Nadvi and Schmitz, 1994: 43–4*]. None of the clusters could truly be characterised as 'high road'. Most show aspects of both high and low roads, usually a combination of innovation and cheap labour. Some fall squarely into the low-road category. Even more common in African countries, are tiny agglomerations of enterprises operating in a semi-subsistence economy. Like their 'low-road' counterparts, they try to minimise costs, but they function even more simply, finding free workspace on public land, using family labour, and keeping capital intensity low [*McCormick, 1988; 1991a; McCormick et al., 1994*].

Nadvi and Schmitz [*1994: 41*] conclude that 'while clustering is not an uncommon feature of industrial organisation for small- and medium-sized firms in the developing world, the consequences for inter-firm production and social relations and ultimately for sustained economic growth of the cluster as a whole is extremely mixed'. They draw out five main findings from existing studies. First, clustering is significant to the industrial organisation of small scale manufacturing in developing countries, particularly in Latin America and South Asia. Second, clustering has brought with it various types of inter-firm relations, ranging from total absence of co-operation to situations with extensive collaborative arrangements in production. Third, clusters in developing countries are often associated with some form of common social identity or social and affective network. Such shared identity provides the basis for interpersonal relations, for notions of trust and reciprocity, and for social sanctions that set boundaries on accepted competitive behaviour. Fourth, although clustering is not usually the outcome of planned intervention by the state, the state can play an important facilitative role for clusters. Finally, the growth experience of industrial clusters is internally uneven. Within a given cluster, some enterprises will grow and others will fail. These conclusions suggest that interfirm relations, social networks, government intervention, and growth of individual firms within the group could provide important insights into the nature and strength of Nairobi's garment clusters.

III. METHODOLOGY

The discussion which follows draws on data gathered during a five-year study of Nairobi's garment industry. Although the study did not set out to deal with clustering, we gradually became aware that interactions among firms and individuals could be important to enterprise survival and growth. By the third phase of the research, some networking considerations were explicitly incorporated into the data-gathering. Nevertheless, it is important to recognise that, at this stage, we lack the comprehensive view that a targeted study of clustering might provide.

Study Design

The study was conducted in three phases. The first phase, extending from early 1989 to the end of 1990, provided baseline information on the entire garment industry in Nairobi. In the second phase, which was carried out in the second half of 1992, researchers revisited the full sample before focusing on what firms in the middle size ranges considered to be the main barriers to growth. The third phase addressed the issue of barriers to growth of firms in greater depth. This chapter draws on material gathered in all three phases.

Each phase had its own methodology. The first phase mainly used structured interview questionnaires administered to business owners in a stratified random sample of garment manufacturing firms. The second phase used an interview schedule to guide informal, probing discussions with a small purposive subsample of entrepreneurs. The third phase combined the usual structured interviews of individual business owners with a participants' seminar that provided for an exchange of views on emerging issues and findings. At every stage of the research, we searched for additional information about the industry and its firms by holding informal discussions with business owners, observing local tailors and dressmakers at work, and scouring newspapers and scholarly journals for relevant material.

Sampling and Data Collection

The first phase began with a census of individuals and groups making or selling new clothing anywhere within the Nairobi city limits [*McCormick, 1989; 1993*]. The census turned up 2,200 garment makers with a total of 11,607 workers [*McCormick, 1993*]. An additional 421 businesses sold clothing at retail, but did no manufacturing [*McCormick, 1991b*]. From the clothing manufacturers, we drew a random sample of 268 firms stratified according to employment size. We chose employment as the measure of firm size because it is easy to apply and is closely correlated to size measured in terms of capital or output [*Little, Mazumdar and Page, 1987*]. Employment is also especially important in the Kenyan context, where unemployment is high and capital costly.

The second and third phases focused on enterprises in the middle size ranges of the garment industry: firms with four to 50 workers. Approximately one-quarter (23.4 per cent) of the industry's firms fall into this category. In 1989, they employed 3,247 workers, or 28 per cent of the industry's labour force. The full sample contained 91 such firms. Between 1989 and 1992, 22 of these closed, moved away, or changed from garment production to other activities. The second phase used a subsample of eight firms chosen as representative of the sizes, ages, and general performance of medium-sized businesses [*Ongile and McCormick, 1995*]. The third phase dealt with a stratified random subsample of 40 businesses in the same size range. The subsample was 7.8 per cent of the 513 firms recorded in the 1989 census as having four to 50 workers. Data collection was done in two parts. The first part used an interview questionnaire to gather information on organisation of production, finance and sources of capital, markets and other linkages, and perceived business problems. The second was a half-day seminar at which participating business owners received and discussed the findings.

IV. NAIROBI'S GARMENT INDUSTRY

Clothing sold in Kenya comes from three sources: domestic production, so-called 'second-hand' clothing, and imported, new clothing. Imported, new clothing probably represents less than two per cent of the market and has little impact on the domestic industry [*Kenya, 1990: 67, 126*]. 'Second-hand' clothing includes imported, used clothing, used items collected locally, and miscellaneous new clothes, complete with foreign labels and price tags. 'Second-hand' clothing competes actively with Kenyan goods, especially with low-priced garments of the type produced by mini-manufacturers.

Garment production in Nairobi, as in the industry world-wide, is labour-intensive with few obvious economies of scale [*McCormick et al., 1994*]. Productivity gains are mainly attributable to increased machine speeds and the use of special-purpose machines, such as buttonholers, button-fixing machines, and machines set for a particular stitch. The lack of scale economies, and the peculiarities of Asian and African capitalism in Nairobi, have enabled firms using different production technologies and having different market relations to coexist [*McCormick et al., 1994*].

Types of Garment Manufacturing Firms in Nairobi

Analysis of the market relations of Nairobi's garment producers in the middle size ranges (4–50 workers), revealed four, quite distinct types of firms [*McCormick et al., 1994; Ongile and McCormick, 1995*]. Figure one lays out the salient features of each type. The typology, which grew out of our Nairobi observations, does not include a 'high road' category of firms. Such firms, although key to industrial districts in developed countries, were missing from Nairobi's garment industry.

FIGURE 1

FIRM TYPES

1. Custom Tailors
* Produce men's and women's garments to order.
* Owner of the business is often a tailor who employs between two and five other skilled tailors.
* Some are mainly providers of labour who require the customer to supply the cloth and, sometimes, other inputs such as buttons, zippers, or lining.
* Others are fabric retailers who employ tailors as a service to their customers.

2. Contract Workshops
* Produce in quantity.
* Sometimes the firm supplies the cloth, sometimes the customer does.
* Use little or no division of labour; cutting the cloth sometimes reserved to one person.
* Skilled tailors expected to sew entire garments.

3. Mini-Manufacturers
* Some specialise in high fashion garments; most produce low-priced garments.
* Generally concentrate on one or two products, such as boys' school uniform shorts, women's petticoats, or men's trousers.
* Use a combination of skilled and unskilled workers.
* Some division of labour: for example, cutting, assembling, finishing, and pressing.

4. Mass Producers
* Manufacture standardised goods using assembly line production techniques.
* Make good quality garments for the middle income market.

Categorisation of firms in the subsample depended mainly on their volume of production, division of labour, and size the workforce. Overall, the most common firm type is, undoubtedly, the custom tailor. Although available data are not sufficient to allow us to categorise all firms in the original sample, it is likely that all of the one-person firms and most of the two- and three-person firms are custom tailors. In the middle size ranges, however, firm types vary, with mini-manufacturers replacing custom tailors as the most common type. Figure two shows the distribution of types across firms with between four and 50 workers. One-third (33.7 per cent) are custom tailors and more than half (54.6 per cent) are mini-manufacturers. The rest are contract workshops (9.6 per cent) and mass producers (2.1 per cent).

Location and firm type are strongly related [*McCormick et al., 1994*].[1] Mass producers are found mainly in Nairobi's industrial area and in the older industrial quarters to the east of the city centre. Contract workshops are located in town, both in city centre office buildings and in the older sections towards the Nairobi River. Custom tailors, the most dispersed of all the firm types, can be found in city centre shops, office buildings, residential estates, and suburban markets and shopping centres. In contrast, mini-manufacturers are highly

114

concentrated, with 89 per cent operating from one of two large City Council markets located in Nairobi's Eastlands. The rest are found in the city centre (3.3 per cent) and other markets or shopping centres (7.7 per cent).

FIGURE 2
DISTRIBUTION OF FIRM TYPES: GARMENT FIRMS WITH 4–50 WORKERS

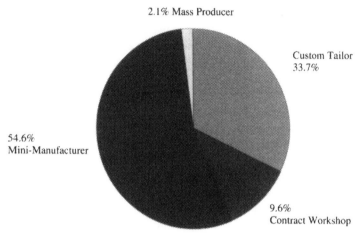

2.1% Mass Producer

Custom Tailor
33.7%

54.6%
Mini-Manufacturer

9.6%
Contract Workshop

Mini-Manufacturers: An Overview

Mini-manufacturers use a scaled-down version of mass production technology and generally specialise in one or two products, such as boys' school uniform shorts, women's petticoats, or men's trousers. Their combination of skilled and unskilled workers allows for some rudimentary division of labour. They may, for example, divide the manufacturing process into cutting, assembling, finishing, and pressing.

Mini-manufacturers make low-quality products, using cheap raw materials and unimaginative designs. The appearance of the final product is often further diminished by a lack of attention to details, like matching of thread, buttons, or zips. For example, we observed red petticoats being sewn with black thread, and dark blue shorts made with light blue zippers. When questioned, entrepreneurs said that 'it doesn't matter' to their customers. Price is mini-manufacturers' competitive advantage. They fear anything, including improved quality, which might raise their costs and force them to increase prices.

Mini-manufacturers tend to sell their products to wholesalers who take them to multiple market areas. A combination of markets, including Nairobi and one or more smaller up-country towns, is most common [*McCormick et al. 1994*]. Over two-thirds (68.8 per cent) of the African entrepreneurs, who sold

115

goods up-country, included their own home area in their market. Although we did not ask business owners why they chose particular market areas, family networks are probably an important consideration in decisions to sell at home.

V. THE GARMENT MARKETS

The garment-making clusters are housed in two large markets, each consisting of several concrete block buildings. The history, physical surroundings, and layout of the markets have had a significant impact on the clusters.

History of the Garment Markets

Uhuru and Quarry Road Markets were built in 1974 to replace older, makeshift premises from the colonial period. The markets were initially designed as retail outlets for groceries and clothing. When open-air markets for green groceries began selling similar goods at cheaper prices, often just outside the market buildings, grocery vendors could no longer compete. As they left the markets, clothing retailers moved in. Since the clothing sellers had somewhat higher profit margins and a product that does not spoil when business is slow, they could more easily afford the stall rents.

At first, these dealers sold mainly second-hand clothing. Then, in the buoyant economy of the late 1970s, businesses began making and selling new clothes, undeterred by the unsuitability of the markets for manufacturing. By 1989, according to our survey, Uhuru Market had 361 garment manufacturers and Gikomba Market, 235. These markets are neither factories nor organised industrial parks. Inside, they are poorly lighted and ventilated. The power supply is hardly adequate for even such light manufacturing as garment production. The markets are subdivided into small stalls of about two square metres. Three or four machines are squeezed into this small space, leaving little room for movement or storage of raw materials. Some innovative founders have built upstairs rooms out of wood to house more workers and machines. Many use the stalls' window shutters as display boards or cutting tables. The surroundings are little better than the market interior. Roads and car parks are inadequate. There are no banks, telephones or other supportive infrastructure to facilitate the evolution of manufacturing. The Quarry Road market is especially filthy and dilapidated, with poor drainage and overflowing sewers.

Entrepreneurs were aware of conditions in the markets when they responded to our question about choice of location. When asked why they chose to locate in the garment market, nearly three-quarters (72.2 per cent) said simply, 'This was where I could get premises.' The tone of resignation in their replies contrasted with responses of entrepreneurs in other locations who spoke of access to their customers or convenience to their place of residence.

Characteristics of the Clusters

A group of producers making the same or similar items in close proximity to each other, does not guarantee economic benefits. The concentration provides opportunities for other developments, such as the division of labour and specialisation among firms; the emergence of suppliers providing raw materials, components, new or second-hand machinery, and spare parts; the emergence of agents who sell to distant markets; the growth of firms providing technical, financial, and accounting services; and the formation of associations of similar producers [*Schmitz, 1993: 4*]. Preliminary evidence suggests that successful clusters in developing countries will be characterised by strong working relations among firms in the cluster, social and professional networks extending beyond the cluster, and a certain internal dynamism and resilience.

Inter-firm Relations

A major strength of industrial districts lies in the opportunities physical proximity offers for linkages among firms. Clustering facilitates vertical and horizontal relations between producing firms and makes producer–trader interrelations easier. Proximity can also promote formation of self-help organisations. Nairobi's garment markets exhibit these inter-firm linkages in varying degrees. We saw some sharing of basic equipment, very limited contracting of specialised services, fairly extensive use of traders, but no sectoral associations. On the product level, relations are clearly more competitive than collaborative.

Vertical subcontracting and a specialised division of labour, whereby a few firms provide specialised services to the others, characterises many developing countries small firm clusters [*Nadvi and Schmitz, 1994*]. Such basic inter-firm collaboration exists to a limited degree in the garment markets. Sometimes, it is as simple as lending scissors or a measuring tape. At a slightly higher level, businesses with specialised machines such as electric cutting shears or a button-holer, perform certain functions for neighbouring firms. The market atmosphere, where firms operate near one another in semi-open stalls, seems also to facilitate informal collaboration. Businesses reported asking colleagues for assistance with machine breakdowns, learning new designs, excess orders, shortage of raw materials, and marketing of new products. The first two of these – assistance with machine breakdowns and with learning new designs and patterns – appear to be the most important, reported instances of collaboration by 62.8 and 49.6 per cent of the market-based mini-manufacturers. In contrast, none of the mini-manufacturers located outside the markets collaborated in these ways. The results are not statistically significant, probably because of the small number of mini-manufacturers located outside the garment markets. The observed instances of collaboration are, therefore, best considered as indicators for further research.

Nadvi and Schmitz [*1994: 22–4*] identify producer–trader interrelations as particularly important in clusters in developing countries. Noting that clustering not only encourages the emergence of specialised suppliers, but also attracts agents who sell the output to distant markets, they connect the features of trader–producer linkages to the targeted market segment. At the predominantly low-quality/low-price end of the market, such interrelations between producers and traders are generally impersonal, hierarchical, and involve little exchange of knowledge and information. When, on the other hand, quality is a determining aspect in a finished product's marketing strategy, the relationship between producers and traders becomes more collaborative, personalised, and involves elements of trust and stability.

As expected, mini-manufacturers use traders for both purchases of inputs and sale of final products. Nearly three-quarters (74.2 per cent) of the mini-manufacturers reported buying cloth from wholesalers. A much smaller proportion (18.0 per cent) bought directly from the factory, while a few (7.8 per cent) went to retail shops. The purchasing pattern for other materials was similar. The use of traders depends, in large measure, on firm size, though organisation also plays a role. Custom tailors and contract workshops (74.0 per cent and 60.5 per cent respectively) also buy cloth from wholesalers, unlike the much larger mass producers who go direct to the factory.

Apart from the fact that suppliers are mostly Asian businessmen, we know very little about these cloth wholesalers or their dealings with firms in the garment markets. Some suppliers visit the markets, bringing samples with them. Most often, however, business owners go to them to purchase materials. Few mini-manufacturers (28.6 per cent) can buy on credit. This is a very small segment compared with, for example, the 87 per cent of the custom tailors who reported being able to buy materials on credit. The difference is all the more remarkable when we realise that the firms are probably dealing with many of the same wholesalers.

Lack of supplier credit is congruent with an expected association of low quality output with impersonal trading relations [*Nadvi and Schmitz, 1994*]. Garment firms with supplier credit were apt to have chosen their suppliers on the basis of some personal contact, while those without credit tended to identify suppliers through advertising, agents, or other intermediaries. Ranking of the reasons for choice of suppliers from the most to the least personal revealed significant differences between those receiving and not receiving credit on the one hand, and between custom tailors and mini-manufacturers on the other.

Field officers for a local non-governmental organisation (NGO) involved in credit and business training offered another reason why mini-manufacturers lack supplier credit. They explained that suppliers generally give credit only on certain types of materials. Typically the older, slower moving stock is available on credit, but the producer must pay cash for goods that are in high demand. Custom tailors stand ready to make a variety of items. Often, customers supply the material, but tailors also stock and display sample fabrics as a sales promotion device. This stock can be a mixture of fabrics, some purchased with cash and others taken on credit. Mini-manufacturers, however, because they produce larger quantities of more standardised goods and because price is a major consideration, have less flexibility in their choice of material. The cheap fabric that they need most is in high demand and, therefore, rarely available on credit. This lack of supplier credit is important because the ability to raise funds through borrowing or supplier credit is one of four variables distinguishing growing from stagnant or shrinking mini-manufacturers [*McCormick et al., 1994*].

Traders are mini-manufacturers' main customers. Firms report selling an average of 62.8 per cent of their products to wholesalers, compared with 18.3 per cent to individuals and 18.9 per cent to retailers [*McCormick et al., 1994: 36*]. Traders visit the markets frequently. When they come, they bring important market information. Most mini-manufacturers (69.4 per cent) said they learn mainly from their customers about the kinds of products people want. Much more research is needed to investigate the nature of the information shared and the level of collaboration between traders and producers. Nevertheless, this preliminary analysis suggests that the opportunity for regular producer–trader interaction may be the clearest benefit offered by location in the garment markets.

Nairobi's small-scale garment manufacturers lack effective self-help organisations. Business owners gathered at the final seminar agreed that they would benefit from forming some type of support group [*McCormick et al., 1994: 110*]. Among the functions envisioned for the group, the most prevalent were looking into the problems of small garment manufacturers, setting industry standards, and developing training programmes for employees. Although about one-third of the seminar participants attended a follow-up meeting to discuss forming a group, no concrete plans have as yet emerged. If, as Nadvi and Schmitz [*1994: 28*] argue, the effectiveness of sectoral associations is directly related to the overall development and formalisation of business practices within the cluster, we might expect Nairobi's garment makers to have difficulty in putting together a strong association.

Despite these limited indications of co-operation and collaboration, the markets are mainly places of competition. The similarity of products and geographic overlapping of markets means that businesses are locked into fierce competition with one another. Entrepreneurs responses to a request to identify

119

their major competitors supports this observation. Nearly two-thirds (62:5 per cent) said that their main competitors are producers in one, or both, of the garment markets. This response far outranked second-hand clothes (20.8 per cent) Asian shops in town (12.5 per cent), and large garment factories (4.2 per cent), indicating that business owners perceive their major source of competition to be within the markets themselves.

Social and Professional Networks

The debate on industrial districts in Europe is rooted in the theory that economic relations between firms are embedded in social relations [*Grabher, 1993; Nadvi and Schmitz, 1994*]. The theory has three dimensions: the belief that specific and interrelated historical, social, and cultural factors generate significantly different processes of development [*Garofoli, 1992*]; the belief that socio-cultural identities provide a basis for trust and reciprocity in inter-firm relations [*Granovetter, 1985; Seierup, 1995*]; and the view that the social milieu strongly influences and is influenced by the processes of innovation and technological change [*Lundvall, 1988*]. Our research dealt specifically with only the second of these aspects. Within the general framework of socio-cultural identities, we examined networks based on three characteristics of the firms' owners: ethnicity, level of education, and gender. The three combine to determine an entrepreneur's family and professional networks.

TABLE 1

ENTREPRENEUR'S ETHNICITY BY FIRM TYPE

Firm Type	Firms		Ethnic Group (%)			
	N	%	Kikuyu	Luo	Other African	Asian
Custom Tailor	13	33.7	29.4	26.0	39.0	5.5
Contract Workshop	4	9.6	6.5	20.6	10.3	62.6
Mini-manufacturer	22	54.6	50.6	36.3	9.8	3.3
Mass Producer	1	2.1	0.0	0.0	0.0	100.0
TOTAL	40	100.0	37.9	30.5	19.2	12.4
Percentage of Kenyan population			20.9	12.8	65.1	0.5

Source: Own survey, 1989.
Notes:
1. Cases are weighted to reflect entire population of firms in 4–50 employment range.
2. The significance of the chi-square statistic for differences in ethnicity by type of firm is .0058; the lambda statistic for dependence of firm type on ethnicity is .2710.
3. Population figures are based on 1979 Census Data [*Kenya, 1991*].

Although the garment industry attracts Kenyans of many ethnic groups, there are noticeable ethnic concentrations. African entrepreneurs predominate in custom tailoring and mini-manufacturing (see Table 1). Asians own over 60 per cent of the contract workshops and all of the mass producing firms in our sample, though small sample sizes may distort the percentages for these types. Asians, though less than one per cent of the population, own 12.4 per cent of the garment firms in this size range. Nearly all (86.9 per cent) of the mini-manufactures are members of Kenya's two largest ethnic groups, the Kikuyu and the Luo. The remainder are divided between Asians and other African communities. No Asian entrepreneurs operate within the garment markets.

Education largely determines a person's professional networks. These networks, which can be crucial for mobilisation of adequate managerial and technical skills, consist of colleagues, schoolmates, the former boss, and stable customers and suppliers from former jobs [*Rasmussen, 1992*]. Professional networks offer access to customers, market information, and production networks that can, in turn, lead to higher profits and better sources of finance. Those with higher levels of education will have better placed schoolmates, former workmates who have advanced to higher positions, and skills that enable them to track friends and colleagues who might be able to assist them.

Gender can also be the basis for networking. Women and men often belong to different social groups, and maintain their social ties in different ways. Even within the same family, the social networks of male and female members may differ. Often social networks are sex-segregated, with men belonging to primarily male networks and women to mainly female networks. Women's generally disadvantaged position in Kenyan society means that women's networks normally provide less access to power and resources than men's networks. Most (79.2 per cent) mini-manufacturers are women. On average, they are the least educated entrepreneurs in the industry [*McCormick et al., 1994*]. Nearly half (46.9 per cent) have a primary education or less. The rest have had some secondary (51.9 per cent) or post secondary (1.2 per cent) education. Since nearly all of the owners of mini-manufacturing firms are female with fairly low educational attainment, we would expect their networks to be limited in working for the business.

All business owners use family and professional networks to some extent. Both the networks' ability to provide positive support, and the nature of that support, vary considerably. At the high end of the spectrum are the Asian owners of mass producing businesses who can take advantage of the entrepreneurial tradition and established business, and the professional networks of their ethnic group. At the other end is the typical mini-manufacturer: a woman with only a primary education whose chief linkages are to a peasant-farming family in a distant rural area.

The evidence on how these networks operate comes mainly from informal observation and secondary sources. Nevertheless, it seems to, at least partially, explain the different operating styles and growth potential among garment manufacturers. African and Asian social structures share one important characteristic: lines of social differentiation tend to be more vertical than horizontal. In other words, the predominant social division is along ethnic or religious lines, with class distinctions within communities being less important [*Gregory, 1993: 356–7; Macharia, 1988*].

Asian family and professional networks reflect the general prosperity achieved by the Asian communities over the past 50 years [*Gregory, 1993: 351*]. Asians are involved in commerce, industry, and specific occupations. Their strength in wholesale trade and industry prompts Himbara [*1994: 158–60*] to call them *the* Kenyan capitalist class. Asian garment producers, therefore, can include in their networks textile wholesalers, shop owners, bankers, other garment producers, sewing machine vendors, and a wide range of middle- and upper-income consumers. These networks can be tapped formally or informally. The entrepreneur buying fabric from a wholesaler in the family network is formally working through the solidarity group. Many times, however, the interaction is informal: a casual conversation at the club or mosque, or a discussion at a family gathering. Formal and informal access to family and professional networks gives the entrepreneur many opportunities to increase technical competence, knowledge of the product and the market, management capability, and understanding of local or national industrial conditions.

Asian networks are generally on a high level, making their effect on business performance overwhelmingly positive. The family and professional networks of African entrepreneurs also support business endeavours, but lack the power to lift them to higher levels. Kinship and ethnicity seem to be most powerful. Epstein's [*1969*] classic study showed how ties of kinship and ethnicity changed but remained important as Africans moved from rural villages to an urban setting. Macharia [*1988*] found that ethnic considerations in Nairobi's 'informal sector' affected entry into business, brought customers, and largely determined who got credit. His finding that certain ethnic groups dominate particular activities was borne out by Ngau and Keino's [*1995*] study of women entrepreneurs in Nairobi. The dominance is often perpetuated by limiting training to co-ethnics, by passing information about business opportunities along ethnic networks, or by 'handing down' market stalls or other business sites to younger relatives [*Macharia, 1988: 9–20*]. In some trades, notably prepared food and garments, customers seemed to prefer patronising businesses run by co-ethnics [*Macharia, 1988: 13, 20*]. In others, such as fresh produce or baskets, networks can be traced from rural villages to urban producers and/or traders [*Ngau and Keino, 1995*].

A typical mini-manufacturer exemplifies the mixed effects of African networks. The business owner is a woman with a primary education. She came to Nairobi after she married, but maintains very close ties with her rural home.[2] She almost always has a young relative staying with her, either attending school or looking for employment. She may have been previously employed at a low-level job. If she is married, her husband may be a civil servant with the same or somewhat more education. Her strongest networks link her to the family in the rural area and people from her home village, now living in Nairobi. Like other African migrants to the city, she brought with her a mode of social and economic interaction characterised by face-to-face relations and contacts based on kinship or personal acquaintance. When she wanted to start her business, she feared the bureaucratic procedures. Thus, instead of going alone to city hall to apply for a licence or obtain a market stall, our prospective entrepreneur looked for someone – a relative, schoolmate, or someone from her village known in city hall – to intercede for her. In this way, the family or professional network facilitated the business start. Our entrepreneur may also use the family network to find a market for her products. She, therefore, produces the low-priced, low-profit garments that rural consumers want.

This discussion of networks has ranged over a variety of issues. Two points bear emphasising. First, mini-manufacturers have effective networks, but their networks usually lead to rural markets where profit margins are necessarily low. Second, the garment markets have an 'air' of socio-cultural identity. In contrast with other segments of Kenyan manufacturing where class and ethnicity separate managers from workers, mini-manufacturing workers and entrepreneurs share a common background that seems to create a cohesiveness and *esprit de corps* in the markets.

Dynamism and Resilience

One of the supposed advantages of clustering is the way in which it fosters specialisation and flexibility that enable individual firms, and the cluster itself, to survive economic declines and/or shifts in consumer tastes and preferences. In developed countries, analysts have unfavourably compared the rigidities of 'Fordist' mass production with industrial districts housing firms of different sizes and specialisations [*Piore and Sabel, 1984; Hirst and Zeitlin, 1989*].

The period from 1989 to 1993 was difficult for Nairobi's garment industry. Not only was the domestic economy declining, but the garment industry was also buffeted by competition from second-hand clothes. The only bright spot – the export market – was accessible to only a minority of larger firms. It was, in some ways, the ideal time to test the supposed benefits of clustering. The data on mini-manufacturers seem, at first glance, to support the hypothesis that clustering helps firms to withstand economic difficulties. Like custom tailors and contract workshops, mini-manufacturers lost workers between 1989 and 1993 (see Table 2). Mini-manufacturers' employment, however, declined less than the other types, suggesting that the location of most of these firms within the garment markets might have positively influenced their performance. Further analysis, however, appears to contradict this conclusion. A discriminant model, designed to distinguish between shrinking and growing mini-manufacturers, shows a negative correlation between location within the garment markets and firm growth. In fact, the three firms located outside the markets were growing, while most of those inside were not [*McCormick et al., 1994: 96*].

TABLE 2

EMPLOYMENT (INITIAL, 1989, 1993) AND EMPLOYMENT
GROWTH BY FIRM TYPE

Firm Type	*Firms*		*Mean Employment per Firm*			*Mean Employment Change 1989–93*
	N	*%*	*Initial*	*1989*	*1993*	
Custom Tailor	13	33.7	3.82	4.09	2.42	−1.67
Contract Workshop	4	9.6	2.75	7.67	5.55	−2.12
Mini-manufacturer	22	54.6	2.50	4.30	3.48	−0.82
Mass Producer	1	2.1	24.33	42.00	47.33	+5.33
TOTAL	40	100.0	3.50	5.37	4.26	−1.11

Source: Own survey, 1993.
Notes:
1. The significance of F-statistics for differences in means is .001 for initial, 1989, and 1993 employment, and .002 for employment change.
2. Cases are weighted to reflect entire population of firms in 4–50 employment range.

This conflicting evidence suggests that location in the garment markets is a mixed blessing. The inter-firm linkages discussed above offer the clearest benefits, but these appear to have been superseded, at least in the recent past, by the markets' negative features. Limitations on growth caused by lack of security of tenure and, more importantly, the inadequate physical arrangements of the markets seem, in this period at least, to have more than offset the benefits of clustering.

The garment manufacturers in the markets have no security of tenure. Instead of being secured by a lease, stallholders' occupation of a space depends only on timely payment, to the Nairobi City Council, of a rent or a stall fee set by the Council (The City of Nairobi By-Laws, 1948, amended to 1967, Section 3). The City Council frequently behaves in a punitive manner and in direct contradiction to the stated policies on small enterprise development. In the recent past, hawkers have been more seriously affected by arbitrary City Council action than market stallholders, but the fact remains that a garment producer whose rent is late could be summarily evicted. Furthermore, should local or national governments decide to enforce codes restricting manufacturing activities to designated industrial areas or apply the onerous provisions of the Factories Act, nearly all mini-manufacturers would face immediate closure. This insecurity adds to the risks inherent in small scale garment manufacture and may make business owners unwilling to expand beyond a level of which they could absorb the losses.

Mini-manufacturers show the highest number of workers per unit of value added and the lowest total factor productivity [*McCormick et al., 1994*]. The cheap products made by these firms undoubtedly explain some of the relationship of value added to labour. Also important, however, is their situation in premises that make efficient manufacturing nearly impossible. The lack of suitable premises may also hamper technological change among the mini-manufacturers. Introduction of specialised machines and new techniques requires space, reliable power supplies, and security from fire and theft, all of which are lacking in the garment markets.

Product quality and design are also affected by poor lighting and the lack of space for cutting and finishing. Introduction of new designs to meet changing consumer tastes requires secrecy. In the garment markets, however, as soon as an entrepreneur begins working on a new design or new product, others copy it, denying the innovators the benefits of their creativity. Profit margins stay uniformly low, and firms cannot grow.

VI. CONCLUSIONS

This analysis has attempted to determine how closely the garment markets resemble successful industrial clusters elsewhere. This final section summarises the findings, points to needs for further research, and outlines interventions that might assist the clusters to develop.

Findings and Research Needs

Like many clusters in developing countries, the garment markets exhibit weak internal and external linkages. The inter-firm specialisation and division of labour, which are supposed to be key to collective efficiency, are almost totally lacking. Those inter-firm linkages that exist are often informal and at a low level. Producer–trader links appear to be important for both inputs and the sale of final products. Traders are clearly important sources of market information, but available data did not allow us to assess the closeness of the relationship between producers and traders, or to estimate the influence of the traders on quality, design, or innovation. Sectoral associations do not exist, though some entrepreneurs seem interested in forming an association.

Evidence on ethnicity, gender, and education suggests that entrepreneurs' social and professional networks are important to their business operations. The mini-manufacturers use their networks well, but most are poorly educated, African women whose networks have limited power to uplift a business. Some networks lead back to rural markets where low incomes and competition with the second-hand clothing market keep profit margins extremely low.

Others encompass the lower ranks of city bureaucrats and professionals who can assist with licences or access to premises in the garment markets, but who cannot help a business to change significantly. Furthermore, these networks appear not to be based in the cluster, but rather are rooted in the entrepreneurs' other social and professional contacts.

Mini-manufacturers' businesses have exhibited a certain dynamism and resilience during the recent economic downturn. Their performance, which was slightly better than that of custom tailors and contract workshops, seems to be the net result of contradictory forces. The clearest benefit of clustering is in the area of producer–trader relations. Unfortunately, poor conditions in the markets, by working against efficient production and product development, largely negate this advantage.

In sum, Nairobi's garment markets are more of a sectoral agglomeration than a true industrial district. Our conclusions are limited, as already mentioned, by a study design that did not focus on clustering. New studies to test our findings and fill in the information gaps are now needed. Such studies could follow the model suggested by Nadvi and Schmitz [*1994: 59–61*]. The most crucial needs are for a better understanding of the role of traders, both suppliers and traders, in final products; a clearer picture of the functioning of entrepreneurs' social networks; and finally, if we are to judge the effects of clustering on firm performance, data on the efficiency implications of clustering.

Possible Interventions

The information gleaned thus far points to the need for interventions that could improve the performance of firms in the garment markets. Government, NGOs, and small and large firms in the private sector all have a contribution to make.

Evidence from European industrial districts and clusters in developing countries suggests that the state, especially at subnational levels, can perform an important function in providing institutional support to industrial districts [*Schmitz and Musyck, 1993; Nadvi and Schmitz, 1994*]. Despite a strong policy commitment to the furtherance of small enterprises, the Kenya government has done little to assist either individual garment producers or their business clusters [*Kenya, 1992*]. One problem seems to be lack of coordination between national policy and its implementation, which is often in the hands of local authorities. The insecure tenure arrangements and poor condition of the garment markets are examples of the inability or unwillingness of local government to implement national policy [*McCormick, 1993; McCormick et al., 1994*]. The Kenya Government needs to review laws governing African markets. The principles of periodicity and temporal conditions, upon which the Nairobi City By-Laws seem to have been based, no longer hold for

126

markets such as Quarry Road and Uhuru. In particular, the By-Laws need to be updated to include a section on the rights of stallholders. The city needs also to commit itself to improved maintenance of the markets.

NGOs in Kenya currently offer many services aimed at fostering small enterprise development. The findings of this research suggest that NGOs could fruitfully continue to aid in providing training and access to credit, but with, perhaps, a slight change in emphasis. Mini-manufacturers have very little access to credit. The lack of banks near the garment markets means that mini-manufacturers, probably, have few other banking services. NGOs could help by locating field offices near the garment markets to enable loan officers to become more familiar with the mini-manufacturers' operations and particular problems. This should result in more firms gaining access to current NGO loan programmes. In the longer term, mini-manufacturers may benefit from the shift on the part of some NGOs from credit delivery to more comprehensive forms of financial intermediation [*Otero, 1994*].

Mini-manufacturers' low-quality strategy is showing signs of failing under competition from better quality, but similarly priced, second-hand clothes. The clothes, which were, at first, mainly available in cities and large towns, have now reached the smallest rural markets. If mini-manufacturers are to alter their market strategy, they will need assistance. In particular, they will require training to enable them to improve their quality without drastically increasing costs. NGOs could assist by offering such training at times and places convenient to the entrepreneurs.

In the private sector, larger garment firms, private investors, and the small firms themselves all have a part to play in strengthening the mini-manufacturers. Larger firms can assist NGOs with training for improved quality. This would be especially appropriate if large and small firms also explore the possibility of mutually beneficial subcontracting relationships. In this event, improving the quality of small firm output becomes the subcontractor's concern. Quality enhancement will probably also require better premises. In the current political and economic climate, it seems unrealistic to expect the Government to renovate the garment markets. It may be possible, instead, to interest real estate firms or other private investors to develop suitable space for rent on commercial terms. Finally, the small firms themselves can form associations that will give them greater bargaining power with City authorities and provide a forum for continuing to explore common problems.

Planned interventions can go only so far in creating sufficient conditions for the development of an industrial district [*Asheim, 1992*]. Trust, loyalty, solidarity, stronger and more extensive networks, and an atmosphere conducive to innovation and specialisation are as crucial to the process as functional external economies. Some of these can, no doubt, be facilitated by purposive action and the creation of new institutions, but whether such

127

positive forces will be enough to enable the mini-manufacturers to evolve into an industrial district remains to be seen.

NOTES

1. The significance of the chi-square statistic for differences in location by type of firm is 0.0001; the lambda statistic for dependence of location on firm type is 0.5089; lambda for dependence of firm type on location is 0.5999.
2. Mini-manufacturers scored highest of the four firm types on an index developed to measure the strength of rural ties [*McCormick, 1988: 323–4*].

REFERENCES

Asheim, B.T. (1992): 'Flexible Specialisation, Industrial Districts and Small Firms: A Critical Appraisal', in Ernste and Meier (eds.) [*1992*].

Brusco, S. (1990): 'Small Firms and the Provision of Real Services', Discussion paper for the workshop 'Flexible Specialisation in Europe', Zurich, Switzerland, 25–26 Oct.

Coughlin, P. and K. I. Gerrishon (eds.) (1991): *Kenya's Industrialisation Dilemma*, Nairobi: Heinemann Kenya.

Dosi, G. *et al.* (eds) (1988): *Technical Change and Economic Theory*, London: Pinter.

Epstein, A.L. (1969): 'The Network and Urban Social Organisation', in Mitchell (ed.) [*1969*].

Ernste, H. and V. Meier (eds.) (1992): *Regional Development and Contemporary Industrial Response: Extending Flexible Specialisation*, London: Belhaven Press.

Garofoli, G. (ed.) (1992): *Endogenous Development and Southern Europe*, Aldershot: Avebury.

Grabher, G. (1993): 'Rediscovering the Social in the Economics of Interfirm Relations', in Grabher (ed.) [*1993*].

Grabher, G. (ed., 1993): *The Embedded Firm: On the Socioeconomics of Industrial Networks*, London: Routledge.

Granovetter, M. (1985): 'Economic Action and Social Structure: The Problem of Embeddedness', *American Journal of Sociology*, Vol. 91, Nov.

Gregory, R.G. (1993): *South Asians in East Africa: An Economic and Social History, 1890–1980*, Boulder, CO: Westview Press.

Himbara, D. (1994): *Kenyan Capitalists, the State, and Development*, Nairobi: East African Educational Publishers.

Hirst, P. and J. Zeitlin (1989): 'Flexible Specialisation and the Competitive Failure of UK Manufacturing', *The Political Quarterly*, 60.

Kenya (1990): *Statistical Abstract*, Nairobi: Government Printer.

Kenya (1992): *Small Enterprise and Jua Kali Development in Kenya*, Sessional Paper No. 2, Nairobi: Government Printer.

Little, I.M.D., Mazumdar, D. and J.M. Page (1987): *Small Manufacturing Enterprises: A Comparative Analysis of India and Other Economies*, New York: Oxford University Press.

Lundvall, B.-A. (1988): 'Innovation as an Interactive Process: From User Producer Interaction to the National System of Innovation', in Dosi *et al.* [*1988*].

Macharia, K. (1988): 'Social Networks: Ethnicity and the Informal Sector in Nairobi', IDS Working Paper No. 463, Institute for Development Studies, University of Nairobi, Nairobi.

Marshall, A. (1890): *Principles of Economics*, London: Macmillan.

Marshall, A. (1919): *Industry and Trade*, London: Macmillan.

McCormick, D. (1988): 'Small Manufacturing Enterprise in Nairobi: Golden Opportunity or Dead End?', Ph.D. dissertation, Baltimore, MD: Johns Hopkins University.

McCormick, D. (1989): 'Garmentmaking in Nairobi: A Research Proposal', IDS Working Paper No. 468, Institute for Development Studies, University of Nairobi, Nairobi.

McCormick, D. (1991a): 'Success in Urban Small-scale Manufacturing: Implications for Economic Development', in Coughlin and Gerrishon (eds.) [*1991*].

McCormick, D. (1991b): 'Nairobi's Clothing Retailers: Preliminary Findings', in Nyong'o and Coughlin (eds.) [*1991*].

McCormick, D. (1993): 'Risk and Firm Growth: The Dilemma of Nairobi's Small Scale Manufacturers', Discussion Paper No. 291, Institute for Development Studies, University of Nairobi, Nairobi.

McCormick, D., Kinyanjui, M.N. and G. Ongile (1994): 'Networks, Markets, and Growth in Nairobi's Garment Industry', Final Report on study of Barriers to Growth of Small and Medium-sized Enterprises, Institute for Development Studies, University of Nairobi, Nairobi.

McCormick, D. and P.O. Pedersen (eds.) (1995): *Small Enterprises: Flexibility and Networking in an African Context*, Nairobi: Longhorn Kenya Ltd. (in press).

Mitchell, J.C. (ed.) (1969): *Social Networks in Urban Situations: Analyses of Personal Relationships in Central African Towns*, Manchester: Manchester University Press.

Mitchell, J.C. (1969): 'The Concept and Use of Social Networks', in Mitchell (ed.) [*1969*].

Nadvi, K. and H. Schmitz (1994): 'Industrial Clusters in Less Developed Countries: Review of Experiences and Research Agenda', IDS Discussion Paper No. 339, Institute of Development Studies, University of Sussex, Brighton.

Ngau, P. and I. Keino (1995): 'The Social Background of Women Entrepreneurs in Nairobi', in McCormick and Pedersen (eds.) [*1995*].

Nyong'o, P.A. and P. Coughlin (eds.) (1991): *Industrialisation at Bay: African Experiences*, Nairobi: Academy Science Publishers.

Ongile, G. and D. McCormick (1995): 'Barriers to Small Firm Growth: Evidence from Nairobi's Garment Industry', in McCormick and Pedersen (eds.) [*1995*].

Otero, M. (1994): 'The Evolution of Nongovernmental Organisations toward Financial Intermediation', in Otero and Rhyne (eds.) [*1994*].

Otero, M. and E. Rhyne (eds.) (1994): *The New World of Microenterprise Finance: Building Healthy Financial Institutions for the Poor*, West Hartford, CT: Kumarian Press.

Pedersen, P.O. (1995): 'Flexibility and Networking in an European and an African Context', in McCormick and Pedersen (eds.) [*1995*].

Piore, M.J. and C.F. Sabel (1984): *The Second Industrial Divide: Possibilities for Prosperity*, New York: Basic Books.

Pyke, F. and W. Sengenberger (eds.) (1992): *Industrial Districts and Local Economic Regeneration*, Geneva: International Institute for Labour Studies.

Pyke, F. and W. Sengenberger (eds.) (1990): *Industrial Districts and Inter-firm Cooperation in Italy*, Geneva: International Institute for Labour Studies.

Rasmussen, J. (1992): *The Local Entrepreneurial Milieu: Enterprise Networks in Small Zimbabwean Towns*, Department of Geography Research Report No. 79, Roskilde University in co-operation with Centre for Development Research, Copenhagen.

Schmitz, H. (1992): 'On the Clustering of Small Firms', in *IDS Bulletin*, Vol. 23, No. 3.

Schmitz, H. (1993): 'Small Shoemakers and Fordist Giants: Tale of a Supercluster', IDS Discussion Paper No. 331, Institute of Development Studies, University of Sussex, Brighton.

Schmitz, H. and B. Musyck (1993): 'Industrial Districts in Europe: Policy Lessons for Developing Countries', Discussion Paper No. 324, Institute of Development Studies, University of Sussex, Brighton.

Seierup, S. (1995): 'Small Town Entrepreneurs and Their Networks in Kenya', in McCormick and Pedersen (eds.) [*1995*].

Storper, M. (1990): 'Reply (to Amin and Robins)', in Pyke *et al.* [*1990*].

Storper, M. and R. Walker (1989): *The Capitalist Imperative: Territory, Technology, and Industrial Growth*, London: Basil Blackwell.

Sverrisson, A. (1992): 'Innovation as a Collective Enterprise: A Case Study of Carpenters in Nakuru, Kenya', Research Policy Studies Discussion Paper No. 189, Research Policy Institute, University of Lund, Lund.

Sverrisson, A. (1993): 'Evolutionary Technical Change and Flexible Mechanisation: Entrepreneurship and Industrialisation in Kenya and Zimbabwe', Ph.D. dissertation, University of Lund, Lund.

Thompson, G., Rosalind, F.J.L. and J.C. Mitchell (eds.) (1991): *Markets, Hierarchies & Networks: The Coordination of Social Life*, London: Sage.

Williamson, O.E. (1975): *Markets and Hierarchies: Analysis and Antitrust Implications*, New York: Free Press.

Williamson, O.E. (1980): 'The Organisation of Work: A Comparative Institutional Assessment', *Journal of Economic Behaviour and Organisation*, 1.

Small Enterprise Associations and Networks: Evidence from Accra

MEINE PIETER VAN DIJK

I. INTRODUCTION

In this chapter, the importance of small enterprise associations and networks of entrepreneurs will be studied. Fieldwork undertaken in Accra, the capital of Ghana, in 1993, focused on the relation between household poverty and the employment situation of the household members [*Alberts and Van Dijk, 1994*]. The main objective of the fieldwork was to identify the economic activities in which the urban poor were involved and the problems they face while developing their activities. In this chapter, particular attention will be paid to the importance of factors such as networking and participation in associations by small enterprises for entrepreneurial success. In dealing with these cases, we do not stay at the enterprise level but also analyse the environment of a small enterprise. The analysis is limited, however, to the interactions of enterprises with family, friends, tribe members and other entrepreneurs.

II. THE RESEARCH METHODS

The fieldwork took place in three neighbourhoods of Accra, where a high incidence of poverty was expected.[1] Qualitative research methods were used to find out how the poor of Accra have adapted during the period of structural adjustment that started in 1983 [*Kumar (ed.), 1993*]. The economic activities in which the households were involved were studied after interviewing randomly selected households in three neighbourhoods. Separate questions about the economic activities of their members were asked. Hence, the sample of economic activities on which the information was collected has not been drawn in a random way and, consequently, may not be representative of all economic activities in these neighbourhoods.

The research for this chapter was undertaken while the author was working with Wim Alberts as consultants for the World Bank, financed by the Netherlands Trust Fund. The results do not represent the point of view of the World Bank, however. Use has been made of Wim Alberts' write-up of his fieldwork in Maamobi.

A parallel research exercise has attempted to assess the functioning of the labour market in a more conventional manner [*Chhibber and Leechor, 1993*]. Our analysis stresses the people's perceptions of labour market issues and, as such, is complementary to a quantitative analysis of the Ghanaian labour market. The more quantitative analysis is based on three rounds of the Ghana Living Standards Survey [*Bureau of Statistics, 1989*]. The Ghana Living Standards Survey household data analysis intends to provide information on issues such as real wage rigidities, sectoral wage differentials, inflexibilities in the market, sectoral reallocation of labour, trends in employment and so on.[2]

The information collected on the economic activities is of both quantitative and qualitative nature. A precoded questionnaire was used to collect standard information on the economic activities of the members of the household. The quantitative data concern employment, income, turnover, level of technology, and so forth. These data are complemented by qualitative findings from the more open, semi-structured part of the interviews. This qualitative information basically concerns the economic environment of poor entrepreneurs, and includes matters such as personal motivation, choice of activity, educational background or training, access to capital, market situation, competition, aspirations, connections and networks, the importance of associations and collaboration, and so on.

In summary, a combination of research methods was applied. A short precoded questionnaire per household and per economic activity, and participatory rapid appraisal methods were used to study the labour market, poor households and the economic activities in which their members were involved. Applying both methods of poverty research gave the fieldwork an innovative aspect. The qualitative techniques were designed to investigate, in a participatory manner, local perceptions and concepts of employment and poverty, while the questionnaire was designed to generate basic information in a systematic way [*Kumar (ed.), 1993*].

III. COPING STRATEGIES OF THE POOR

A multi-criteria poverty definition is derived from the perceptions and descriptions of poverty as elicited from respondents. During each interview, people were requested to elaborate on what they considered to be poverty and whether they considered their own household to be poor. The research teams subsequently grouped the wide variety of poverty definitions around eight common characteristics; these form the basis of the multi-criteria definition, with each household scoring on those criteria.[3]

A classification of coping strategies, that is, activities of poor households that enabled them to cope with their resource poor conditions was made.

Consumptive strategies, involving adjusting expenditures and falling back on the support of others were distinguished from productive strategies, involving intensified and more diversified economic activity. Adjusting expenditures was a first reaction to a reduction in income. Less nutritious foods were chosen and cold or cooked food bought in the street instead of being prepared at home. Families also cut back on expenditure for health care and their children's education: children were taken from private schools resulting in eventually, due to cutbacks and rising pupil intakes, public schools being undermined, while spending less on food and delaying medical treatment had substantial effects.

Appealing to family members, to other households in the community, to friends and people from one's tribe or region was a fallback mechanism, and constituted the second coping strategy. These networks were used for obtaining money and food; similarly, people used their social network to find work. However, in an urban context, where many face similar problems and where traditional ties are becoming less important, it may no longer be possible for a number of the poor to fall back on their family, friends, tribesmen or people from their region.

Poor households have also tried to push more of their members into economic activities; this is the third coping strategy. This led to more child labour and to an increasing share of women participating in the labour force. Starting from a disadvantaged position, however, makes it more difficult to turn their work into rewarding activities: investments are minimal, the location may not be optimal and the person concerned may not have the appropriate skill and experience to start a new activity. Female traders often sell very small quantities with low margins. Often, too many sell the same product, which makes it difficult for any one individual to earn a living from the trade. Further, the tendency to use working capital for necessary daily household expenditures may lead to what is called 'eating into profit'. At the end of a week the discovery would be made that there is not enough money left to buy new stock, to pay certain charges or pay for transportation.

Diversifying existing activities, the fourth type of coping strategy, can be seen as a form of risk spreading. Female traders will sell additional products, or metal workers may venture into the production of new models or products. Participating in a collective savings system (Rotating Savings and Credit Associations, ROSCAs, called 'susu' in Ghana), buying and selling on credit, selling very small quantities and using a different way of packaging may be considered diversification strategies as well. Other examples are renting out rooms, having children take up apprenticeships, investing in their education and training, gambling, and lending money to others.

The challenge for the formulation of good policies is to find the means to alleviate poverty by building on positive actions of the poor. Instead of merely providing some material support, it is necessary to find ways in which the poor may successfully harness their efforts to improve their situation.

IV. ECONOMIC ACTIVITIES OF THE URBAN POOR

Tables 1–3 give an overview of all economic activities studied. This will be followed by a breakdown of activities in which the poor and non-poor are more active, and a description of their income ranges. The overview of economic activities studied is presented in Table 1, disaggregated by gender and location. The activities categorised are listed as food processing, textile-related activities, trade activities, construction-related activities, metal-related activities and, a general category, other. Food processing activities include the creation of a wide variety of foods: *banku, fufu,* soup (groundnut and palm-nut), *kokonte*, riceballs, rice and sauce, fried fish, grilled fish, *kenkey, gari* and beans, beer (*broukoutou* and *pitou*), stew, *waayke*, bread, *kokoo*, pepper soup and *agidi*, and cornmilling. These activities are clearly dominated by women; only two out of 35 are carried out by men. The heterogeneity of economic activities is an important aspect of the economic environment of the poor. The table gives an indication of the variety across and within the selected categories of activities.

Textile-related occupations include seamstresses, tailors, tie and dye manu-facturers, weavers and knitters; shoemakers and cobblers are also included in this category because the activities are quite similar. In our sample there are twice as many men involved in textile-related activities than women. The category, trade, again covers a wide spectrum, including herbal medicine, charcoal, groundnuts, cooking-oil, table-cloths, material (cloth), icewater, ice-blocks, fish, cars, cereals (maize, rice, sorghum and millet), tubers (cassave, yam and cocoyam) and *akpeteshie*. This category is also dominated by women, a little over 80 per cent of the traders being female.

TABLE 1

OVERVIEW OF ECONOMIC ACTIVITIES BY GENDER AND AREA

Area	Food		Textiles		Trade		Construction		Metal		Other		All	
	M	F	M	F	M	F	M	F	M	F	M	F	M	F
Abeka	–	7	4	2	4	9	5	–	4	–	11	6	26	24
East-Maamobi	2	10	3	3	2	15	5	–	5	1	16	2	33	31
Jamestown	–	16	3	–	1	6	4	–	5	–	6	4	19	26
Total	2	33	10	5	7	30	14	–	14	1	33	12	80	81

Construction-related occupations include blockmakers, potmakers, carpenters, woodhewers, masons, builders and hardware store owners; these activities are all carried out by men. The fifth category of activities are the metal-related activities, metal being defined in a very broad sense. Occupations include bicycle repairmen, mechanics, fitters, welders, engineers, moulds and parts makers, body worker and painters, spare parts and brake-fluid sellers, and electric mechanics. Metal-related activities are dominated by men. The category, other, covers the wide variety of occupations: drivers, a lotto ticket seller, hairdressers, a barber, a nurse, a telephone operator, an electrician, a videohouse operator, watchmen, fishermen, students, sanitary workers, a loud speaker repairer, sanitary brush makers, a vulcaniser, teachers, civil servants and a computer programmer. Close to 75 per cent of these activities are carried out by men.

So far we have made no distinction between economic activities carried out by members of poor households and those carried out by members of non-poor households. Incorporating the poverty classification used by Alberts and Van Dijk [*1994*] into the analysis enables us to distinguish between the economic activities of poor and non-poor households. Table 2 shows how many activities are carried out, respectively, by poor and non-poor household members. The tables point to three important aspects of the economic activities of the poor. The first impression to be derived from this information is that poverty is spread across all activities. All categories include poor household members. In relative terms, the largest number of poor are to be found in the food and trade sectors. Between 70 and 90 per cent of these activities are carried out by members of poor households. The poor and non-poor are more evenly distributed in the textiles, construction and metal sectors.

TABLE 2

ECONOMIC ACTIVITIES IN RELATION TO THE POVERTY STATUS OF THE
HOUSEHOLD

Area	Food		Textiles		Trade		Construction		Metal		Other		All	
	P	NP	P	NP	P	NP	P	NP	P	NP	P	NP	P	NP
Abeka	5	2	1	5	7	6	1	4	1	3	10	7	25	25
East-Maamobi	11	1	4	2	14	3	2	3	2	3	12	6	45	17
Jamestown	15	1	2	1	6	1	4	–	5	–	7	3	39	6
Total	31	4	7	8	27	10	7	7	8	6	29	16	109	51

Note: P stands for poor households and NP stands for non-poor households.

The majority (59 per cent) of the economic activities carried out by poor household members is carried out by women. On the contrary, the majority (69 per cent) of the economic activities carried out by non-poor is carried out by men. A little over 40 per cent of the female activities are carried out by women who are considered heads of households. The remaining 60 per cent is carried out by women who come from male-headed households. Our qualitative survey revealed, however, that the distinction between male and female-headed households is not as clear-cut as convential household surveys have

TABLE 3

ECONOMIC ACTIVITIES AND INCOME IN ABEKA AND EAST-MAAMOBI

Poor Households Activity (occupation)	*Monthly Income (cedis)*	*Non-Poor Households* Activity (occupation)	*Monthly Income (cedis)*
Rice and beans seller	12,000–15,000	Banku etc seller	125,000–150,000
Banku processor	15,000	Rice and fish seller	20,000–30,000
TZ and stew seller	12,000–15,000	Kenkey seller	30,000–40,000
Cornmiller	2,500	Kenkey seller	80,000–100,000
Broukoutou brewer	10,000–20,000	Kokoo and koose seller	25,000–37,500
Kenkey seller	20,000		
Fish fryer	8,000–10,000		
Pitou brewing	16,000		
Gari and beans	10,000–15,000		
Waakye seller	12,000		
Seamstress	3,000		
Tailor	30,000–40,000	Tailor	35,000–45,000
Cobblar	10,000–15,000	Weaver	40,000
Cobblar	20,000		
Provisions/ jewelry trader	15,000–20,000	Materials trader	70,000–100,000
Herbal medicine trader	3,000	Fishmonger	50,000–60,000
Charcoal trader	15,000–20,000	Spare parts trader	100,000–120,000
Provisions trader	12,000–15,000	Sugar and rice trader	45,000
Groundnut/ firewood trader	3,000–9,000		
Provisions trader	20,000–30,000		
Fruit trader	3,000		
Charcoal trader	15,000–20,000		
Water trader	15,000		
Sugar trader	12,000	Hairdresser	60,000
Cereals	5,000	Videohouse operator	120,000–240,000
Carpenter	4,000–8,000	Carpenter	180,000–200,000
Woodhewer	15,000	Hardware store owner	100,000–200,000
		Hardware store owner	100,000–200,000
Electric apprentice	5,000–9,000	Car mechanic	360,000
		Potmaker	70,000
Driver	28,000	Electric mechanic	60,000–80,000
Barber	30,000–40,000	Electrician	100,000–120,000
Telephone operator	29,000	Bus driver	160,000–200,000

indicated. In quite a few male-headed households, women are actually responsible for meeting basic need requirements. An issue then arises concerning who should be considered the head of the household and, closely linked, how to deal with income derived from alternative sources (men and women) in households.

Economic activities of poor households generate less income and are less rewarding than those of non-poor households. The relation between income derived from the economic activity and the poverty level of the household is very clear. Table 3 summarises the available information on the range in monthly income of a set of economic activities. It indicates whether an economic activity is undertaken by a member of a poor or a non-poor household. Income ranges are related to a particular activity and, therefore, do not represent total household income. The table does not list all the economic activities of each member of the household; certain households have more than one source of income and certain members are engaged in more than one activity.

It was difficult to obtain a clear picture of the income of all members of the household and to determine exactly how much each member contributed to the household expenditures. An unwillingness to disclose exact amounts, the uncertainty among participants of the total amount of income, profit, earnings or remittances (the husband's income tended to be a well-kept secret), the variable size of the household even within short time periods, and the fluctuations in income and expenditure patterns were all factors which resulted in inconclusive income and expenditure data. Determination of monthly or weekly averages involved assumptions on the part of the researcher at various levels. However, efforts to collect this type of information consistently throughout the survey resulted in a fairly accurate and reliable picture in Table 3 of the actual income derived from each particular activity.

The picture arising from the table confirms the findings of our poverty classification. The monthly profit of the self-defined, poor households does not exceed 40,000 cedis and ranges on average, from 12,000 to 20,000 cedis.[4] The monthly profits of the non-poor households from 20,000 to 30,000 cedis and, on average, from 90,000 and 110,000 cedis. In the case of East-Maamobi, the activity is the only activity undertaken by 15 out of 22 poor households, the remaining poor households undertake additional activities.

V. CHARACTERISTICS OF THE ECONOMIC ACTIVITIES OF THE POOR

Only the most typical features of each category of activities will be described; case studies will be used to provide illustrations. The focus is on the activities of the poor but, in order to put their activities into a dynamic perspective, the analysis will also compare them to the activities of some of the more successful entrepeneurs. Activities are considered as formal or informal. In formal activities entrepeneurs must pay registration fees and/or income tax on a regular basis, they are licensed to operate and they must submit to formal labour regulations [*Van Dijk, 1987*]. The basic characteristics of the economic activities of the poor can be described as follows:

Heterogenity

The basic feature of the informal sector is its heterogeneity: at one end of the spectrum, informal sector activities include viable and thriving small-scale industries) which appear to have growth potential; at the other end, there are individuals such as hawkers and street vendors whose income merely reaches the subsistence level and whose prospects for growth seem minimal. In between the two extremes, there exists a whole range of more or less productive and income-generating activities.

Differentiation

The fieldwork brought out the heterogenic picture of micro-enterprises in the informal sector. However, it also pointed to a differentiation process within the informal sector and within specific activities. There are large differences in the economic activities studied, and even within one particular activity, one may find stagnating as well as booming micro enterprises.

All economic activities studied in detail provide similar evidence of differentiation within activities. The food processing activities of the poor are predominantly marginal. Most activities take place in a vicious circle and do not create much surplus income. However, some examples show that there is a way out of this marginality. Product diversification and efficient management have led some of these poor entrepeneurs on to a path of dynamic growth. For the textile-related activities, there exists a tremendous glut in the market, though successful cases show how specialisation and a good location can create opportunities in this overcrowded market. The activities of most poor traders have a very limited scope. The success stories of some of the traders reveal that the ability to seek and discover niche markets does generate growth. Metal-related activities give a similar picture of constraints and potential for growth. Increased competition and diminishing demand can work against entrepreneurs who may sometimes find niches and benefit from locational advantages. Construction-related activities may be characterised by the same heterogeneity. Poor and marginal construction workers may be found besides non-poor and dynamic small-scale construction enterprises. There is little demand for the services of the poorer more labour-intensive construction entrepeneurs, while more dynamic firms may obtain their share from the booming construction activity in Accra.

The Poor are at the Bottom End

The market for the activities described is very competitive. Most of the poor entrepeneurs are situated at the lower end of the continuum of informal sector activities. An important distinction between the two ends of the continuum is that the economic activities of the poor are mainly driven by the supply of labour, while the economic activities of the non-poor are mainly driven by consumer demand for their products.[5] The poor basically struggle for subsistence and seek income for survival. The economic activities of the non-poor go beyond income generation to building enterprises and the accumulation of profits.

Most of the poor entrepeneurs are involved in micro-enterprises that operate from temporary structures and informal settings. The level of technology that they apply is generally low and, very often, traditional. They seem not only to adapt slowly to changing market circumstances, but also to lack the ability to improve the quality of their work. This tends to exclude poor entrepeneurs from the dynamic part of the market, and keeps them in the highly competitive lower end of the activity spectrum.

The Importance of Networks

Networks may be built through family relations, friends, and connections from one's tribe or region, and all kinds of associations are very important. The importance of family members has already been mentioned in relation to coping strategies; the most common way of finding a job is through family members and friends. Some claim that difficulties finding employment stem from a lack of connections. Ethnic segmentation of the labour market takes place when certain activities are open only to certain ethnic groups. Such is the case for charcoal selling, beer brewing and palm oil processing.

In many branches, there are associations of small entrepreneurs, some of which work reasonably well (for example, those for hairdressing, garages and textiles), while some have already existed for a long time. In certain cases, the initiative to set up the associations was taken by entrepreneurs; in other cases, the government required the set-up as, for instance, in the import of certain products. An association may function as a platform for discussion, and for the exchange of new ideas and experiences. Associations may also be the inter-locuteur for negociations with the government.

As an example of the activities of associations, a female entrepreneur, involved in seamstressing as a member of the seamstress association, mentioned that at their last meeting they tried to handle the issue of the glut in the dressmaking market by raising the initial apprenticeship fees up to 100,000 cedis. So far she has not done so yet, as she collects only 30,000 cedis in bulk when they start and 400 cedis each month.[6] The problem of a glut of dress-makers does not seem to bother her too much. In her view, they produce children, and all of them need to be dressed at some point in time. The small entrepreneur considers having many apprentices as compensation for the decline in demand. By doing so she is able to meet her short-term consumption needs. However, she also trains her own competition in the near future. In two to three years' time all ten girls will have finished their apprenticeship and will try eagerly to enter the overcrowded seamstresses market.

Another example of the importance of associations can be seen in hair-dressing, a typical female activity. A hairdresser interviewed explained that the association fixes the prices for pomades, creams, etc. However, in the market in which she works she collects an income for her services which is lower than the cost of purchasing materials. The fixed prices, set too high, benefit only saloons at the high end of the market. Many women, it seems, tend to spend their money in these places.

Low Productivity

The most striking difference between the two ends of the spectrum of activities appears to be the level of productivity. For micro-enterprises, the level of productivity tends to be low, while for dynamic enterprises it tends to be higher. Conventional measures of productivity measures of productivity of an enterprise can be expressed as a ratio of output to a selected input (labour or capital). The picture that emerges from various informal sector surveys carried out since the introduction in 1983 of the Economic Recovery Program is one of falling long run productivity in the micro-enterprise sector. In particular, the studies of Dawson [*1992*] and Steel and Webster [*1989*] conclude that the majority of firms surveyed have experienced a fall in demand for their output since 1983. It is quite likely that the decline in output at the firm level is consistent with growth of output of the micro-enterprise sector as a whole. The aforementioned studies depict a situation in which it appears that a slowly growing pie is being cut into ever smaller pieces. This seems most certainly to be the case for the segments of the micro-enterprise sector in which the poor mainly work.

More recent information on enterprise productivity is provided by the preliminary results of the Ghanaian enterprise survey, conducted on behalf of the Regional Program for Enterprise Development in 1992.[7] A comparison of capital–labour ratios across firms of different sizes reveals that the capital intensity in large firms is seven times greater than in micro firms. Differences in capital–labour ratios are also reflected in the labour and capital productivity ratios. The value added per unit of labour is three times higher in large firms than in micro firms, while the value added per unit of capital is nearly 20 times higher in micro firms than in large firms. Hence, smaller firms have a much lower labour productivity, but use their capital equipment more intensely!

The survey also found that large firms pay workers significantly higher wages than in micro firms. Average earnings for all workers rise with the size of the firm, and earnings are also highly correlated to the firm's profitability. These findings confirm the picture of low labour productivity and low returns to labour for micro-enterprises in Ghana.

With the data collected in our survey, it is not possible to apply either one of these productivity approaches. More precise input and output data are necessary. Within a typical neo-classical analytical framework of competitive and unregulated markets, income may also be taken as an indicator for productivity. The demand side of labour market analyses are strongly embedded in the marginal productivity approach. This reflects the behaviour of profit-maximising entrepeneurs within highly competitive market structures; the framework yields relatively precise outcomes for earnings structures. The earnings differentials subsequently reflect variations in productivity. In our sample, the working poor are located at the lower end of the activity continuum and score poorly within these activities. They operate in a highly competitive market under unregulated conditions.

The available income data are derived from individual economic activities and many therefore, be taken as an indicator of their productivity. The income received reflects the productivity of the person involved in that activity. Marginal economic activities suffer from low productivity as measured by the income of the owner. A comparison between incomes derived from economic activities of poor and non-poor is presented in Table 3, indicating differential productivity levels. The economic activities of poor households are less productive and, hence, generate less income than the economic activities of non-poor households.

Conclusion

The informal sector does provide employment and income for the poor. However, its heterogeneous nature makes it difficult to assess the potential contribution of the informal sector to overall economic growth. The capacity of the different segments or sub-sectors to reduce poverty varies substantially. To increase that capacity and to raise the various sub-sectors above the marginal level requires the identification of constraints that block the enhancement of the productivity of the poor. Without removing the constraints to access for the poor to productive assets, and without a strategy that both encourages the enhancement of the productive resources of the poor and increases their resource endowments, the most vulnerable groups in society will not be able to enhance their productivity and generate more income.

VI. CONSTRAINTS FOR GROWTH

This section aims to point out what basic constraints the selected activities face, while the following looks at which factors contribute to the dynamics of other activities and enterprises. Low productivity is a key impediment for poor entrepeneurs. Other constraints discussed are the lack of connections or networks, ethnic factors, lack of access to capital, existing barriers to entry in the informal sector and the cost of formalisation. Finally, constraints such as competition, increased costs and seasonality will be discussed.

Low Labour Productivity

Monthly income at the lower end of the spectrum usually does not exceed 20,000 cedis. Entrepeneurs are economically active in an environment where profit is generally eaten up, and cannot be saved or utilised to expand the business.

Lack of Connections or Networks

In many cases, connections or networks are important to the survival of a poor family in finding a job or in making an initial investment. There are also examples to the contrary, however. The preference of enterprises to remain independent can be seen in the limited role trade associations play in the areas studied. Only about a third of the entrepeneurs are members of an association, and the influence of decisions taken at association meetings does not appear to be very far-reaching. An exception to this is the influence of the dressmakers' and hairdressers' associations.

Ethnic Factors

Modern trades are not segmented along ethnic lines in the sense that tailoring, for instance, would only be undertaken by Ashantis. Ethnic affiliations, however, do play quite a substantial role in labour networks and different forms of co-operation. Looking for jobs and effectively exploring employment opportunities is hardly feasible without the assistance of tribesmen. Masters usually hire apprentices of their own kin, subcontracting is delegated to tribemembers, and co-operation between different masters is quite often based on kinship. Acces to jobs or apprenticeships and participation in clusters are highly influenced by ethnic affiliations.

Limited Access to Capital

Most of the entrepeneurs complain that they lack access to capital. However, none of the respondents considered the formal banking system a viable option, 'unless you know someone'. Reputation and connections seem more important than collateral. In addition, bank procedures are considered too cumbersome, too long and interest rates too high. Borrowing money through informal moneylenders is also not very popular. The fear of defaulting and the subsequent 'noise', restrains most entrepeneurs from making any effort in that direction. 'Usury' interest rates further discourage this source as a plausible venue for investment in a business. Financial support for start-up costs is almost entirely conceived through spouses, relatives or friends. Connections are used to access capital for starting as well as expanding a business. In the more marginal activities, collateral is virtually non-existent. Connections, therefore, seem the viable option.

Two types of informal credit arrangements play an important role in many economic activities. The first venue is buyer's and supplier's credit. 'Ladies' agreements', for instance, play a crucial role in small-scale trading and food processing. These kinds of agreement entail informal credit relationships which form the backbone of the small-scale trade in Accra [*Alberts, 1993*]. Connections and good relations are crucial for these arrangements. Paying back suppliers after sales are made is a very common practice. Customers, also, quite often pay for their purchases in instalments. The advantage of this informal credit system is that it enables people to become engaged in business. The disadvantage is that it reduces profit margins in the case of supplier's credit, and it entails the risk of defaulting in the case of buyer's credit.

The second credit venue is saving money through the 'susu' system. This is a long-established informal savings system, whereby entrepeneurs save small amounts of money on a daily, weekly, or monthly basis with a susu collector, and get reimbursed after an agreed term, usually a month. For most marginal enterprises in East-Maamobi, the money is usually diverted to expenditures like school fees, rent, and medical bills. What is left may be used to build up stock, increase working capital, pay off debts and so on.

Barriers to Entry

It is not as easy to enter the informal sector as conventional theories suggest. Even in the case of marginal trading or food processing activities, one needs the equivalent of a lower echelon civil servant's monthly salary to get involved in such an activity. For the more productive activities, the cost of apprenticeship, tools and, eventually, machines are all major constraints. Barriers to entry may also be substantial because of the necessary investments, for instance, the down payment for a shop in a good location, the necessary bribes to obtain a licence or a site, or the high costs of equipment. The other side of this picture is that the impediments to entry actually restrain the increase in competition in already saturated markets.

Cost of Formalisation

Many small entrepreneurs consider the increasing costs related to registration fees, licence fees and income taxes an impediment to the expansion of their businesses. According to most of micro entrepeneurs, they must divert a substantial part of their surplus to settling the aforementioned formal arrangements. This constrains their potential for growth. Other formal costs incurred stem from the activities of the Accra Metropolitan Authority (AMA) task force on behalf of the 'beautification' operation. Besides being thoroughly involved in the formalisation process, the AMA has repeatedly been accused of seizing goods, breaking down structures and evicting people from their sites. Entrepeneurs complain they have never received any compensation for

143

the damage done to them by members of the task force and, in certain instances, they have been arbitrarily victimised.

Processes of formalisation and informalisation are simultaneously occurring in Accra. Poor entrepeneurs are increasingly becoming formalised as they enlarge their economic activities or start operating from more permanent structures. The Accra Metropolitan Authority has fairly rigorously improved its registration system. As a consequence, it has become more difficult for entrepeneurs to escape the regulations and the revenue collectors. On the other hand, there continues to be an inflow of poor households into informal activities. This growth in the participation in the informal labour force continues to reinforce the extensive informalisation process. The net result of these simultaneous processes, however, cannot be verified by our research.

Competition

Most of the product markets are oversaturated. The survey showed that for East-Maamobi, there exists a glut in food processing, textiles, small-scale trade, hairdressing, repair activities and transport markets. This intensifies the aforementioned productivity problem. The negative effects are, among others, a downward pressure on prices and profit margins. People encouraged or forced to become engaged in economic activities keep joining these already saturated markets, although returns to investment are decreasing substantially. Competition has become fiercer since the introduction of the 'killer budget', an action for which the government is to blame and which has reduced the level of trade activity.

Increased Costs

The term 'killer budget' refers to the negative impact of the 60 per cent petrol price increase felt throughout most economic activities, not just directly in activities such as food processing, but also indirectly in trade, metal-, wood- and construction-related activities. The depreciation of the cedi has also been blamed for having increased prices of imported inputs such as textiles, spare parts, tools, machines, or other productive assets such as cars, deepfreezers, TVs and VCRs. Immediate effects are felt, for instance, by food processors. Wholesale and retail prices of most cereals and tubers have gone up due to higher transport costs. Entrepeneurs, however, have not been able to raise their product prices accordingly. The purchasing power of customers has been squeezed because wage increases lag behind price increases. The most bitter complaint concerned the fact that there is 'no money in the system'. The indirect effects are felt as soon as a greater portion of the household budget has to be allocated to basic need requirements, and a smaller portion remains available for other expenditures. Consequently, people adjust their expenditure pattern and postpone spending on things such as car check-ups, instalment payments to dressmakers, more expensive hairdressing saloons, the acquisition of durables and so on. Demand diminishes, competition becomes harder and the level of activity becomes depressed.

Seasonality

In general, respondents indicated that their incomes and profit margins fluctuate considerably over the year.[8] This seasonality was closely linked to climatic variations and to the social calendar (festivities). Food processors and fish traders experience fluctuations in the supply and prices of their inputs, and profit margins vary accordingly. For most enterprises, festive occasions such as Christmas, Easter or Sallah, marriages, outings and funerals mark peak business periods. Quite often, the rest of the year is marked by minimum operations. Market traders commented that, although people buy food all the time, higher quantities are purchased on festive occasions. In contrast, when food prices shoot up in the rainy season, before the next harvest, people tend to buy smaller quantities of food and of less variety.

Entrepreneurs selling cooked food have an inverse pattern in relation to festivals. These are the periods when women cook a lot of food at home. Serving portions decrease at certain times because of the high costs of inputs. Some customers switch accordingly from more expensive foods (for example, *kenkey* and fish) to cheaper foods (such as *gari* and beans). Car mechanics and welders mentioned that they service more cars in the periods before festivals and during the rainy season. Dressmakers and hairdressers noticed that few women sew clothes and set their hair regularly. A large number only incurs such expenses on special occasions. Seasonality has two major consequences, firstly in the variation of profit and, second, in the sense that productivity during the good season is not always sufficient to build up stores for the off-season.

VII. OPPORTUNITIES

A number of factors explain the success of the dynamic enterpreneurs and enterprises: diversification, finding niche markets, using networks and relations, occupying a favourable spot, an entrepreneurial drive and efficient management, and access to informal financing. These will be discussed in that order.

Diversification

Diversification occurs when a firm undertakes the production of a new product without ceasing production of its existing products. Entrepeneurs attempt to spread risk or compensate for fluctuations in demand. They very often change their product mix in response to changing consumer demand. The development of new markets or the changes in existing markets tend to be fruitful testing grounds for diversifying and upgrading production. An excellent example of how diversification may turn a marginal economic activity into a very rewarding business may be found in one woman's *banku* business; after expanding her range of products from just *banku* to *fufu*, *kokonte*, riceballs and different types of soup, she became quite successful. The increase in the variety of dishes and the high quality of food spurred the growth of her business.

Diversification creates new opportunities in an overcrowded product market. So far, the success of the woman in the example above is the exception to the rule in the processed food market in her neighbourhood, but the fact that this woman is outwitting her competition is forcing other food processors in close proximity to anticipate and introduce innovations in their product cycles. In the short term, these kinds of developments may endanger the position of some marginal producers, but in the long run this venue offers many opportunities.

Other diversification and risk spreading strategies have been discussed under the coping mechanisms where diversification was presented as a generally productive way of coping with poverty. It builds up resources that may be used preventively to avoid poverty, or curatively to deal with poverty.

Discovering Niche Markets

Several entrepeneurs were able to spot niches or anticipate new developments in otherwise overcrowded markets. In the 1980s, the business environment changed drastically: imports were liberalised and the cedi devaluated. Entrepeneurs jumped at the opportunity to supply product markets with low-cost substitutes. They sought ways to develop locally available raw material, and dynamic entrepeneurs anticipated these new developments. In response to the changing economic environment, a large number were able to build their enterprises often from scratch.

Good Relations

Networks of interpersonal relationships and reputation are essential ingredients of the labour market within the city. Networking for employment opportunities, for example, continues to operate along ethnic lines. Networks are also important for small businesses. However, there are again examples of the contrary. One female entrepreneur rides alone and has no trust in others; according to her, the business is not registered, she pays no taxes or licence fees, and manages to escape import duties. In life she manages a lot without collaborating with others!

Many people seem to face a psychological barrier in the sense that, in many instances, they depend on relations. They lack the initiative to search for other opportunities and rely totally on family and friends. Additionally, they quite

146

often restrict their networking to their own ethnic group. Further, men, look for job opportunities in traditionally gender-dominated trades. Women search for jobs in food processing, small-scale trading, dressmaking or hairdressing, and men search for jobs in metal-, wood-, construction- or repair-related economic activities.

Location

For numerous enterprises, the location of the business is important for their success. Direct accessibility to customers is important and a good location can sometimes allow entrepreneurs to tap the market potential outside the neighbourhood. In one case, an electric mechanic who is part of a cluster had a comparative advantage from the fact that he is the only one within the cluster who owns a charging machine to test batteries. The enterprises are located at the edge of Abeka, along the ringroad and beside the main road to Kumasi where the more dynamic enterprises are located.

Entrepeneurial Drive

Entrepeneurs engaged in marginal activities occasionally lack the entre-peneurial drive to improve the productive and income-generating capacity of their business. In these cases, being engaged in an economic activity is merely a means to an end, a way to survive, and is not aimed at maximising profit or growth. The absence of the initiative to seek access to capital, more training or skills, or to consider other employment opportunities is quite striking in many cases. Such entrepeneurs appear to lack access to information about alterna-tives and see no ways to improve their productivity. Their aspirations are vague, and they have no clear ideas on how to develop their businesses or achieve growth. This most likely does not only stem from a lack of knowledge on business operation methods or management practices. Most of these very marginal 'entrepeneurs' seem to be satisfied with their type of small-scale businesses and prefer not to embark upon risky expansions. An additional problem for some of these entrepeneurs is the claims made on their earnings by friends and family which way seriously erode their working capital.

Virtually all dynamic activities in East-Maamobi are characterised by the drive of the entrepeneur to strive for economic growth. Entrepeneurial drive may almost be described as the inverse of what was described as a negative business attitude. This drive manifests itself in clear aspirations: risk-taking behaviour, anticipation, initiative, innovative mentality, specialisation, skill acquisition and sound business plans.

Informal Financing

A number of examples of informal financial agreements were found during the analysis of the trading activities. Traders receive goods on credit from suppliers and issue payments after sales are made. One such case involves a female trader who buys on a short-term credit basis. The relationship with her 'madam' has been established for more than ten years. It is a typical 'Ladies Agreement', which very closely resembles the traditional patron–client relationships, and one of trust and mutual benefit that forms the backbone of much of the small-scale trade in Accra. Besides the informal credit agreement, this kind of relationship quite often also entails a personal understanding that the 'madam' will assist in emergencies, for instance, with medical bills. Traders and craftsmen also sell on credit, and get either a lump sum payment after an agreed period of time, or get paid in instalments.

VIII. POVERTY, LABOUR MARKETS AND ECONOMIC ACTIVITIES

Incorporating the respondents perceptions into our assessment of poverty reveals that poverty in Ghana is not merely a rural phenomenon. According to the criteria of those interviewed, poverty is widespread in the three neigbourhoods of Accra studied. Individuals emphasise that beyond material deprivation, there are important qualitative dimensions to poverty. Relevance is attached to non-material values such as dignity, independence, moral standards, security and, most of all, vulnerability. Poverty is not seen as just a lack of control over certain goods and services, but, in a broader sense, as a deprivation of basic human rights.

The link established between urban household poverty and the economic activities of the household members enhanced our understanding of vulnerability. A household's resource endowment and, therefore, the capacity of the members to cope is determined by what they initially own and can acquire through exchange. The urban poor in Accra lack access to productive resources, and the productivity of the resources at their disposal is low. An improvement of their resource endowment is a precondition for sustainable poverty reduction. Households have already adopted various coping strategies to overcome the implications of their poverty. Existing productive coping strategies need to be strengthened and supported in poverty alleviation policies.

The major objective of the World Bank's Ghana Extended Poverty Study is to develop a long-term and Ghana-specific poverty alleviation framework that would be consistent with the broad themes of the outward-oriented macroeconomic policies espoused by Ghana 2000 [*Chhibber and Leechor, 1993*]. We focused on urban poverty and attempted to establish links between poverty and employment. An important conclusion is that, for economic growth to reduce poverty, it should to a large extent be labour-intensive. The link between economic growth and poverty reduction in Ghana has to be productive, labour-intensive employment.

The Ghana 2000 study assumed smoothly functioning labour markets. This seems to be the case in Accra as far as wage, time, spatial, occupational and sectoral flexibility are concerned. It does not mean, however, that the market provides a reasonable wage for those who are willing to be flexible. In fact, households require several incomes not to be poor. The conclusion must be that more productive employment will be created if the macroeconomic environment remains positive and if specific labour-intensive policies and pro-grammes can be put in place. It has become attractive for employers to employ more Ghanaian labour at the present wage level, and this will continue to happen if liberal economic policies continue. Ghana will then cash in on its favourable location, its low level of wages, its relatively high literacy level and its entrepreneurial population.

Labour markets would benefit from a good information system. The present employment services do not function in that way. Information on changes in skill demands, employment opportunities, and training capacity in the economy is crucial for developing flexible labour market policies. Improved investment in a labour market information system would greatly strengthen the links between labour market policy and human resource strategies.

Monitoring of labour market developments is very important. The extent of segmentation and flexibility in the labour market influences the responsiveness of the market to economic stimuli. Bottlenecks, for example, in the acquisition of skills, such as high apprenticeship fees, and imbalances and irregularities that constrain the qualified from accessing employment opportunities, such as bribery and favoritism, need to be removed. Education and training need to be geared more to the market, in this case, the needs of micro enterpreneurs. Although agricultural extension services seem to be an integrated part of a policy environment that attempts to raise rural productivity, an urban equivalent attempting to raise the productivity of the poor micro entrepeneurs barely exists, but is vitally important for urban poverty alleviation.

Employment is often the only possibility for the poor to escape poverty, hence it is desirable to take a number of measures to increase the productivity of the economic activities in which they are involved. The fact that some activities are mainly helping the poor to survive, while others are seed-beds of entrepreneurship means that different policies and projects may be needed to stimulate the various categories of activities.

IX. INCREASING PRODUCTIVE EMPLOYMENT

For activities which seem to be the seed-bed for entrepreneurial development, it is particularly important that the government creates the appropriate policy context for their development. It is also necessary to provide targeted assistance to specific activities and those who cannot find employment in the informal sector. For those who do not be benefit from these policies, assistance should be given through safety net constructions. These three types of assistance will be elaborated below.

The Appropriate Policy Context

Structural adjustment has created new opportunities for a large number of people in Ghana. Many Ghanaians launched themselves in the informal sector, most often through self-employment. Examples of this can be seen in the increasing number of female traders, chop bars, hairdressers, tailors and repair shops. Not all of these will survive. Some may grow and develop into small enterprises, some may merge and a number will disappear.

Typical for poor households is their limited resources endowment. This includes the low productivity of available resources, as well as the limited access to productive resources, human resources, credit and inputs, stores and claims. Increased opportunities for productive and renumerative employment are important for poverty reduction. A critical precondition for both productivity and employment enhancement is the enhancement of the productivity of the poor producers, which would also require an improvement in their access to physical resources and other productive inputs.

Targeted Assistance

At present, many rules and regulations make the life of small entrepreneurs complicated. Selective deregulation may help the development of this sector. Similarly, a large number of taxes needs to be paid. It is not always clear to the entrepeneurs which taxes need to be paid, for what, at what point and in what amount. The government should clarify the system and redesign it in such a way that small enterprises are not driven by the complexity to illegal behaviour.

A more positive attitude should be taken to the economic activities of the poor and attempts should be made to contribute to the necessary increase in the productivity of these activities. Appropriate macroeconomic policies help the development of micro and small enterprises. Physical planning policies can help to make land and appropriate infrastructure available. Private sector development programmes should include micro and small enterprises.

In addition, policies and projects may be designed specifically to support the economic activities of the poor. A whole range of projects and policies can contribute to the labour-intensive development of the economic activities of the poor. Often, the private sector will have to be stimulated to start these activities, to provide access to markets for micro entrepreneurs and to subcontract to them. So far, most micro-entrepeneurs are not familiar with institutional delivery systems promoting productivity enhancement or facilitating access to credit, inputs or markets. To develop a coherent policy framework for micro-enterprise and productivity development, it seems appropriate at this stage to initiate a stock-taking exercise on the capacity and the constraints of existing institutional delivery systems.

Micro-enterprise development projects in other countries reveal very positive experiences with such innovative concepts as technology development and innovation diffusion centers, the development of clusters of economic activities (such as, for instance, Suame-Magazine in Kumasi), or the improvement of subcontracting and other relations between micro, small, medium and large enterprises.[9] Policies and projects addressing the economic activities of the poor directly could incorporate these innovative strategies and gear them to the specific needs of the Ghanaian situation.

Safety Net Constructions

Research at the household level also showed that there is a group which is not benefiting from the new opportunities created by structural adjustment. We do not refer to those who were disadvantaged by cut-backs in government jobs or trade monopolies. We point to a large number of elderly who can no longer rely on their children for support, to female-headed households with large numbers of children and to those who are sick or otherwise handicapped. There is no social security for the vulnerable of the urban population and the traditional mechanisms are fading away. For these groups special programmes will remain necessary.

Safety net constructions are necessary for those poor who are not able to undertake rewarding economic activities. People who lack skills, are not sufficiently entrepreneurial or lack initiative need help. Refugees and women left by their husbands are also vulnerable. A general improvement of the economic situation will also eventually create more possibilities for these people. However, in the short run, some kind of targetted aid is required.

A number of productivity-enhancing priorities could be established through a Social Investment Fund (SIF) *[Van Dijk, 1992]*. Incorporating the lessons learned from implementing Pamscad, the Ghanaian government and the international donor community could consider establishing an institutional structure or mechanism that facilitates the channeling of resources directly to poorer communities to build economic and social infrastructure. Experiences with Social Investment Funds in Latin America have been very positive. SIFs are designed to fund local organisations, public or private, in a more flexible and transparent manner than regular government line ministries normally do. SIFs are demand driven, they respond to funding requests from local agencies but are not involved in the identification or implementation of projects *[Marc et al., 1993]*.

X. RECOMMENDATIONS TO DEVELOP THE ACTIVITIES OF THE POOR

Many of the constraints mentioned are related to the macroeconomic environment, such as the policy context and the impact of taxes and regulations. Others are related to the entrepreneur, such as a lack of relations, education, training and business skills; or related to the enterprise, such as initial investments, chosen technology and location. Still others are related to the market, such as competition and weak demand for these products and services. The most pressing problems seem to be related to how the productivity of these micro-enterprises can be increased. The constraints and suggested solutions are summarised in Table 4.

TABLE 4

POLICIES FOR ECONOMIC ACTIVITIES OF THE POOR

Constraint	Suggested Policies	Project Activities
1. Low labour productivity	Training and technical assistance Create technology centres	Use existing training facilities Use universities and laboratories
2. Limited access to capital	Stimulate access to existing formal and informal credit institutions	Use existing formal and informal credit facilities; try to link them
3. Barriers to entry	Deregulate Avoid legal barriers	Help entrepreneurs to deal with the requirements
4. Cost of formalisation	Facilitate administrative procedures	Help entrepreneurs to deal with formalities
5. Competition	Stimulate specialisation Train in design	Assistance to find niche markets Improve quality
6. Lack of networks	Stimulate networking by using those for consultations	Create special purpose cooperatives Stimulate trade associations
7. Seasonality	Stimulate diversification	Help with storing
8. Marketing	Stimulate diversification	Make available good locations
9. Lack of appropriate technology	Stimulate the development of labour-intensive technologies	Promote clustering and technology centres
10. Unclear tax system	Explain different taxes and their use	Train entrepreneur to take taxes into account

The strongest impact on generating growth is to be expected from the level of the entrepeneur. In a very competitive and profit-maximising environment, the initiative and the ability to seek and recognise opportunities can be considered prerequisites for any micro-entrepeneur who desires to enlarge the scope of his/her business. What the dynamics have in common is that they facilitate the accumulation of resources and make the surplus required for productive investment available.

Given the above mentioned constraints and factors contributing to the success of certain activities and entrepreneurs, the recommendation is to stimulate specialisation, to help entrepreneurs to find niche markets and to diversify their products. Good locations can be made available through urban authorities and efficient management can be enhanced through education, training and technical assistance. Technology centers can play an important role in this respect. Credit supply should be improved, and formal and informal institutions can play a role. Administrative procedures are not a major hurdle in Ghana, but entrepreneurs do need to be stimulated to achieve development from below.

The development of associations for micro and small entrepreneurs could improve access for individual entrepeneurs to productivity enhancing techniques, credit and markets. In many branches, there are already trade associations, some of which work reasonably well (for example, those for hairdressing, garages and textiles). Functional associations can function as a platform for discussion, and exchange new of ideas and experiences. They can also function as the interlocuteur for negociations with the government.

Similarly, stress can be placed on the need to create clusters and networks, and to develop organisations of small entrepreneurs. The constraint analysis showed that it is necessary to stimulate micro entrepreneurs to specialise. Training at existing vocational training and technology centres would help in the process. Secondly, it is desirable to help entrepreneurs to find niche markets and to diversify their products. An inflow of new designs, better quality products and different colours would help many to sell more. Good physical locations should also be made available by the urban authorities. Ghana has a tradition for regrouping activities. This can be succesful if the locations are not too far away and the transition does not take too much time. Finally, efficient management can be enhanced through education, training and technical assistance.

The development of networks and associations of small entrepreneurs should be stimulated. Credit supply should be improved and formal and informal institutions should be stimulated to provide access to small entrepreneurs. This is a new and lucrative market. Particularly female entrepreneurs are known to pay back regularly. Administrative procedures are not a major hurdle in Ghana, but efforts need to be made to stimulate entrepreneurs to comply with the rules and regulations, given they understand them and benefit from them as well. In such a way a development from below can be promoted, benefiting particularly the poor working in the informal sector.

NOTES

1. The fieldwork in Abeka was carried out by the author with Daniel Inkoom from the Technology University in Kumasi.
2. Suggestions on how to apply the qualitative findings in the design and conceptualisation of the quantitative analysis, and how to integrate the qualitative results into the overall labour market analysis have been made [*Van Dijk, 1996*].
3. The criteria used for the subjective poverty definition are to be found in Van Dijk [*1996*]: no money for basic needs, no assets, bad appearance, un- (or under-) employed, a bad family situation, misfortune, misconduct and vulnerability.
4. One US dollar equalled C. 650 at the time of the research.
5. A similar observation was made by Steel and Webster [*1989*].
6. The girls do not receive chopmoney anymore like they used to.
7. Baah-Nuakoh [*1993*].
8. I would like to thank E.B. Dorku for her account of seasonality, based on the Participatory Poverty Assessment fieldwork in East-Maamobi in May 1993.
9. In this respect compare suggestions in Rasmussen *et al.* (eds.) [*1992*] and Pedersen *et al.* (eds.) [*1994*].

REFERENCES

Alberts, W. (1993): 'Ladies Agreements', unpublished MA thesis, University of Utrecht.

Alberts, W. and M.P. van Dijk (1994): *Urban poverty and employment in Ghana, a qualitative assessment*, Washington DC: World Bank.

Baah-Nuakoh, A. (1993): *The Informal Sector in the Social and Economic Development of Ghana*, Frankfurt: GTZ.

Bureau of Statistics (1989): *First year report of Ghana Living Standards Survey 1987–88*, Accra: Bureau of Statistics.

Chhibber, A. and C. Leechor (1993): 'Ghana: 2000 and Beyond', *Finance and Development*, Sept., pp.24–8.

Dawson, J. (1992): 'Flexible Specialization in Ghana', in Rasmussen *et al.* (eds.) [*1992*].

Dijk, M.P. van (1987): *Le secteur informel de Ouagadougou*, Paris: L'Harmattan.

Dijk, M.P. van (1992): 'Socio-Economic Development Funds to Mitigate the Social Cost of Adjustment: Experiences in Three Countries', *European Journal of Development Research*, Vol.4, No.1, June, pp.97–112.

Dijk, M.P. van (1996): 'Economic Activities of the Poor in Accra', in D. Bryceson and V. Jamal (eds.), *De-agrarianization in Africa*, Leiden: Africa Studies Centre (forthcoming).

Kumar, K. (ed., 1993): *Rapid Appraisal Methods*, Washington, DC: World Bank.

Marc, A., Graham, C. and M. Schacter (1993): *Social Action Programs and Social Funds*, Washington, DC: World Bank.

Pedersen, P., Sverrisson, A. and M.P. van Dijk (eds.) (1994): *Flexible Specialization: The Dynamics of Small-Scale Industries in the South*, London: Intermediate Technology.

Rasmussen, J., Schmitz, H. and M.P. van Dijk (eds.) (1992): 'Flexible Specialization: A New Paradigm for Small Enterprises?', *IDS Bulletin*, Vol.23, No.3, July.

Steel W. and L. Webster (1989): *Small and Medium Enterprises in Ghana*, Washington, DC: IBRD.

World Bank (1994): *Adjustment in Africa: Reforms, Results and the Road Ahead*, Oxford: Oxford University Press.

PART III

8

Trust Building in Tanzania's Informal Credit Transactions

M.S.D. BAGACHWA

I. INTRODUCTION

This chapter examines some of the mechanisms used by informal financial institutions (IFIs) in Tanzania to build trust among transacting parties. IFIs have developed a number of innovative informal arrangements through which externalities that are intrinsic in the highly imperfect residual market have been internalised. These include the use of a web of interpersonal relationships, market interlinkage, credit layering and specialised, custom-tailored, small-scale services in which formal financial institutions have a cost disadvantage. The chapter is based on a recent survey covering 30 money lenders (22 trader-lenders and 8 landlords), 19 savings and credit societies (SCSs) and 10 rotating savings and credit associations (ROSCAs). The value of loans and deposits are measured in Tanzanian Shillings.[1]

II. TYPE OF INFORMAL FINANCIAL INSTITUTIONS

The analysis of the existing literature revealed four important types of informal finance in Tanzania, which will be discussed. The four are: financial arrangements among relatives, neighbours and friends; commercial money lenders (landlords or farmer-lenders and traders or trader-lenders); savings and credit societies (SCSs), and rotating savings and credit associations. A distinction should be made at the outset, between informal financial institutions and the real informal sector enterprises or micro enterprises. IFIs are primarily involved in the mobilisation of savings and or in the intermediation of credit. These financial institutions are informal in the sense that they are not subjected to the regulatory powers of the Central Bank of Tanzania with respect to capital, reserve and liquidity requirements, interest rates, and so on. The real informal sector or the micro-enterprise sector consists of small-scale units producing and distributing goods and services for sale. They are informal in the sense that they are, for the most part, unregistered, unrecorded in official statistics and have little or no access to organised markets. Micro-enterprises are one of the potential clients for the IFIs. Another useful distinction to be made is that between rural and urban areas. Rural settlements are defined broadly to include (as in the 1988 population census) villages and small towns which are not under the jurisdiction of the regional headquarters. Urban areas are confined to regional headquarter towns.

Arrangements among Relatives, Neighbours and Friends

Financial arrangements among relatives, neighbours and friends have a long tradition in Tanzania. Such arrangements operate based on the exchange of money among relatives, friends and neighbours but are non-commercial in the sense that no interest charges are involved. The exact quantitative magnitude of these transactions is not known, but the limited evidence available suggests that it is substantial. Various studies show that credit from friends and relatives is an important source of initial capital for many micro-enterprises in urban areas and for farmers in rural areas, and that it constitutes, in some cases, up to 55 per cent of the total initial investment funding. This evidence is corroborated by the studies on informal finance by Amani *et al.* [*1987*], Malkamaki [*1990*] and FAO [*n.d.*]. The FAO study was undertaken in selected villages in Moshi, Pare and Kurogwe districts in Tanzania. The survey found that 40 per cent of all informal loans were from friends. The importance of credit from relatives and friends can be explained by the fact that this kind of arrangement is deeply rooted in the Tanzanian culture and stems from the existence of strong social linkages within the local community. Such types of mutual help schemes are considered as social obligations. Other considerations include the locational proximity of the lender/borrower, the likelihood of persuasion and the prospects of leniency in the event of non-repayment. In addition many of these loans involve no interest or collateral, tend to have openended repayment arrangements are based on reciprocity. They are thus popular.

Commercial Moneylenders: Landlords and Traders

Apart from the non-commercialised money lending from friends and relatives, there is also evidence suggesting the existence of various types of commercial-oriented money-lenders in the urban and rural segments of the Tanzanian society. Landlords or farmer-lenders are reported to exist in the rural areas of Iringa. In another rural informal finance survey carried out by Malkamaki [*1990*] in the Dar es Salaam, Morogoro and Mtwara regions, about five per cent of the respondents stated that they borrowed from professional money/ equipment lenders. Professional money-lending in Tanzania does not seem, however, to be as developed and extensive as in some parts of West Africa. Evidence gathered and the surveys by the FAO [*n.d*] and Amani *et al.* [*1987*], tend to suggest the absence of an active role b professional money-lenders in the intermediation of informal finance. This, however, could be an under-estimation. The relatively low profile allegedly assumed by money-lenders in the channelling of informal credit, could just be a camouflage, partly a reflection of traditional habits which regard commercial lending as exploita-tive, and partly a result of the previous socialist policies and ideology which discouraged all forms of private capitalist entrepreneurship. Because of this rather hostile attitude, Malkamaki [*1990*] revealed that though money-lenders exist, most of them do not admit to being money-lenders. This may result in the underestimation of their numbers and their role in the provision of informal credit.

Undoubtedly, recent trade liberalisation reforms have not only allowed existing informal lenders to transact business more openly, but have also stimulated the emergence of new ones. As Gordon [*1989*] documents, follow-ing the dismantling of the grain trade restrictions, informal operators have reacted vigorously:

> In volume terms, open market sales grew seven-fold between 1980/81 and 1987/88. The growth in volume has been accompanied by an increasing number of market participants both in assembling grain and wholesaling and retailing in urban centres. In Dar es Salaam wholesale markets a new class of traders has emerged that provides short-term financing for crop purchasing and financing and who, in addition to trading on their own account act as brokers, provide buying and selling services to others for a fee. The number of these traders has grown from 15 in the early 1980's to nearly 100 now. Similarly the number of traders active in rural market has grown significantly Gordon [*1989*] in World Bank [*1991*].

Savings and Credit Societies

Another important form of informal finance comes from savings and credit societies (SCSs). These associations consist mainly of mutual groups of indi-viduals linked together by a common bond (for example, ethnic, residential, occupational and so on) and are subject to internally-set rules and regulations. Most of these groups are formed spontaneously although, in some cases, the government has tried to influence their formation. In Tanzania, SCSs can be defined according to two broad types, SCS proper and saving and credit schemes. The SCSs proper are independent, legal co-operative entities and primary societies whose main purpose is to raise money from their individual members on a systematic and continuous basis, and to distribute portions of the money as loans to the members. The SCSs proper operate mainly in urban areas.

Savings and credit schemes have similar objectives to SCSs proper but are not independent legal entities, but the savings and credit activities of the primary co-operative societies. These societies, in addition to mobilising savings and providing credit, perform other functions to their members. Presently these schemes operate mainly in the rural areas [*Keddie, 1992*].

Under the Cooperative Societies Act of 1991, primary co-operative societies can raise money from their members in both share and deposit accounts. In practice, SCSs proper do both. Saving and credit schemes, however, raise money almost exclusively on deposit account because they lack shares. While money on deposit constitutes voluntary savings and can be withdrawn at the depositor's discretion, money in a share account cannot be withdrawn from the society unless a member is leaving the cooperative society entirely.

Membership is open for persons aged 18 years and above, who have a regular source of income and who are known to other members of the society. The minimum group size for a society is ten members. The groups operate in occupational areas, working places, parishes, villages, etc. Normally, members can save as much money as they are able to, though none of the members may own more than one-fifth of the total savings of the group. Participants in these groups contribute on a periodic (monthly or fortnightly) basis.

Rotating, Savings and Credit Associations

Rotating, Savings and Credit Associations generally combine savings and credit arrangements. They explicitly pool savings and tie loans to deposits. ROSCAs, like the savings and credit societies, operate from mutual ownership and control. They resolve problems with loan collateral and borrower information by enroling only members who have mutual confidence in each other or by having sponsors who can guarantee the performance of the individual enroling Loan recovery is not a problem since defaulting members not only lose the opportunity to remain in the association, but may also be shunned by other members, losing social and business ties altogether. This acts as an incentive for assuring loan repayment. Various studies have revealed that ROSCAs, known in Tanzania as 'Upatu' or 'Mchezo', are wide spread in both the urban and rural areas of Tanzania [*Ndanshau, 1990; Malkamaki, 1990*].

Types of Borrowers and Use of Credit

The major recipients of informal credit include farmers, traders, micro enterprises, wage employees and members of various informal associations. In general, traders tend to lend primarily to other traders and landlords to farmers. ROSCAs and SCSs tend to confine their loans to members. Traditionally, the loans from the SCSs in Tanzania have been used for consumer goods. However, because of the growing economic difficulties, societies now provide three types of loans: productive loans for income generating activities, housing, etc.; provident loans for school fees, medical fees, etc. and emergency loans for funeral, wedding or other disasters.

III. THE NATURE OF INFORMAL SECTOR CREDIT

Trust, Adverse Selection, Moral Hazard and Enforcement

Credit, whether formal or informal, involves an intertemporal relationship between borrower and lender with a promise to repay the borrowed amount in the future. Since repayment is not always guaranteed, credit transactions generally involve an element of trust. In formal credit transactions, trust is enhanced by a system of well developed, financial and legal infrastructure: availability of legally recognised collateral, information networks, well-established financial regulations, court systems and so on. Such infrastructure facilitates the provision of the necessary information and helps to ensure contract enforcement, and collateral liquidation and transfer. By doing so, some of the transactions costs, such as those relating to the gathering of information about clients, negotiation, coordination, monitoring and contract enforcement, are significantly reduced. IFIs are, however, characterised by the absence of such trust-building market infrastructure.

Besides the issue of trust, and especially when information is asymmetric and the disbursement and repayment of credit are separated in time, lenders, whether formal or informal, tend to face three other related problems. The first problem is that of adverse selection, which arises from a lender's failure to distinguish a potentially good borrower from a bad one, at a reasonable cost. The second is moral hazard, which is associated with prohibitive monitoring costs, arising from the uncertain environment (random production and consumption shocks or bad luck) that might negatively affect the returns from the activities of the borrower and hence his/her capacity to repay. Lastly, the lender faces a potential problem of enforcement since, when the loan falls due, the lender must recover the principal and interest either out of the borrower's returns and/or out of collateral specified in the loan contract [*Bell, 1990*].

However, within the limits imposed by the inadequately developed market and the associated transaction costs, a number of IFIs covered by the survey appear to have developed a variety of alternative informal methods for enhancing trust among transacting parties, minimising incidences of adverse selection, and mitigating the problem of moral hazard, thereby reducing transaction costs. These methods have included the following:

(1) the use of personal ties to build intimate knowledge of the borrower's character and circumstances, thereby enhancing trust among transacting parties;

(2) the use of interlinked contracts to increase information, improve contract enforcement, and adapt to the moral hazard implicit in many loan transactions;

(3) the use of collateral pledge to reduce moral hazard and alleviate the problem of adverse selection;

(4) specialisation in small decentralised transactions for which management information and other transaction costs are relatively high for formal financial institutions;

(5) the use of intermediary agents (credit layering) to reduce the costs of monitoring credit and gathering information; and

(6) the use of quantity rationing to allocate credit funds on the basis of differing criteria for creditworthiness.

IV. THE USE OF PERSONAL TIES TO ENHANCE TRUST

Since credit involves trust, increasing the level of confidence in the borrower's ability to repay in the future is an essential component of any credit programme. Trust-building in the informal credit transactions appears to revolve around personal relationships. Personal considerations seem to be a necessary (though insufficient) condition for qualification for a loan. This aspect is reflected in many forms. In much of the previous literature, small farmers and owners of micro enterprises turned first to relatives or friends if they wished to borrow [*Bagachwa, 1993*]. This appears to be the case whether borrowing is for securing start-up capital or for capital expansion. Potential borrowers tend to behave this way for various reasons which include, the lender's locational proximity, the likelihood of persuasion, the chances of obtaining low interest charges (or none at all) and the prospect of leniency in the event of non-repayment [*Mrak, 1989; Shipton, 1991*]. The lender may also prefer to lend to a relative or friend because proximity reduces information and monitoring costs, kinship ties constitute potential social pressure to repay and/or fulfils a long and well-established tradition of mutual help also considered as a social obligation. It is perhaps not surprising that with most loans between friends, relatives and kin, no guarantee or collateral are required. There is always the social pressure to repay and the threat of being refused future loans in the case of default.

The findings of our survey revealed that personal ties were also important where loans to non-relatives were involved. Clients, in this case, when choosing a lender for a loan, have to lean on ties with other village residents, ethnic or other social ties such as age-set, school ties, recommendations from a reliable and established relative, friend, or client. According to the survey, 77.8 per cent of the urban informal clients and 90 per cent of the rural informal clients relied mainly on friendship, ethnic connections and recommendations from relatives, old clients or contacts to acquaint themselves with a lender.

Likewise, the lender's familiarity with the borrower's economic and social behaviour appears to be essential in facilitating the loan screening and selection processes. Survey responses revealed that, on average, 85.9 and 63.3 per cent of the urban and rural informal lenders, respectively, personally knew the people who applied for loans (this proportion was almost 100 per cent for ROSCAs). Only 8.5 per cent indicated not always having known the people who came to apply for loans. The rest indicated that they sometimes had knowledge of their applicants. In general, over two thirds of the successful applicants were known to respective lenders before applications were made. Furthermore, the fact that, in 1992, almost all (about 95 per cent) repeat loan applicants in 1992 were successful suggests that money-lenders prefer to deal with known, long-standing clients in order to mitigate the problem of moral hazard.

Thus the extended family, friendship, kinship institutions and other social relations such as either village members, school ties and networks of contact persons are instrumental in shaping personal ties that not only enhance trust between transacting parties but also facilitate simple loan processing and monitoring. This, thereby, makes burdensome and time-consuming documentation and other paper work unnecessary. This also reduces the lender's costs in the screening, processing, and monitoring of a loan. For example, 27 (87.1 per cent) and 25 (84.3 per cent) the urban and rural informal lenders, respectively, indicated that they did not test applicants before granting them the required loans (for example, by giving them a small initial loan to study the response). Prior knowledge of and trust in the applicants explain the lack of need for such tests. It is also important to note that because of trust and flexibility in operation, lenders usually grant clients the amounts requested.

IV. THE NATURE AND TYPES OF LOANS

Interlinkage of Loans

The survey identified two main types of informal credit contracts: unlinked and linked loans. Unlinked loans involve a contract between borrower and lender which relates to one market exchange. The interlinkage of credit transaction occurs when the process of contracting between the borrower and lender involves two or more market exchanges [*Braverman and Srinivasani, 1980*]. In poorly developed credit markets, the interlinking of contracts is said to have three main advantages. First, it helps to increase information (by reducing bounded rationality[2]) and to improve contract enforcement (since it reduces opportunism[3]). Second, it reduces uncertainty by improving the lender's forecast of the individual's behaviour and, hence, the ability to select risk appropriately from a number of potential borrowers. Finally, it expands the control variables and strategies available to lender, enabling them to influence the borrower's actions. An interlinked transaction may thus be seen as a disguised form of collateral and may serve to reduce moral hazard or adverse selection [*Udry, 1990*].

Four main types of market interlinkage were identified during the survey of rural money-lenders:

(1) loans linked to sale of output to the lender;
(2) loans linked to the purchase of inputs or equipment from the lender;
(3) loans linked to transfer of land rights; and
(4) loans linked to provision of labour services to the lender.

The first two sets of transactions were prevalent among the trader-money-lenders who would often lend to farmers who are linked to them through purchases of inputs or sales of output. Loans linked to output are generally linked to the agricultural cycle and require borrowers to sell their output to their lenders. The sale of crop through a lender enables the lender to exercise first claim on proceeds at the disadvantage of the borrower's other creditors. In such cases, credit interlinkage is sometimes used to close the borrower's access to other lenders. The last two sets of transactions were exclusively carried out by landlords. In all cases, the loan was linked to the primary occupation of the lender. The most dominant form of informal credit contracts among rural money-lenders appears to be linked loans. In 1992, this constituted 86 per cent of their total credit volume. Out of the total volume (TShs. 21.4 million) of loans issued by trader-lenders in 1992, 87 per cent (TSh. 18.6 m) were linked. Among landlords, 71 per cent of their total credit volume was linked.

Farmer-lender loans tied to land were generally of two types. Richer farmer-borrowers could borrow by pledging highly productive land as collateral. The lender could then use the mortgaged land for cultivation or could receive an agreed upon portion of the borrower's harvest from the land. Once the contractual time (one to two years) ended the land-use rights returned to the borrower and the loan was considered to be repaid in full, both principal and interest. Alternatively, for small loans, a lender could issue a loan against the mortgaged piece of land which he then could use indefinitely until the loan principal was paid in full. In both cases the lender acquires rights to the land in the event of default.

Loan Sizes and Maturity

In general, linked loans tend to be larger than unlinked loans. In 1992, for example, an average linked loan by a trader-lender was five times larger than a non-linked loan. In the case of a landlord, it was twice as much. Average urban loan amounts were consistently larger than those in rural areas. Likewise, trader-lender loans tended to be larger than those granted by other lenders. Overall, informal loan sizes vary enormously but they are generally very small. In 1992, the largest loan issued (in the sample) was TShs. 4 million (about US$10,000) while the smallest loan was TShs. 2,000 (about US$5).

Loan maturity periods vary from one lender to another, ranging between one to 24 months. Trader-lenders grant loans of between one to 12 months with a typical, unlinked loan maturing in three months and a linked loan maturing in six to 12 months. Loans linked to land tend to have the longest maturity period (sometimes up to 24 months) and are expected to be repaid during harvest. Most loans from ROSCAs mature in three months. Although a few loans granted by SCSs were reported to mature in 24 months, the average loan matures in three months.

Pledging of Collateral

According to Udry [*1990: 252*], collateral pledged in exchange for receipt of a loan serves three important functions. First, it directly reduces the cost to the lender of a default on a loan. Second, it serves as an added incentive for the borrower to repay, thereby reducing moral hazard. Lastly, it can mitigate the problem of adverse selection by screening out borrowers most likely to default. The fact that the majority (62.7 per cent) of the informal lenders inter-viewed indicated that they always asked for security against loans granted, suggests that they take the problems of moral hazard and adverse selection seriously. Thus, although most of the loans are transacted within the same village or town, the existence of contractual interlinkage and pledging of collateral indicates that information asymmetries between the transacting partners are important. This contrasts with the situation in Northern Nigeria where they have been found to be unimportant [*Udry, 1990*].

Use of Intermediary Credit Agents

There were two cases in which trader-lenders use landlords as their inter-mediaries. Typically, a trader-lender advances capital to a farmer-lender for re-lending. The loans were to be repaid in the form of output, normally during the harvest period. The built-in advantages of such informal credit layering is that it reduces the number of borrowers served by a lender to a manageable number. By so doing, it directs credit to clients that are well known and hence, can be observed closely. It is another kind of trust-building mechanism and an important way of reducing transaction costs.

The analysis in this chapter has shown that IFIs in Tanzania do not rely heavily on the institutional and market infrastructure to build trust and reduce transaction costs. Rather, they rely mainly on interpersonal relationships and credit interlinkage. Such strong social ties have been able to ensure extremely low loan default rates. Furthermore, credit interlinkage reduces the transaction costs of lenders and producers thereby facilitating both production and financial contracts. IFIs follow a sort of market *niche* strategy by specialising in small size loans of which for formal institutions risk and management information and other transaction costs are relatively high. However, this *niche* strategy has its own limitations. The small size of the transactions, their short term nature and the fact that operations are confined to locational proximity limits access to information about markets and, in some cases, it may restrict competition.

V. RATIONING, CLIENT SORTING AND LOAN MONITORING

Information from our survey, appears to suggest that different categories of informal lenders have different objective functions and hence different perceptions of risk. This fact has led some of the lenders to exercise quantity rationing by allocating credit funds on the basis of their own selective criteria of creditworthiness instead of clearing the market by charging what the traffic will bear.

As already pointed out, ROSCAs and SCSs prefer unlinked loans and target members of their associations as clients. They are mainly interested in maximising savings because loans are usually tied to deposits or shares. This implies that they tend to sort out potential borrowers, not necessarily on the basis of liquid or tangible collateral, but on the basis of a good track record in fulfilling their deposit obligations. As stated before, the associations resolve the problems of loan collateral, creditworthiness and borrower information by enroling only members in which other members have confidence or for which sponsors can provide a guarantee.

Trader-lenders and landlords also tend to have different objective functions and different perceptions about risk. As pointed out earlier, trader-lenders have trading as their main occupation. Trader-lenders, therefore, seek to maximise returns on their main (trading) activity. They like to see farmers sell their output right after harvest and pay their loans in terms of output as soon as possible. The need to have a high volume and reliable supply of trading inventory makes traders, prefer as a priority linking credit with the output and/or purchases of farm inputs. This practice assures the trader-lender of a future supply of goods and the continued loyalty and dependability of the borrower.

This all minimises market risk. Second, this practice tends to make traders more concerned with the borrower's repayment capacity and implies that they prefer to lend to borrowers with a lower default risk, in particular richer borrowers.

Landlords behave differently from trader-lenders. Since most landlords farm as their main activity, informal lending plays two important roles. First, it adds interest income to incomes from farming. Second, it can be used as a means of acquiring land. This happens when credit is tied to land and the borrower fails to repay the loan. Money-lending has, in fact, become an important form of acquiring land in Tanzania since both the customary and state laws in Tanzania prohibit the sale of land. Poor farmers are the most vulnerable, and may be forced to give up a part of their landholdings to pay accumulated debts.

Landlords would behave in such a way so as to maximise the joint returns from farming (acquiring land for cultivation) and lending (interest income). Since access to land is possible in event of non-repayment of loans, landlords are inclined to lend to poor farmers (who have smaller marketable surpluses and are, hence, vulnerable to the vagaries of weather and market fluctuations). The poor farmers are more likely to default and, therefore, likely to be forced to release their mortgaged land. It is not surprising that 72 per cent of the landlords' loans are tied to land.

Sorting Behaviour: Screening Costs

As discussed earlier, personal ties, market interlinkage, and quantity rationing are some of the peculiar features characterising the process of screening and sorting of borrowers among IFIs. Such unique features help IFIs to internalise some of the externalities that are inherent in the highly imperfect, residual credit market and in the absence of developed market-support infrastructure.

Transaction costs can stem from the costs associated with the screening process for loan applications and applicants. It has already been pointed out that 100 per cent of the ROSCAs, 85.9 per cent of the urban trader-lenders, and 63.3 per cent of the rural money lenders personally knew the people who came to them to apply for loans. As a consequence, over 80 per cent of the informal lenders never tested applicants before granting them the required loans.

In addition, only three of the 31 (about 9.7 per cent) urban trader-lenders and two of the 28 (7.1 per cent) rural money lenders employed an extra person to deal with loan screening. This suggests that screening costs are, most likely, kept low. In estimating screening costs for money lenders, the most important costs taken into account were the cost of time spent on the screening process, estimates of transport costs and travel expenses.

A typical urban trader-lender incurred screening costs equivalent to 1.2 per cent of each loan granted. This proportion was two per cent in rural areas. Landlords had relatively higher costs (0.6 per cent of the loan amount) than rural traders. This is because most loans by landlords are tied to land and must be physically monitored to check its suitability and productivity. SCSs had screening costs equivalent to 1.95 and 2.4 per cent of the loan amounts in urban and rural areas, respectively. SCSs had relatively higher screening costs per average loan because loan appraisals are carried out by a credit committee (which normally sits quarterly) and some members of the committee have to visit personally the project sites. ROSCAs, on the other hand, can be assumed to have almost zero screening costs. In general, screening costs are higher in rural areas than in urban areas. This is mainly due to high transport costs which raise the direct cost of communication between transacting parties.

Loan Monitoring

Typically, project follow-up such as regular visits to project sites, auditing of books and writing progress reports, is an essential component of formal credit monitoring and administration. This does not seem so in the case of informal credit in Tanzania. Only two of the ten ROSCAs, two of the 19 SCSs and three of the 22 traders covered by the survey reported having carried out any form of loan monitoring. Furthermore, only two of the 22 trader-lenders and only three (37.5 per cent) of the eight landlords indicated having visited clients for loan monitoring. It appears that the existence of informal trust-enhancing mechanisms, especially personal and social ties, mutual confidence, and market interlinkages help to reduce, almost to zero, screening costs and other costs associated with loan monitoring.

One of the reasons why small (informal) borrowers are normally excluded from the institutional market for credit is that they are perceived to have a higher risk of default and, therefore, to be high risk clientele. The survey results however, do not corroborate this conventionally perceived notion. Between 1990–92 there were 12 cases reported by SCSs of borrowers who had failed to repay the principal and interest on loans contracted during that period. ROSCAs reported only nine such cases (out of 354 clients or 2.5 per cent), traders reported nine such cases (out of 195 clients, or 4.6 per cent).

IV. CONCLUSIONS

How can one explain the relatively low default rates observed among informal borrowers? Contract enforcement in the financial informal sector is normally facilitated by the use of social ties (and hence social pressure) and market interlinkage. For example, where credit is linked to the sale of output to the lender, it becomes easier for the lender to exercise first claim on the proceeds compared with other borrowers. Similarly, when credit is tied to land, the pressure to repay is great, because the borrower fears to lose most valuable property. Thus, market interlinkage serves as collateral and improves contract enforcement by reducing post-contract opportunism.

It was not surprising, therefore, that the majority (72 per cent) of the landlords and traders preferred output and input control as measures for avoiding default. However, 63 per cent of SCSs and 84 per cent of ROSCAs would prefer to persuade, advise and encourage defaulters to repay. Collateral confiscation and court action are rare, and wherever they were mentioned, they were ranked lowly.

The preceding sections have described and analysed the complex informal financial and institutional arrangements through which various categories of informal lenders (traders, landlords, SCSs and ROSCAs) transact with individual traders, farmers and small firms in both the rural and urban areas of Tanzania. In particular, it has been shown that in the absence of formal institutional and market infrastructure (for example, government regulations, the court system, information networks and so on.), IFIs have developed a number of innovative informal arrangements through which externalities that are intrinsic in the highly imperfect residual credit market have been internalised. The use of a web of interpersonal relationships, market interlinkage, credit layering and specialised, custom-tailored, small scale services, in which formal financial institutions have a cost disadvantage, have helped many of the IFIs to enhance trust and to reduce problems associated with moral hazard and adverse selection. These mechanisms have also helped them to extend credit efficiently beyond the narrow confines of the project feasibility and bankability that characterise the rigid and overregulated formal financial institutions.

Informal financial intermediaries exist partly because they are able to adapt to the prevailing market conditions. This flexibility and adaptability explain their resilience and their ability to operate with lower transaction costs than formal financial institutions. The policy implication of this is that if funds are channelled into formal financial institutions and away from IFIs, intermediation costs are likely to rise. Moreover, the cost of the remaining funds would presumably be higher thereby reducing investment.

NOTES

1. About 1 US$ equalled TSh. 335 at the time of the survey in 1992.
2. In this context, bounded rationality refers to lack of access to information about market opportunities and, hence, the inability to predict in advance future outcomes of certain events contracts.
3. Opportunism refers to the possibility that mutually reliant parties may mislead, distort, disguise or confuse in order to expropriate wealth from one another. For example, control over the

borrower's assets constitutes some form of dependence and can be one way of reducing post-contract opportunism.

4. The perceived high risk is due to the fact that most financial institutions have little knowledge about small, poor borrowers with no established track record, who cannot afford to pledge full collateral and may, therefore, require substantially more supervision costs per shilling of credit.

5. These default rates were much lower than those experienced by the National Bank of Commerce when extending loans to micro enterprise – which averaged 60 per cent in 1991 [*Keddie, 1992*]. In case of default the transfer of land-use right may involve a considerable time of negotiations and/or legal proceedings.

REFERENCES

Adams, D.W. and D.A. Fitchett (eds), (1992): *Informal Finance in Low-Income Countries*, San Francisco CA: Westview Press.

Amani, H.K.R., Msambichaka, L.A. Lundhl–M. and S. Hedlund (1987): 'Agricultural Credit in Tanzania: A Peasant Perspective', *Savings and Development*, Vol. XI, No. 4, pp. 379–401.

Bagachwa, M.S.D. (1994): 'Financial Integration and Development in Sub-Saharan Africa: A Study of Informal Finance in Tanzania', Report to ODI and World Bank.

Bagachwa, M.S.D. (1993): 'The Rural Informal Sector in Tanzania', Economic Research Bureau, University of Dar es Salaam (mimeo).

Bell, C. (1990): 'Interactions Between Institutional and Informal Credit Agencies in Rural India', *The World Bank Economic Review*, Vol.4, No.3 (Sept), pp.297–327.

Braverman, A. and T.N. Srinivasan (1980): *Interlinked Credit and Tenancy Markets in Rural Economics of Developing Countries*, Washington, DC: World Bank Development Research Centre.

FAO (n.d.): 'Agricultural Credit in Three Village Areas in North Eastern Tanzania', FAO Agricultural Credit Studies unpublished Working Paper No. 2.

Keddie, J. (1992): 'Financial Services to Informal Sector Enterprises', Dar es Salaam: ILO.

Malkamaki, M. (1990): 'Financial Intermediation for Micro-enterprises in Bangladesh, Kenya, Tanzania and Zanzibar', Dar es Salaam (mimeo).

Mrak, M. (1989): 'Role of the Informal Financial Sector in the Mobilization and Allocation of Household Savings: The Case of Zambia', *Savings and Development*, Vol.XIII, No1, pp. 65–83.

Ndanshau, O.M. (1990): 'Informal Finance in Africa: A Case of Upatu Groups as ROSCAS in Dar es Salaam, Tanzania', Paper presented at the Economic Research Bureau, Staff Seminar, University of Dar es Salaam.

Shipton, P. (1991): 'Time and Money in the Western Sahel: A Clash of Cultures in Gambian Rural Finance', in M. Roamer and C. Jones (eds.), pp.113–39.

Udry, C. (1990): 'Credit Markets in Northern Nigeria: Credit As Insurance in Rural Economy', *World Bank Economic Review*, Vol.4, No.3, Sept., pp.251–69.

World Bank (1991): *Tanzania's Grain Markets*, Washington, DC: IBRD.

9

Enterprise Networks and Technological Change: Aspects of Light Engineering and Metal Working in Accra

ARNI SVERRISSON

I. INTRODUCTION

This chapter considers technical change in small and medium-sized light engineering and metal working enterprises in Accra, and mechanisation among their customers. After a brief statement of the theoretical context of this paper, the main attributes of the enterprises visited are described. Training, forms of mechanisation, co-operation between light engineering enterprises and the product range of the firms are discussed next. The networks external to the light engineering and metal working sector are analysed under the sub-headings local relations, input networks, output networks and user-producer interaction.[1] The interrelations between light engineering networks and other local production networks is discussed using examples from carpentry, bakeries and building. The concluding section highlights the close relation between technological configuration, work organisation and cooperation between enterprises in the light engineering sector in Accra, and discusses the conclusions which can be drawn from this study about technology policies, trade and development.

Up to now, industrialisation in Africa has taken place along three major paths, which roughly correspond to similar paths elsewhere. One of these paths has been based on public sector enterprises and subsidiaries of multi-

The interviews on which this chapter is based were carried out with Walter Atubra and Godfred Frempong at the Policy Research and Strategic Planning Institute (PORSPI) in Accra, Ghana. Both made valuable suggestions during the fieldwork, and in discussions on other occasions, about the planning and implementation of the fieldwork and the interpretation of data collected, although other commitments prevented them from joining me in writing this report. The fieldwork was conducted within a research project carried out in cooperation between (PORSPI) and the Research Policy Institute, University of Lund in Sweden. The chapter has benefited from comments and criticism from colleagues at both institutes, and special thanks are due to Dr M.N.B. Ayiku, former director of PORSPI, for his support and encouragement during all phases of the work. The project was funded by the Swedish Agency for Research Cooperation with the Developing Countries (SAREC), the support of which is gratefully acknowledged.

national corporations. Another path is characterised by the improvement of small and micro-enterprises of an 'informal' type. Large differences in capital investment, technological sophistication and scale of operations have arisen between the sectors created by each of these development paths.

However, a third, intermediate sector has also emerged, either through gradual mechanisation of small enterprises, or through the efforts of private entrepreneurs, who have started small manufacturing enterprises which are from the outset, partially or completely mechanised. These intermediate enterprises are usually flexibly organised and are parts of highly adaptable enterprise networks [*Sverrisson, 1993; 1994*].

The current problems created for African economies by structural adjustment policies, particularly for the public sector, will probably increase the opportunities for privately owned enterprises. Expansion of the private sector can either result in the proliferation of very small enterprises working with basic techniques, mostly hand tools, or in an increasing role for partially or completely mechanised enterprises, medium or small size. The reduction of employment opportunities as well as the decline of real wages in the public sector may, in particular, result in the proliferation of 'informal' micro-enterprises, and such tendencies have already appeared as a consequence of real-wage decline in several instances [*Sachikonye, 1996*]. With declining purchasing power customers also tend to prefer very cheap products which are usually provided by the 'informal sector'.

However, due to the relatively advanced competence and ambitions of former public sector employees venturing into private business, partially or next to completely mechanised enterprises are likely to increase in numbers, judging from previous experiences [*Kondowe, 1992; Billetoft, 1989*]. Competition from cheap imports can also be a threat to endogenous enterprises, but the effects of imports vary between activities. Small-scale carpentry is hardly affected, for instance, whereas weavers, tailors and dressmakers suffer greatly.

An expansion of small enterprises occurred before as a result of crisis in Africa [*Havnevik, 1987; Dawson, 1990*]. However, this did not necessarily lead to long-term growth. In this regard, recent studies of enterprise networks in the Third World have brought into focus four related issues which have not been adequately addressed [*Knorringa, 1991; Van Dijk, 1994; Rasmussen, 1992; Weijland, 1994*]. They are:

(1) The role of middlemen and brokers of various descriptions, as well as of the private provision of various services and inputs,

(2) The relation between technological leaders and laggards in small enterprise networks, and the potential of networks which combine enterprises at different levels of technological sophistication and scale of operations,

(3) Technological consequences of subcontracting and other co-operation arrangements between enterprises in adjacent positions in the sequence of production operations,

(4) The specific role of the light engineering and metal working sector, and the local production and maintenance capacity in this sector.

This chapter takes the last issue as its point of departure and considers how the capability of local producers of tools and machines to provide appropriate equipment to private small and medium-sized firms depends on local social networks, which become manifest through co-operation among firms as well as in the diffusion of technical experience and skills. In the analysis, the other three issues will be addressed in so far as they relate to the potentials of light engineering activities in Accra and in its general vicinity. We will return to them in the conclusion.

II. A BRIEF DESCRIPTION OF THE ENTERPRISES VISITED

In Accra, metal working enterprises can be found in great numbers, but not all of them are equally important for other manufacturing activities. Some are mainly directed towards vehicle maintenance and others are auxiliary to construction networks. However, most of them tie in one way or another into other manufacturing processes.

The fieldwork reported on here consisted of visits to 25 privately owned enterprises of different sizes and sophistication, which produce or recondition machinery and provide maintenance services to local industries. Some of these enterprises also produce agricultural implements and/or household goods. Enterprises which were exclusively engaged in basic vehicle maintenance were not visited. The enterprises were selected through strategic sampling in order to ensure adequate coverage of different types, including the relevant size categories.[2]

The enterprises visited were all located in the Accra metropolitan area (Accra and Tema). Five were limited liability companies, four were partnerships and the rest were owned by a single owner. The age of the enterprises ranged from less than a year to 35 years, and the average age was 13.7 years.

Eleven of the enterprises operated from a wooden structure and an adjacent lean-to, the rest had access to brick or concrete buildings of varied descriptions, usually surrounded by sheds. Every enterprise had access to electricity, though seven did not have water on the premises. Three had difficult access to streets or roads and only eight had telephones.

Accounting methods can be an indicator of that elusive quality, 'modernisation'. Six enterprises did not have any accounts whatsoever, 11 registered transactions and eight used the double entry method. Hence, six would be considered 'traditional', eight would be considered 'modern' and the rest classified as 'transitional'.

The enterprises visited employed 382 persons, of which 207 were skilled craftsmen or 'masters' in local parlance. The last number included a number of persons which were mainly involved in supervisory activities. 148 apprentices were regularly tied to the enterprises. The balance included night watchmen, secretaries, drivers and other auxiliary staff. The enterprises, therefore, employed on average, 15.3 workers, of which 8.3 were 'masters'. Total employment per firm ranged from two to 75, however.

The work was usually organised around master craftsmen, who were assisted by apprentices and daily labour. Among the skill categories, welders were the most common, followed by machinists. In a number of cases, a certain specialisation had developed in the machine shops in that lathe-operators, milling machine operators, boring machine operators, etc., would concentrate on a particular moment in the process. Generally, however, every craftsman in the shop was able to use the available machinery if the need arose. Further, most of the proprietors were concerned that their apprentices be suitably trained across the board and saw to this in various ways.

III. TECHNOLOGY AND NETWORKS IN LIGHT ENGINEERING

In this section, a number of selected socio/technical issues are discussed, starting with the training of proprietors/managers, moving on to spacing mechanisation and co-operation, and lastly, to the product range.

Training and Tacit Knowledge

Historically, craftsmanship and tacit knowledge gained through practical experience have played a large role in light engineering and metal working, and the role of craftsmanship has not diminished quite as fast during indus-trialisation processes in this sector as in many others [*Isacson and Magnusson, 1987; Sabel and Zeitlin, 1985*]. This general observation is still valid and applies directly to the light engineering network discussed here.

Half of the proprietors/production managers interviewed, or 12 out of 25, had attended some kind of technical school for a period of between two and five years. Three had university level training; of these two had degrees in engineering. However, 20 proprietors, or 80 per cent, had worked as apprentices for periods between two and six years. The persons who had both been apprentices and attended technical school (seven of those interviewed) had become apprentices at their present work place, with one exception. In addition, 17 owners/managers had working experience ranging from one to to 22 years from other firms.

This brief summary of the careers of those interviewed shows that they were generally well prepared for their job. The least prepared proprietor had only had a two year apprenticeship before starting on his own, the most experienced proprietor had spent five years in a technical school and then worked for 22 years before he became his own boss. Another had been apprenticed for five years and then worked 20 years before setting out on his own.

But how important were the different components of the training received? In spite of the considerable number which had been to technical school every respondent maintained, when asked, that he had learned most of his skills, both technically speaking and in terms of running a business, either from his master or from working experience after school. This reflects the importance of various concrete skills, which cannot be learned in school, for running a business of the type discussed here. Making do with less than adequate raw materials, catering to customers who want to keep prices low but still expect the product to serve adequately, and using machinery which demands constant attention and maintenance, all definitely hone survival skills which are very different from those needed in large organisations, commercial or parastatal. Sometimes it is also necessary to deviate, sometimes drastically, from the norms of quality and workmanship which are cultivated in schools. These tend to be abstractions of entirely different circumstances, the kind which prevail in large organisations.

This is not to say that vocational training is unimportant. Although cumulative experience is seen, in retrospect, as the main prerequisite of success, that accumulation process must start somewhere, and for many, that happens at school. Further, theoretical knowledge must be acquired before it can be applied and adapted to concrete problems arising in the production of simple machines, and again, this learning process starts in school. Hence, in light engineering as in other small and medium scale manufacturing, vocational training which provides basic theoretical insights as well as an introduction to the culture of good workmanship is a seed, which only bears fruit later on if provided with a suitable environment. Vocational training does not guarantee success, but without it, progress is very difficult. Hence, a combination of apprenticeship and formal training in school is appropriate, and this is the prevalent model in Accra. However, the training provided tended to be geared to preparations for employment in fairly advanced establishments rather than a career in the small enterprise sector. This explains why proprietors who had spent many years acquiring a technical education none the less valued highly the instruction they had received from their masters.

Gradual Mechanisation

The machine-making and maintaining enterprises in Accra can be classified into two main categories: welding enterprises and machine shops. Of the 25 enterprises visited, ten were welding enterprises and 14 were machine shops.

One electrical motor reconditioner was also visited. Welding enterprises or welding shops, as the label indicates, mainly assembled machines, and the technical interrelations between tasks in the shop are centered on the welding unit. Machine shops, in contrast, specialised in the shaping of components, and the central piece of machinery in this instance is a lathe. All the machine shops visited also had welding facilities, however, with one exception. In a number of cases assembly, including welding, or 'manufacturing' as it is termed locally, was a large part of the work even in the machine shops. On the average, welding enterprises were of more recent origin than machine shops (11.6 years compared to 16.1).

This flexibility of the enterprises is reflected in the character of the production instruments used. Generally, these workshops can be characterised as combinations of multi-purpose machinery [*Sabel and Zeitlin, 1985*]. Further, co-operation among enterprises is common (more about this later) and any specialised machinery which is available in one enterprise in the area is, therefore, in principle available to them all.

This in turn creates the possibility for gradual mechanisation. It is possible to start out with the essential machine, a lathe or a welding unit, and then add on new machines as the business takes off. Until then, equipment can be borrowed or rented, or specific tasks can be farmed out to better equipped enterprises. Hence, at any point in time, many enterprises will have incomplete sets of machinery but remain functional because of co-operation among firms. This was also the case here. Table 1 shows the number and percentage of firms in possession of each type of machine. The machinery currently available had, with two exceptions, been acquired gradually over a number of years.

TABLE 1

FREQUENCY OF MACHINE TYPES

Machine type	Number of firms	Percent of firms
Welding Unit	23	92
Grinding Machine	20	80
Drill	16	64
Center Lathe	14	56
Power Saw	9	36
Capstan Lathe	7	28
Milling Machine	4	16
Shaping Machine	7	28
Block Boring Machine	4	16
Crankshaft Machine	2	8

The possibility of gradual mechanisation is particularly relevant for machine shops. A complete machine shop consists of a collection of expensive and relatively complex machinery which must be imported. Most machines currently in use had been imported several years or even decades ago, and then bought second hand and reconditioned by their present owners. The original owners were usually parastatals or other organisations (educational establishments or foreign companies) with access to foreign exchange.

However, from our interviews we could ascertain a growing trend in the purchase and import by Ghanians of second hand machinery from Europe or the USA. The middleman would typically be a relative of the shop-owner, or actually own the workshop, using his savings (or borrowing) abroad to invest at home. In addition to this, a number of machines had also been acquired by two respondents from a recently initiated donor-financed hire/purchase scheme.

In contrast, to start a welding shop one only needs a welding unit which can and often is made locally, sometimes by the proprietor himself. One also needs access to a simple grinding machine. Hence, the import dependence of this activity is not quite as absolute as that of the machine shops.

Co-operation in Light Engineering Networks

Co-operation between enterprises in the light engineering business in Accra is predicated given the incomplete sets of machinery in many enterprises described above. Of the 14 machine shops, seven had a more or less complete set of machining, milling, shaping and grinding machines, but seven were less well equipped. This subcategory would best be described as turning shops. The other machine shop subcategory, combining machining and assembly, will in the following be called 'combined shops'. Hence, we have, in effect, three enterprise categories: welders, turning shops and combined shops.

Because of incomplete sets of machinery in many enterprises, welders and turners must interact continuously with each other and with the combined shops. The welding enterprises would, for example, routinely approach machine shops of both types for work they could not carry out themselves, such as machining of shafts and milling work, particularly gears.

The combined shops, however, are less dependent on this interaction, because their equipment is relatively complete, and some interviewed indicated that taking work for other proprietors was rather a nuisance when in full production. Such work was only welcomed in times of low demand. Conversely, farming out work to others was only practised in times of exceptionally high demand. Even these combined enterprises did, however, with two exceptions, subcontract casting and black smithing work to other enterprises, large or small.[3]

From the analysis above, the close interrelationship between technology and organisation appears clearly. Having an incomplete sets of machinery creates the basis of cooperation, and because of co-operation, technical self-sufficiency is not necessary for enterprise survival. This, in turn, makes evolutionary technical progress, and particularly gradual mechanisation, a realistic alternative to strategies which are predicated on the import of complete production units.

Product Range

Table 2 shows the 'frequency', or number of main products manufactured by the firms.[4] A number of products show up most frequently in this table: the most commonly found are gates and burglar-bars which are the main focus of seven enterprises. Four enterprises counted block-making machines or flour mixers and dough rollers among their main products. Somewhat less commonly found were wood-saws, wood lathes and aluminum spinning machines which were produced regularly by three enterprises. Coal-pots were produced in significant batches on a regular basis by two enterprises and cassava graters were also among the main products of two other, firms. The rest, 16 different products in all, were the main products of only one enterprise.

FREQUENCY OF MAIN PRODUCTS
(NUMBER OF ENTERPRISES PRODUCING EACH PRODUCT
ON A REGULAR BASIS)

1	2	3	4	7
Gears	Coal-pots	Wood Saws	Spares	Gates
Planers	Feed Mills	Wood lathes	Block Machines	Burglar
Pot-stands	Cassava Graters	Aluminum	Flour Mixers	Bars
Bread Ovens		Spinning	Dough Rollers	
Chair/table Frames		Machines		
Roof Tile Machines				
Gravel Shakers				
Spindle routs				
Block Linings				
Petrol Tanks				
Rice Polisher				
Bolts and Nuts				
Cake/pie displays				
Wheelbarrows				
Carbide Pots				
Gas-burner Heads				

The table reveals considerable specialisation. In some cases, enterprises specialise in the production of more advanced machinery, such as wood planers or routs, due to the superior skills of the proprietors. In other cases, enterprises focused on simple products such as petrol tanks (for service stations) because the proprietor (a former petroleum company employee) had developed a contact network which brought him prospective customers. In contrast, only two enterprises produced a large number of coal-pots (simple cooking stoves), although they were among the most elementary products mentioned and could readily be sold in local shops and market-places.

176

Most interviewed mentioned a number of products which they could produce, had produced, or planned to produce beyond what is listed above. Hence, in most firms, the potential product range in each enterprise more or less included all the products listed above, although the actual scope of production was much less.

This type of flexibility is essential for the survival of small and medium-sized enterprises of the type discussed here. Proprietors usually attempt to establish and maintain a network through which orders are channelled and material obtained. However, if the flow of work from one network turns to a trickle for some reason, the technical capability exists to make different products and from that, to develop new networks. Successful proprietors in Accra are also connected to several types of networks, for example, carpenters' networks, bakers' networks and builders' networks, at the same time. Through a diversity of contacts, they expand and stabilise their businesses, and avoid excessive reliance on the fortunes of a particular customer category. In the next section, we will turn to these external networks of light engineering enterprises.

IV. EXTERNAL NETWORKS OF THE LIGHT ENGINEERING SECTOR

In this section we focus on the external networks of the light engineering sector. The importance of local relations is discussed first. Input networks, output networks and user-producer interaction are then analysed in turn.

Local Relations

Generally, manufacturers have two options when they acquire new machines, namely import or local production. Imports may be cheaper and of better quality, but spares can be difficult to get and can be expensive. The non-availability of foreign exchange, import controls, customs duties, and the extra work and other costs related to importing also pose considerable obstacles. The purchase of local products can therefore be, in practice, the only realistic possibility, even if their quality is in some sense inferior.

In Ghana, manufacturing enterprises in, for example carpentry, brick-making and bread-making, are not quite as dependent on imported machines as the light engineering sector. A cursory examination of the machinery used by the customers of those interviewed reveals, however, that this is only partially true. Imported and rehabilitated machinery can be seen everywhere, and such rehabilitation work was, indeed, a major part of the activities in the light engineering enterprises visited. New machinery from abroad is rare, however. The local products, being both available and cheap, were preferred although they were usually inferior in terms of quality and finish. Further,

177

establishing contacts with purveyors of machines abroad is difficult, obtaining credit is almost impossible, and importers of small machines in Accra focus their business on development co-operation projects which are reliable customers. Accordingly, most respondents in the light engineering sector maintained that they did not face serious competition from imports, and in their view, trade liberalisation had not changed this. Consequently, the relations between the light engineering network and other small manufacturers' networks are quite stable. Most small enterprises rely on local producers for the more elementary and commonly available machines, such as bench-saws, brick-moulders and mixers. The situation is different *vis-à-vis* larger enterprises. They are able to import, and may even be compelled to do so by the terms of financing, both in the case of direct foreign investment and because of tied aid. In addition, the 'modern sector' enterprises do not emphasise co-operation with others and aim for maximum self-sufficiency. This is an essential part of the technological culture associated with mass-production, which calls for effective control of entire production chains in order to minimise insecurity [*Piore and Sabel, 1984*]. This technological culture is the paradigm on which most parastatal activities as well as subsidiaries of multinational enterprises are modelled in Africa [*Bagachwa, 1992*].

Accordingly, most large enterprises in the Accra Metropolitan Area have their own in-house service units rather than utilising maintenance services from the outside. The repair work available to local light engineering enterprises, and the competence development linked to such work, is therefore limited to what is available in other small and medium-sized enterprises. In spite of this general rule, a number of large companies, mostly privately and locally owned, occasionally used the services of five of the enterprises studied here, which had developed specialised niches, machining gears and crankshafts, as well as engine boring and lining. These tasks call for specialised machinery which is not widely available.

Input Networks

Material sources come, in most cases, from scrap of all kinds. The widespread use of scrap material calls for a qualification of the concept of production in which 'production' equals reconfiguration and assembly of parts from junkyards, engine and motor reconditioners, machine shops, blacksmiths and foundries as well as retailers. The most important type of unused components acquired from retailers were bearings, which many customers found prudent to demand new. Other inputs such as welding rods and paint were also acquired from the same source.

However, a variety of components are acquired from the junkyards in addition to scrap metal, sheets or profiles. Pulleys, gears, bearings and bearing seats, shafts of varied descriptions, etc., are available and often used, sometimes after adjusting their dimensions. Production in such cases could (and did) consist of finding a worn-out mixer, replacing the bowl, shafts, gears and pulleys that were not serviceable, and 'recycling' it once more. The line between producing and rehabilitating is thin indeed in such cases.

Due to the limited working capital available to most of the manufacturing enterprises visited, they are unable to maintain input stocks.[5] They depend entirely on retailers and junkyards. Collectors and purveyors of scrap material and reusable components are, therefore, very important in the local light engineering network. A multitude of small shops are found in areas where small enterprises operate, selling just about everything pertaining to the particular activities carried out in the vicinity. These ironmongers, etc., in turn run their shops on a cash and carry basis and rarely give credit to manu-facturers. When this occurs, however, it is based on a long-standing relation-ship, initiated on cash-and-carry basis.

Output Networks

In Accra, middlemen such as traders and travelling salesmen are virtually absent on the output side in the light engineering sector. Products are mainly sold directly to final users: bakers, carpenters, brick-makers, etc. Production in the enterprises studied generally took place in response to orders from customers, who generally paid half of the anticipated price in advance. Only few (four to five) of the enterprises visited had any realistic prospects for leaving this kind of arrangement behind in order to produce continuously for sales in outlets located elsewhere.

However, in the absence of traders who distribute the products, a different kind of networking was practised by light engineering enterprises in Accra. A carpenter contemplating investment would visit another carpenter, who already had mechanised equipment. The visitor would ask where the equip-ment had been bought, if it was reliable and functional and so on. If the answers were encouraging, he would call on the machine-maker and initiate negotiations. User networks are, in other words, a major means of promotion for light engineering enterprises.

Successful entrepreneurs in the light engineering sector would, therefore, actively arrange such visits to prospective customers, if they had not taken place already. Representatives of NGOs and envoys from grass-roots co-operatives in rural areas would, for example, be supplied with the names and addresses of customers in Accra and vicinity, where machinery from the workshop could be observed in real life working conditions. These customers could also answer questions about issues such as the general quality of the work, the availability and reliability of maintenance service and so forth. In this way, capable entrepreneurs consciously built a reputation for quality, robustness, fast service, installation support, etc. This strategy paid off in the

long run. As noted above, many enterprises were relatively old and well established. In these cases, the recommendations of satisfied customers who had
used the products for years, and received advice and maintenance services in
the process, were a significant asset.

The initial steps in this process are rather typical of how information is
transmitted through networks, and represent what Granovetter [*1973*] has
termed 'the strength of weak ties'. New information, according to this view, is
mainly diffused through networks supported by occasional interaction. In
contrast, in closely tied networks characterised by frequent interaction, the
information passed along is either of routine character or originates outside the
network most of the time. In Granovetter's study, the information was about
jobs, and would eventually lead to the establishment of a new, strong tie, that
is, employment. In our case, a similar process occurred. Information about a
possible supplier of machinery was passed through intermittent contact networks, but eventually lead to a long-term relation between the maker and user
of a piece of machinery. Although this relation was not quite as strong as the
employment relation, repairs and even routine maintenance performed by the
machine-maker or his employees kept the relationship alive, and orders for
more machines were likely to follow, strengthening the relationship.

In the network literature, active brokerage between otherwise unconnected
groups is usually seen as a position of power, power which then can be turned
into profits [*Burt, 1992*]. This is what happened in the case of merchants who
subcontracted (the so-called 'putting-out system') in Europe. In the Accra
light engineering networks, and other similar cases (for example, Sverrisson
[*1990; 1992; 1993*], the role of the trader in negotiating prices is taken
directly by the workshop proprietors themselves. In addition, the more enter-
prising proprietors have actively taken over the role of network broker, creating connections which bridge the gap between groups which were previously
unconnected. This is done selectively: prospective customers are not referred
to previous customers who have not been satisfied with the product or the post-
installation service provided. In this way, creating a reputation becomes more
than an issue of maintaining good workmanship and quality and hoping that
the word will spread. Rather, reputation is constructed socially through active
networking which connects the 'right' people with each other.

User–Producer Interaction and Product Design

As could be expected, most designs are the result of imitation or reverse
engineering.[6] The changes in design effected through the latter were usually
derived from the necessity to make do with available material and simple components. More formal designing or the use of blueprints and sketches found in
books, magazines, etc. occurred, but was rare. In recent theories of innovation,
interaction between users and producers has been increasingly emphasised

[*Lundvall, 1992*], and given the absence of brokers on the output side, this issue is highly relevant in the case of light engineering networks in Accra. The role of users in suggesting, for example, material substitution, simplification of the design and other adaptions is considerable in the cases studied here. Customers are actively included in the process of deciding on the properties of the product.

In the case of wood-saws, for example, the customer and the manufacturer discuss how heavy work is that the saw is intended for, and how intense utilisation is anticipated to be. The provision of facilities such as tilting of the blade, the possibility to move it up and down, additional controls and the size of the bench is all subject to discussion and negotiation as well as is, of course, the price.

This calls for innovative adaption. Components which require machining are reduced to a minimum or acquired by other means, for example, by reusing parts of broken down equipment. Welded frames are used rather than cast foot-pieces. The number of functions and controls is reduced. Although technically inferior, such solutions can be well suited to the requirements of the customers, as well as their purses, and are, therefore, economically superior to more advanced constructions [*Takeuchi, 1991*].

However, in order to establish exactly which corners should be cut, as it were, negotiations between customers and producers must take place on the type of products provided and services rendered. When dealing with importers, customers are often compelled to take what is offered whether it responds exactly to their needs or not. When dealing with local producers, however, users can specify exactly the complexity and capacity of the product.

Interactive design of this kind, as well as the organisation of trade through networks rather than the anonymous markets discussed above, are not limited to the light engineering sector in Accra or elsewhere. It is a common occurrence in construction, for instance, where it is also linked to what Stinchcombe [*1959*] has called 'craft administration of production', in contrast to 'bureaucratic administration of production'. A similar type of interaction can also be observed in the furniture business and between tailors and their customers, and at another level, between shipbuilders and their customers. Interactive design obviously places specific demands on the technology used: dedicated machinery turns out standard products or a limited range of products, whereas multipurpose machinery enables producers to respond to the wishes of their customers. Hence, interactive design is possible only in particular socio/technical contexts and not others, and the efficiency gains accruing to the users and created by flexible production can, therefore, only materialise if the technological culture prevailing in a particular activity empowers the user *vis-à-vis* the producers. It is, therefore, no coincidence, that flexible production, craft organisation and interactive design tend to remain a strong feature of machine-making networks, in which the users are technically competent and economically powerful relative to the producers.

V. MECHANISATION IN OTHER PRODUCTION NETWORKS

In view of the reliance of small and medium sized enterprises in Ghana on local providers of machinery, the *form* of mechanisation in other manufacturing activities largely determines what *kind* of machines are in demand and are produced by the light engineering network. A closer look at mechanisation processes in other activities, therefore, contributes to a more detailed picture of the potential of light engineering and metal working.

Let us first analyse more closely how the problem of mechanisation can be made amenable to network analysis. Our point of departure is that production in most activities such as small-scale carpentry, bread-making and construction (to consider the prime examples available in Accra) proceeds in separate, identifiable steps, which are, however, closely interrelated on the basis of the relevant technical attributes of the process.

This type of production sequence can be analysed from a number of viewpoints. One way is to reconstruct the work-flow network, in which information moves and tasks are allocated according to the logic of the underlying production sequence. This in turn leads to a concept of empowering connections, or, which amounts to the same, a concept of power as a function of central location in the work-flow network, rather than in the production sequence *per se* [*Ibarra, 1992; 1993*]. The question then arises whether mechanisation changes the relative importance of positions in the work-flow network, which can happen quite independently of changes in the interrelations among the production practices which make up the production sequence itself.

In gradual mechanisation processes, as discussed above with reference to the light engineering sector, each step in the sequence of operations can be mechanised more or less independently of the others. This observation also applies to the enterprises or branches from which the customers of machine manufacturers come, such as building, baking or furniture-making. The production sequence in these instances tends to remain the same or be only slightly modified during mechanisation processes. The same cannot be said of the work-flow network as it is defined above, however.

Changes in the work-flow network can, for example, happen in the following way in the type of context we are discussing here: A machine is acquired by the proprietor of a workshop (for example, a mortise cutting machine, in the case of carpentry) and a worker is assigned to operate this machine.[7] By acquiring superior skills in handling the machine, the worker moves from being only one of the staff to a more important position within the workshop. He cuts mortises in all pieces to be assembled by other carpenters and the number of his work-related connections therefore increases. Although mortises can be cut by using a hammer and chisel, the absence of the mortise-cutting-machine-operator would obviously create problems for the other workers and for the proprietor.

However, the proprietor can decide to teach all and every carpenter in the workshop to operate the mortise cutting machine (a process which in this case demands perhaps a day's work or so on the part of the proprietor or whoever else is doing the training). In this case, no worker is indispensable. If every worker cuts his own mortises with the machine, the benefits of task specialisation are lost. The proprietor can, therefore, decide to teach two or three workers how to use the machine, avoid dependence on one worker but still reap the benefits of specialisation.

Hence, there are three options for reconstructing the work-flow network when a machine is introduced, and examples of each can readily be found within any small and medium-sized enterprise network. The combination of the work-flow network and the production sequence is what is usually understood by 'work organisation'. Over the long term, the organisation of work tends to move from a multiple-task organisation to specialisation, from relatively independent workers to an interconnected labour force. However, that does not mean that all enterprises within a branch or all branches in a country have to follow this general trajectory at the same speed. Indeed, they manifestly do not.

Another way to develop the analysis of production sequences is to focus on the structure of commercial transactions, or in other words, the social organisation of trade in production and services [*Berkowitz, 1988*]. Referring back to the definition of the production sequence above, it can be observed that the different steps of, for example, furniture making, can be carried out within a single workshop or working unit. However, each step can also be carried out in a separate enterprise. It is essential to note, that in both cases the same technical practices and the same combinations of such practices are involved. The work is the same, the sequence of steps is the same and the interdependence of the steps is created by the same technical relations, whether the steps are all carried out in one work place or the process is divided among several work places.

Hence, mechanisation does not always imply the introduction of a machine into a workshop which otherwise carries on pretty much as before. Another option is the establishment of a workshop which specialises in a mechanised service or services. A third variant is that a workshop provides services to other workshops as a sideline to the main production activity. In Accra and its vicinity, both variants can be found. However, specialised 'mechanised service workshops' are strikingly common.

In carpentry, such enterprises provide one or more of the following services:

sawing, planing, moulding, mortising and turning. What happens is this. Prospective customers approach a cabinet maker. After negotiations, an order is placed. The cabinet maker buys the necessary material and arranges transport to the 'service' workshop.[8] The material is then formed into the components of the piece of furniture being produced. Assembly of the components, their ornamentation with woodcarving or other means, and varnishing is then carried out in the carpentry workshop proper, from which the product is also delivered to the customer.[9] This phenomenon is most visible in the Timber Market in Accra and the area around it, but the tentacles of carpentry networks crisscross the entire Accra Metropolitan Area.

A similar type of networking can be observed in small-scale bread-making. In Nsawam, a nearby town, specialised enterprises provide flour-mixing and dough-kneading services to small-scale bakers. Either these enterprises do the work or they rent out the right to use their rollers and mixers. These machines have, in many cases, been made or rebuilt in the very light engineering workshops visited in Accra.

Lastly, in the building sector, mechanisation of brick-making is also based on specialisation. Small-scale brick-makers who acquire their machines from small-scale local machine makers operate independently and sell their products to builders or house-owners who, in turn, employ the builders. This type of brick-making enterprises can be observed all over Accra, in areas where building activity is high and along the main thoroughfares in residential suburbs. The welders also have a more direct relationship with the building sector, in that they produce metal gates and burglar-bars for builders or households.

Obviously, there are baking, building and carpentry enterprises in which the vertical integration of technical functions and the inclusion of a large number of mechanised functions have been more or less successfully attempted. However, due to the capital scarcity mentioned above as well as the prevalence of a network-based economic culture, the network mechanisation is more suitable in many instances.

The insertion of a machine into an entire local production network through a specialised service enterprise or an enterprise which carries services for others on demand is obviously cheaper than introducing a similar machine in every enterprise, not to mention the option of introducing it in one or a couple of workshops and 'isolating' it there. This possibility, however, obliges students of technical change to reconsider their conceptions of efficiency, as suggested by Schmitz [*1989*], and consider efficiency as a function of inter-action within the network. The process of mechanisation itself must be envisioned in a similar fashion. It does not merely or even primarily bring about changes pertaining to the organisation of work within individual enter-prises, or a change in the competitive position of individual firms. Rather, entire production networks, such as bread-making networks or furniture networks, are reconfigured by seemingly minuscule changes such as the arrival of a couple of simple machines [*Sandee, 1995*]. Although these machines can be considered to belong to a single enterprise, this can easily become a misleading construct, because they enhance the opportunities of everybody within the network. The networks, in turn, operates as a quasi-integrated production unit or 'meta-enterprise'. The capability to locally produce at least the most common and simplest machines is, therefore, extremely important, however limited it may be qualitatively and quantitatively.

VI. CONCLUSION

The analysis above has focused on the social network aspects of light engineering and metal working in Accra. The light engineering sector is not only a major provider of equipment and services to other sectors, but also depends on a range of traders for its inputs. On the output side, however, direct interaction with users is the rule, which creates opportunities for interactive design and adaption of the equipment produced. We have shown that co-operation among enterprises, flexible scope of production and gradual mechanisation are essential preconditions for the viability of light engineering enterprises in an extremely inhospitable business environment. Further, active creation and maintenance of local networks, both on the input and the output side, was shown to be an important strategy in the struggle for survival in the light engineering sector.

In the social networks which link together the small and medium-sized enterprises in Accra, the small machine shops and other metal working ventures are central. In addition to network ties they are also part and parcel of a multitude of other production networks, providing equipment to bakers, carpenters, cutlery makers, etc. Further, because most of these latter enterprises do not have the necessary facilities and skills to repair their own equipment without help from the outside, local machine shops and other metal working enterprises provide a lifeline to other small enterprises.

This constellation of relations exhibits strong similarities to production networks elsewhere in Africa [*Sverrisson, 1990; 1992; 1993*], which, in turn, share a number of essential characteristics with early industrialisation experiences in Europe and elsewhere [*Kriedte et al., 1981; Takeuchi, 1991*]. It would take us too far afield to explore the implications of these similarities, and of the important differences as well. However, two issues will be briefly considered. The first pertains to technology strategies, the other relates to the role of merchants and other middlemen.

In Sweden, small workshops in metal working activities developed during the eighteenth and nineteenth centuries into proto-factories similar to the

185

workshops considered here in terms of work organisation. Indeed, the morphology of the internal technological networks of the enterprises, with limited specialisation and an emphasis on broad skills combined with multi-purpose equipment, changed little in light engineering and metal working in Sweden until well into the twentieth century even in relatively large and technically advanced metal working enterprises [*Sabel and Zeitlin, 1985*]. Due to the strong continuity, observed *in this particular activity* both over time and over technological sophistication levels (which sometimes amounts to the same), evolutionary technology strategies seem most appropriate for developing capacity in light engineering and metal working in Ghana as well. This conclusion is strengthened by the findings of this report, which emphasise the gradual character of mechanisation in manufacturing activities which, in turn, determine the demands placed on the light engineering sector.

In earlier proto-industrialisation experiences in Europe, merchants and traders played an important role. Generally, enhanced techniques were the result of capital accumulation initiated by merchants on the basis of trade in various products. Credit to producers was an important strategy through which the producers were tied to particular merchants. Ensuring adequate supply in this way, the merchants could establish themselves in the relevant markets as reliable providers of essential goods, and could build up their positions and profits accordingly [*Kriedte et al., 1981*]. Trade was the vehicle of an effort to organise and maintain networks which connected producers and users, and for this, both paid a price. In Africa, in general, and in the case of light engineer-ing in Accra in particular, this matter is put altogether differently. Traders in Africa are pre-industrial rather than proto-industrial. They are either importers or they connect urban and rural areas, much in the way traders have always done. They do not intervene in the organisation of production, much less finance it. Hence, they do not energise production networks in the same way as in other times and places, and production networks in Africa, as a result, tend to be extremely underdeveloped compared to those we find in other parts of the world [*Anderson, 1974; Kay, 1975; Anderson, 1986*].

Limited growth in private trade, private accumulation, and hence, privately organised production in Africa has largely been the result of the policies of governments which, as with the Nkrumah government in Ghana, have pursued other and different roads to development. Public corporations of the most varied kind were entrusted with both production and trade, and what happened beyond their purview was largely ignored. However, in Ghana and elsewhere, these hopes were frustrated. Eventually, permanent crisis lead to the family of policies known as structural adjustment programmes, but their effect on local production has so far mainly been negative, mainly because these policies, like earlier ones, are based on the false premise that the wellspring of development in Africa is to be found in external trade rather than domestic production.

Hence, instead of importing machines from abroad which can be used by local private producers, the traders which are born of structural adjustment in Ghana import second hand television sets, old cars and cheap clothes. These signs, somewhat dilapidated to be sure, of affluence are imported rather than the cornerstones of real affluence in the future.

This situation is likely to remain in the foreseeable future, and the substitution of machinery for manual work will, therefore, in most manufacturing activities, proceed at a rate which is determined by the capability of the local light engineering workshops. This might seem a gloomy prospect. Numerous studies testify to the low skill level generally observed in both small and medium sized enterprises in Africa, both in terms of organisation and management, and in terms of technology. The light engineering firms in Accra and the workshops in other branches which they serve are no exceptions [*Baark, 1989*]. However, behind the picture provided by averages another reality exists. A minority of small scale entrepreneurs are able to lead the way towards gradual enhancement of productivity and designs, through organisational as well as technical development.

This potential has been documented above. The light engineering firms relate to other local manufacturing networks mainly through local technological leaders, who buy and use relatively advanced tools as well as simpler machines. These leaders are either advanced general purpose workshops or workshops specialising in mechanised services. Above, we have focused on the latter. The development potential of entire networks which flows from the activities of the technological leaders can, to be sure, only be manifested in an evolutionary process. This will be very different from the great strides envisioned earlier as well as from the quick-buck rationale currently feeding on undiscriminating trade liberalisation. However, as this is the only path that leads forward at the moment, it certainly deserves serious consideration as well as support.

NOTES

1. A social network is an iterative pattern of social interaction which constitutes a social relation (tie, connection, link), as distinct from systems of physical connections (such as the telephone network or an electricity distribution grid [*Scott, 1991*].
2. Hence, we are not dealing with a random sample in this case. The general characteristics of the frequency distribution of size categories in enterprises of this sort is by now well known and documented [*Lubell, 1991*]. The overwhelming majority is very small and the larger are few indeed. A distribution in terms of technological sophistication would undoubtedly be skewed in the same direction, but surveys generally avoid measurement of this aspect [*Aboagye, 1986*]. An exception is King and Aboudha [*1991*].
3. The enterprise categories above constitute what has come to be called structurally equivalent positions in the enterprise network. This concept is central to network analysis of the kind developed here, and a short explanation is therefore in order [*Burt, 1983*]. Consider enterprises A, B, and C, which constitute a network among themselves as follows: A and B are related to

C and not to each other. From this follows (within this limited world of three enterprises and two mutual relations with unspecified content) that A and B are in structurally equivalent positions: They both occupy 'one-relation-positions' as distinct from C which occupies a 'two-relation-position'. In worlds where relational content and positional attributes (which should be seen as two sides of the same coin) are more complex, structural equivalence becomes a more complicated affair as well. However, it always refers to a family of positions which share basic relational attributes, and in this case, these attributes are the 'necessity' or 'non-necessity' to relate to welders or turning shops respectively, in order to construct or participate in the construction of a simple machine.

4. By asking how many of each had been made since the same time last year, the list was verified, and initial entries which represented potential rather than actual products were deleted.
5. Merchants and traders in Ghana generally do not risk their money in manufacturing. Instead, working capital is provided by the customers. The manufacturing enterprises demand and get advances when orders are placed, and this money is then used to buy materials. It is virtually impossible for small-scale manufacturers to borrow in banks and the real interest rate, which fluctuates between 15 and 20 per cent, is prohibitively high.
6. The term reverse engineering denotes a process in which a machine or another technical artifact is studied and disassembled in order to see 'how it works'. A new machine which retains the relevant functions is then designed. It can be smaller, be made of different materials or represent a separation of functions which were combined in the model technology.
7. A mortise is a slot cut in one piece of wood into which another suitable formed piece of wood is fitted and fixed by glue, a nail or a screw when a piece of furniture, for example, a chair or table, is assembled.
8. This creates need for specialised transport services, as all workshop proprietors do not possess suitable means of transportation.
9. In addition to transporters, upholsterers and makers of tools such as wooden planes, chisels, etc. also belong to this network.

REFERENCES

Aboagye, A.A. (1986): *Informal Sector Employment in Kenya: A Survey of Informal Sector Activities in Nairobi, Kisumu and Mombasa*, Addis Ababa: ILO/JASPA.
Anderson B.L. (1986): 'Entrepreneurship, Market Progress and the Industrial Revolution in England', in Anderson B.L. and A.J.H. Latham (eds.): *The Market in History*, London: Croom Helm.
Anderson, P. (1974): *Lineages of the Absolutist State*, London: New Left Books.
Baark, E. (1989): *Strengthening the National Capacity for the Transfer, Utilization and Development of Technology: Report on Capital Goods Sector Study*, Accra: UNDP/TTC.
Bagachwa, M.S.D. (1992): 'Choice of Technology in Small and Large Firms: Grain Milling in Tanzania', *World Development*, Vol.20, No.1, pp.97–107.
Berkowitz, S.D. (1988): 'Markets and Market Areas: Some Preliminary Formulations', in Barry Wellman and S.D. Berkowitz (eds.): *Social Structures: A Network Approach*, London: Cambridge University Press.
Billetoft, J. (1989): *Rural Non-farm Enterprises in Kenya: Spatial Structure and Development*, CDR Project Paper 89.3, Center for Development Research, Copenhagen.
Burt, R.S. (1983): 'Cohesion vs Structural Equivalence as a Basis for Network Subgroups', in R.S. Burt, M.J. Minor and Associates: *Applied Network Analysis: A Methodological Introduction*, London: Sage.
Burt, R.S. (1992): *Structural Holes: The Social Structure of Competition*, Cambridge, MA and London: Harvard University Press.
Dawson, J. (1990): 'The Wider Context: The Importance of the Macro-Environment for Small Enterprise Development', *Small Enterprise Development*, Vol.1, No.3, Sept., pp.39–46.
Dijk, M.P. van (1994): 'The Interrelations between Industrial Districts and Technological Capabilities Development: Concepts and Issues', in *Technological Dynamism in Industrial Districts:*

Enterprise Networks and Technological Change

An Alternative Approach to Industrialization in Developing Countries, Geneva: United Nations.

Granovetter, M. (1973): 'The Strength of Weak Ties', *American Journal of Sociology*, 78, pp.1360–80.

Havnevik, K.J. (1987): 'A Resource Overlooked – Crafts and Small-Scale Industries,' in Boesen, Jannik, K.J. Havnevik, J. Koponen and R. Odgaard (eds.), *Tanzania: Crisis and Struggle for Survival*, Uppsala: Scandinavian Institute of African Studies.

Ibarra, H. (1992): 'Structural Alignments, Individual Strategies, and Managerial Action: Elements Toward a Network Theory of Getting Things Done', in Nitin Nohria and R.G. Eccles, *Networks and Organisations: Structure, Form and Action*, Boston MA: Harvard Business School Press.

Ibarra, H. (1993): 'Network Centrality, Power and Innovation Involvement: Determinants of Technical and Administrative Roles', *Academy of Management Journal*, Vol.36, No.3, pp.471–501.

Isacson, M. and L. Magnusson (1987): *Proto-industrialization in Scandinavia: Craft Skills in the Industrial Revolution*, Lemington Spa: Berg Publishers.

Kay, G. (1975): *Capitalism and Underdevelopment: A Marxist Analysis*, London: Macmillan.

King, K. and C. Abuodha (1991): *The Building of an Industrial Society: Change and Development in Kenya's Informal Sector 1970–1990*, Edinburgh: University, Centre of African Studies, Occasional paper No.30.

Knorringa, P. (1991): *Small Enterprises in the Indian Footwear Industry: A Case Study of the Cluster Agra*, Amsterdam: Free University.

Kondowe, M. (1992): *Small-Scale Entrepreneurship in an Emerging Open Market Economy: Preliminary Findings on the Performance of Retrenched Government Workers in Zambia*, Working Paper, National Institute of Public Administration, Lusaka.

Kriedte, P., Medick, H. and J. Schlumbohm (1981): *Industrialization before Industrialization*, Cambridge: Cambridge University Press and Paris: Editions de la Maison des Sciences de l'Homme.

Lindberg, S. and A. Sverrisson (eds.) (1996): *Social Movements in Development: The Challenge of Globalisation and Democratisation*, London: Macmillan Press.

Lubell, H. (1991): *The Informal Sector in the 1980s and 1990s*, Paris: OECD.

Lundvall, B. (1992): 'User–Producer Relationships, National Systems of Innovation and Internationalisation', in B. Lundvall (ed.): *National Systems of Innovation: Towards a Theory of Innovation and Interactive Learning*, London: Pinter.

Pedersen, P.O., Sverrisson, A. and M.P. van Dijk (eds.) (1994): *Flexible Specialization: The Dynamics of Small-Scale Industries in the South*, London: Intermediate Technology Publications.

Piore, M.J. and C.F. Sabel (1984): *The Second Industrial Divide: Possibilities for Prosperity*, New York: Basic Books.

Rasmussen, J. (1992): *The Local Entrepreneurial Milieu: Enterprise Networks in Small Zimbabwean Towns*, Research Report No.79, Department of Geography, Roskilde University with CDR, Copenhagen.

Sabel, C. and J. Zeitlin (1985): 'Historical Alternatives to Mass Production: Politics, Markets and Technology in Nineteenth Century Industrialization', *Past and Present*, No.108, Aug., pp.133–76.

Sachikonye, L. (1996): 'Structural Adjustment and Democratization in Zimbabwe', in Lindberg, S. and A. Sverrisson (eds.) *[1996]*.

Sandee, H. (1995): *Innovation Adoption in Rural Industry: Technological Change in Roof Tile Clusters in Central Java, Indonesia*, Amsterdam: Vrije Universiteit.

Samuel, R. (1977): 'The Workshop of the World: Steam Power and Hand Technology in mid-Victorian Britain', *History Workshop*, Vol.3–4, pp.6–72.

Schmitz, H. (1989): *Flexible Specialisation – A New Paradigm of Small-Scale Industrialization?*, Discussion Paper 261 Institute of Development Studies, University of Sussex, Brighton.

Scott, J. (1991): *Social Network Analysis*, London: Sage.

Stinchcombe, A.L. (1959): 'Bureaucratic and Craft Administration of Production', *Administrative Science Quarterly*, 4, pp.168–87.

Sverrisson, A. (1990): *Entrepreneurship and Industrialisation: A case Study of Carpenters in*

Mutare, Zimbabwe, Research Policy Studies Discussion Paper No.186, Research Policy Institute, Lund.

Sverrisson, A. (1992): *Innovation as a Collective Enterprise: Case Studies of Carpenters in Nakuru, Kenya*, Research Policy Studies Discussion Paper No. 186, Research Policy Institute, Lund.

Sverrisson, A. (1993): *Evolutionary Technical Change and Flexible Mechanization: Entrepreneurship and Industrialization in Kenya and Zimbabwe*, Lund: Lund University Press.

Sverrisson, A. (1994): 'Gradual Diffusion of Flexible Techniques in Small and Medium Sized Enterprise Networks', in Pedersen *et al.* (eds.) [*1994*].

Takeuchi, J. (1991): *The Role of Labour-Intensive Sectors in Japanese Industrialization*, Tokyo: United Nations University Press.

Weijland, H. (1994): 'Flexible Trade Networks for Small Rural Enterprises', in Pedersen *et al.* (eds.) [*1994*].

10

From SMEs to Industrial Districts in the Process of Internationalisation: Theory and Evidence

MICHELLE BAGELLA and CARLO PIETROBELLI

I. THEORETICAL HYPOTHESES AND THE 'STAGE' OF INTERNATIONALISATION

Many studies have shown that Italian small and medium-sized enterprises (SMEs) have recently been prone to international involvement, but only in the simplest form of exporting. The absence of a more complex internationalisation has been explained with the existence of numerous obstacles of technological, informative and financial nature. The aim of this chapter is to analyse the hypothesis that inter-firm relationships in the form of a group of firms or of an 'industrial district' (ID) may enhance the perspectives of the internationalisation of SMEs, especially in developing countries. A simple theoretical model of an ID is presented. Then the hypothesis of the internationalisation of the ID driven by a 'leader firm' is studied. In our model, co-operation with the developing country's firms may ease the productive undertaking in that country. With the aim of preliminary testing this hypothesis in the social and economic context of Latin America, we analysed the experience of groups of SMEs and of 'quasi-IDs' in some countries (Argentina, Brazil, Mexico), with the prospect of future co-operation with the Italian IDs, and further international expansion.

The idea of the existence of different 'stages' in the process of internationalisation of firms has been acknowledged in the literature for some time [*Rullani and Vaccà, 1983*]. These stages range from simple access to the inter-

This study was financed by the Italian National Research Council CNR-PFI Project 3.5.2. Preliminary versions were presented at CNR seminars at the university 'Tor Vergata Roma' in Milano, at the Economic Commission for Latin America (ECLAC), Buenos Aires, Argentina, at the Federal University of Santa Catarina (USFC), Florianopolis, Brazil, and at an EADI workshop on industrialisation in Vienna. The authors wish to acknowledge useful comments by Professor G. Bacattini and of B. Chauduri, M.P. van Dijk, R. Rabeleotti and H. Schmitz. The study is the outcome of a joint effort by the authors, and responsibility for errors and ommissions remain the authors'.

national market through the exports of goods and services, to export consortia and joint ventures, to foreign involvement in production in the form of 'foreign direct investment' (FDI).[1] A *continuum* of 'intermediate' forms ranges between these extremes, including equity and non-equity agreements.[2]

From this approach it follows that trade theory and the theory of FDI may be considered within the same theoretical context [*Ramazzotti and Schiattarella, 1989*]. This is further confirmed by the new approach that emphasises firm-level sources of comparative advantage and international competitiveness. Thus, in addition to the more conventional explanations based on industry- and country-level factor endowments, the inter-firm gaps in technological capabilities, and the duration and effectiveness of the learning process may determine a competitive edge internationally

Moreover, these intermediate forms of internationalisation cannot be regarded as *second best* entrepreneurial choices, but actual *first best* options depending on the specific firm's and market's characteristics. In this perspective, the choice of the preferred 'stage' of internationalisation takes in a 'strategic' dimension.[3] However, the 'strategic' choice of international expansion of a Small and Medium-size Enterprise (SME) is crucially different from that of a large corporation. This reflects the different capabilities to influence and cope with a complex external environment characterised by asymmetric information, different risk propensities, and different opportunities to exploit economies of scale and scope. Sometimes these capabilities are available in-house, but often they need to be purchased from outside. It is well known that a large corporation is often capable of internalising these capabilities. In contrast, a SME will have to rely on real and financial services purchased from the market, and these services will be more varied and complex the more 'developed' the 'stage' of internationalisation. For these reasons, and due to the high transaction costs involved in the process, *ceteris paribus*, SMEs are expected to confine their activities to the simpler stages of internationalisation

The aim of this chapter is twofold. First, we describe the forms that foreign involvement of Italian enterprises has taken in Latin America on the basis of some recent and new empirical evidence. Second, we explore, at a theoretical level, the possibility that belonging to an Industrial District (ID) may improve the internationalisation perspectives of SMEs. Some experiences of the foreign involvement of Italian firms in Latin America, and the policies designed to promote this process, are analysed in sections II and III. In section IV, the central thesis is explored, and some case studies of Latin American IDs are assessed from the perspective of international co-operation with the Italian IDs in section V. Section VI summarises and concludes.

II. EVIDENCE ON INTERNATIONAL EXPANSION OF ITALIAN FIRMS IN LATIN AMERICA

Two recent studies analyse the forms of productive involvement chosen by a sample of Italian SMEs in Latin America, and their sources of competitive strength and weakness [*Carisano, 1994; Pietrobelli, 1994b*].[4] The population from which the evidence was drawn was made of 1000 firms belonging to the 23 export consortia dealing with Latin America and associated with the National Federation of Export Consortia (Federexport). These firms were reached by a postal questionnaire, and 126 firms responded. From them, only the SMEs having some relationship in 1989 with Latin America were selected, to generate a sample of 30 enterprises well representative of the universe.[5] The main results of these studies were the following:

(i) the sample firms show a good attitude towards the international market, with an export propensity of over 40 per cent of their overall sales. However, the empirical evidence shows only a relatively 'easy' stage of foreign involvement, confined to exporting. FDI is virtually non-existent, and only ten per cent of the sample firms set up some kind of agreement with local producers, mostly of a commercial nature.[6] Over 50 per cent of total exports go to the nearer and more accessible markets of the European Community (EC), 23.7 per cent to other industrial countries, and 11.4 per cent to Latin America. Latin America is by far the most important market among the Less Developed Countries (LDCs) broadly defined to include non-OECD countries. Exports are concentrated in intermediate and investment goods, mainly in machinery and metal working, rubber and plastic products. This is consistent with what one would expect on the basis of country endowments (and the ensuing international specialisation).[7]

(ii) The main obstacles to exports are related to the complex customs and administrative procedures, and to the scarce information on foreign markets.[8] The more export success depends on 'non-price' factors, such as product and firm reliability, trade marks, good product and process technology, the more valuable is information on the market and for the characteristics of demand. However, price-based competitiveness is especially relevant for exports to Latin America and East Asia, while exports to the US and Japan rely on technology and product quality to a greater extent. Thus, specialised real services could be more beneficial for the latter markets. Additional obstacles are related to the fragmented sale and distribution network.[9] Efficient production is often not sufficient to ensure stable export competitiveness in the absence of adequate distribution networks. The small firm size and the lack of economies of scale and scope represent a clear obstacle in this sense. The firms often emphasised the inadequacy of Italian public policies to specifically support with financial and real services distribution and sales in overseas markets.

In contrast, the presence of *large* Italian companies in Latin America is much more extended and takes various forms. Becchetti [*1994*], in an analysis focused on the experiences of IRI and ENI (the two largest state-owned conglomerates), shows that these firms have been much more active in Latin America than the SMEs, both in the form of FDI, and interfirm agreements and exports. Contrary to the evidence for SMEs, the main obstacles to large firms' international expansion have been of a financial nature, related to the foreign debt crisis and to the macroeconomic instability in the region. In fact, these large corporations have had the capabilities in-house to operate in the 'imperfect' South American markets, characterised by limited and asymmetric information.

Furthermore, there is evidence that belonging to a 'group' led by a large corporation has been a critical condition to set up international agreements of various kinds. This is shown by Vitali [*1994*], on the basis of evidence concerning the agreements between Italian and Latin American firms during 1987–90 in the clothing and food industries. Out of 26 agreements, nine were signed by enterprises that are part of the Benetton group, five of the Stefanel group, and all the others by firms of other industrial groups (for example, Ellesse, IRI, Zegna, Tachella, Armani).

III. SUPPORT POLICIES FOR SMES FOREIGN INVOLVEMENT: CASE ARGENTINA

In recent years, Italian foreign aid policies have had two related sets of objectives: the promotion of international collaboration in production, especially through international joint ventures, and the use of development co-operation as a strategic tool of foreign economic policy [*Cortellese and Pietrobelli, 1993*].

However, the explicit target of supporting the joint ventures between Italian and LDCs' firms has not been reached. Article No.7 of the law regulating development cooperation (L.49/1987), provides specific support for the setting up of international joint ventures, but it has been applied only in very few circumstances, and the financial incentives offered have not been sufficient to boost the active involvement of the Italian partners.

Within this context, the innovative mechanism of the 'Treaty of Privileged Relationship' between Italy and other newly-industrialising Latin American countries was introduced [*Angori, 1995*]. The first of these treaties was signed by the Italian government with Argentina in 1987 (*Tratado de Relación Asociativa Particular entre Argentina e Italia*), followed by others with Brazil and Venezuela [*Pietrobelli, 1990*]. However, it is acknowledged that the results have generally been very limited and far below expectations.[10] A central weakness, that has been detected by an empirical assessment of the results and the procedures of the Treaty with Argentina, is the excessive emphasis on financial aspects, with a general neglect of the need for real production-related services [*Pietrobelli and Cortellese, 1994*].

A survey based on a sample of 400 enterprises in Argentina usefully highlights the different expectations of and obstacles to Italian and local partners [*Feinstein, 1994*]. Major obstacles have been the complex bureaucratic procedures and the lack of an established relationship between the partners. Argentina's enterprises expected to gain easier access to new product and process technologies, and modern equipment, while offering the Italian partners low labour costs, raw materials, and a quick access to the regional market and to the *Mercosur*. However, the small size of Argentina's partners, their limited technical and marketing capabilities, and their limited access to credit, have all contributed to the establishment of only very few successful joint ventures. Financial support proved insufficient to ensure their success.

The experience of the Italy–Argentina Treaty prompts several interesting considerations, especially on the methodology employed. Thus, when assessing the interest of a SME to set up a joint venture in a developing country, one has to particularly take into consideration the environment of origin, as well as its capacity to introduce technological changes and its sources of competitive advantage.

To summarise, given the evidence that the Italian SMEs' internationalisation is only confined to exporting, and that they have experienced difficulties in undertaking a more complex international expansion, an alternative route needs to be taken. In view of these considerations, SMEs' international expansion may benefit from concepts and analyses that, especially in Italy, have contributed to a better understanding of the organisation and operation of these enterprises. To our present aim, the concept of the Industrial District and the evidence from some concrete historical examples may be useful and promising.

IV. A THEORY OF THE INTERNATIONALISATION OF INDUSTRIAL
DISTRICTS

In addition to the difficulties that Italian SMEs faced in expanding the scope of their activities internationally, the productive involvement of clusters and groups of foreign SMEs[11] is constrained by many difficulties. These include the coordination of individual actions and the structure of incentives to collaborate in all the activities related to product and process design, raw material and equipment procurement, technology selection, adoption and adaptation, the management of production, marketing and distribution. Collaboration in exporting poses fewer problems, and is often efficiently carried out through organisations such as the export consortia.

We discussed above the structural difficulties the SMEs face proceeding to the more complex stages of internationalisation. The difficulties are due to problems of insufficient and asymmetric information, diseconomies of scale and of scope and high transaction costs. Given the existence of these obstacles, the internationalisation of SMEs *together with* other SMEs sharing a tradition of fruitful collaboration on the home market may provide an easier alternative. The Italian IDs provide a clear and successful example in point, where the SMEs interact in a consolidated manner by sharing a common productive specialisation, location, and through the high social and cultural homogeneity of the workers and entrepreneurs.[12]

Some of these conditions may be represented in a simple analytical model that helps to single out those factors which affect the competitiveness of the IDs, defined as its average productivity. Such factors, in the case of a single-product ID, are the following:

$$(1)\ P = f\ (K, L, RSERV, XEFF)$$

$$(2)\ \frac{P}{L} = f\left(\frac{K}{L}, \frac{RSERV}{L}, \frac{XEFF}{L}\right)$$

$$(3)\ RSERV = f\left(\frac{P}{L}, NF, \frac{X}{P}, \frac{M}{P}, Ypc\right)$$

$$(4)\ XEFF = f(HK, COOP, PAR)$$

Symbols stand for:
P = production
K = physical capital
L = labour
RSERV = real services for the SMEs belonging to the ID;
XEFF = 'X-efficiency';
P/L = average labour productivity in the ID;
HK = human capital;
COOP = inter-firm co-operation;
PAR = principal-agent relationships;
Ypc = per-capita income;
NF = number of firms in the industry;
X = exports of the ID;
M = imports of the ID;
All variables refer to the aggregate of the ID.

This model refers to the production (P) in a single-product ID, calculated as a function of labour and capital, some real services needed in various phases of production, and an index of 'X-efficiency'. One hypothesis is that real services (for example, providing information on goods and factors markets) are available within the ID, and that they are an important input of production. We assume that production is positively related to the quantity (and/or quality) of such services, which also lowers transaction costs. Similarly, the expected sign of K and L is also positive, as well as of the index of 'X-efficiency'. This concept [*Leibenstein, 1966*] may be useful to determine the existence of an ID. In fact, when the business environment is positively affected by individual habits, routines and procedures, as happens in an ID, each enterprise's production process is enhanced. Methods, routines, procedures, implicit and explicit codes, schedules and plans, are all central determinants of efficiency, and in an ID these dimensions make an important contribution to the rise in global productivity.

Equation (2) expresses an ID average productivity as a function of a number of variables. Among them, the variable of 'belonging' to an ID operates as a result of numerous positive externalities (primarily of a technological kind), and is the one that most positively affects the productivity of each enterprise, and thereby, of the whole ID. If this applies, then $P_d/L_d > P_i/L_i$ (where d and i stand for district and industry, respectively). In other words the ID average productivity must be higher than the national industry average. This constraint implies that the high geographical concentration of many firms active in the same industry or with substantial backward and forward linkages, enhances collective efficiency through the working of many 'external economies'. In addition, co-operation may also contribute to raise collective efficiency. This is explicitly considered in equation (4).

Equation (3) is a supply function of real services, which is positively influenced by some variables, including the ID's average productivity. One can expect that higher productivity in IDs may itself spur the offer of increasingly more appropriate services, that are, in turn, capable of raising productivity. In other words, a positive and dynamic cumulative interaction would be sparked. Other relevant variables are: the number of firms active in the industry within the same ID, the international orientation of the ID, summarised by the export and import ratios (X/P and M/P), per capita income, as a proxy for the development and complexity of the socio-economic environment. The international orientation of the ID firms positively affects the endogenous offer of real services within the ID, due to the increased flow of knowledge that a wider international openness allows, and to the stronger inducement to compete.[13] Moreover, this itself has a positive and direct linkage to the degree of foreign involvement of the ID. We expect that the number of firms in the ID is correlated with the supply of RSERV, as the demand from a higher number of firms will itself induce a more intense response on the part of the same enterprises and of different agents in a co-operative interaction. In other words, the supply of real services depends on the existence of a critical mass of firms, not necessarily of small dimension. Thus, all the partial derivatives of equation (3) are expected to be positive. To these variables, one could add more policy variables (for example, industrial policies and other selective support policies) that could exogenously raise the quantity and quality of services, and, indirectly, also ID productivity.

Equation (4) makes explicit some of the determinants of X-efficiency. In general, it may depend on the quality of human capital that is available in the productive and service sectors within the ID (HK). Moreover, X-efficiency depends on the extent and quality of inter-firm co-operation (COOP), that, in addition to the prevailing external economies, may improve collective efficiency. Inter-firm co-operation itself reflects the prevailing environmental conditions, that include, among other things, the quality of social life, the firm–union relationships, the co-operative attitude that is shared by every participant towards some common purpose, and the quality of the organisational settings, the routines and procedures. It is bound to improve XEFF in the ID. In a hierarchically structured ID, where some kind of 'leadership' emerges, X-efficiency also depends on the relationships between the leader-firm and the others. As it is well known, such interaction may be portrayed as a 'principal–agent' relationship.[14] This theory argues that there may be a contrast of interests between the two agents, so that in our case the agent-firms may not be induced to seek productivity gains as actively and with as much effort as the leader firm. The agent-firms are often only subcontracted, whereas the leader-firm may hold the responsibility to the entire project. In such instances, fulfilling all the requirements of a project of internationalisation may demand an effort which is higher than the 'routine' effort demanded of the subcontracted firms. For example, product design and realisation should be faster than is usually required, but the leader-firm may not be in the position to perfectly observe and monitor the agents' activity. Insofar as these potential contrasts create difficulties, the X-efficiency of the entire ID-system would be hindered, and relevant to our aims, the project of internationalisation would be delayed. Therefore, a good principal–agent relationship (PAR), where it applies, may improve XEFF, and thereby the ID average productivity.

Concluding this, a group of firms may be considered a real ID if the following relationships apply:

(i) $P_d/L_d > P_i/L_i$, given K/L, is fulfilled, subject to:
(ii) $RSERV_d > RSERV_i$
(iii) $XEFF_d > XEFF_i$

The second and third conditions imply that real services and X-efficiency in the ID must be of a quantity and/or quality that is higher relative to the industry at the national level. If (ii) and (iii) *ceteris paribus* apply, (i) also is satisfied.[15]

Equations (1)–(4) may represent a starting point to measure some statistical indicators of the existence of an ID. A first attempt in this direction was made by Bagarani [*1994*], along the lines first set by Sforzi [*1987*], with a model that allows the overlap of statistical indicators related to the characteristics of the population with the distribution of enterprises in the area, in order to emphasise the existence/absence of some of the necessary elements, although not sufficient, for the existence of an ID. A principal components and cluster analysis highlighted areas in the territory which are homogeneous in terms of the structure of population and the specialisation of industrial activities. This method was successfully applied to the regions of Umbria and Emilia Romagna in Italy. It could also be applied in some newly-industrialising country with the aim of determining a priori the potential for establishing an organisational set-up for an ID, which might spur the internationalisation of an Italian ID, or which might allow the local ID to interact successfully with an Italian ID.

The studies of the Latin American experiences with clustering of firms and ID-like settings, presented in the following section, represent original and interesting material to test the hypothesis concerning the foreign involvement of Italian IDs in developing countries. In a co-operative setting, some Italian SMEs belonging to an ID might be able to get access to some real services that a local cluster may offer.

Having described a simple analytical tool to incorporate all the main features of an ID, and the factors giving it competitive advantage, we come to the central hypothesis which this paper aims to discuss and test with the empirical evidence available: can the network of collaboration and relations existing among the SMEs in an ID or a cluster boost more complex stages of internationalisation (for example, joint ventures or FDI)? In other words, can these external economies foster the process of international expansion? Inter-firm communication and interaction may, in fact, produce important 'clustering' advantages, related to the acquisition of information of product and factor markets, to the use of human capital and training, to the adoption of advanced technologies (and to the learning, adaptation and improvement efforts that are necessary with it), to technology diffusion, to the development of new products and processes, to access to new markets. Do these advantages also give a competitive edge in the process of international expansion?

First, we must define what we mean by 'internationalisation of the ID'. To do this, we need to distinguish conceptually between the internationalisation of the individual firms in an ID, and the internationalisation of the entire ID (in its unity). Bagarani [*1994*] argues that the latter case requires some kind of 'formalisation' of the ID, for example, through a consortium, an association, a trade-mark, or in the case of Italian ID the Law No.317/91, which initially required some degree of formalisation for an ID to get access to soft loans to finance technological innovation. This is not needed for the internationalisation of individual SMEs, even if they belong to an ID. In this paper we do not adopt a rigid definition, and we will examine the case of internationalisation of clusters of SMEs not necessarily formally united, but all sharing a strong interest to collaborate in the international market. The 'strength' of the interest on the part of the individual SME to collaborate may be evaluated on the basis of a cost-benefit assessment, as costs and benefits can be measured. Yet, their measurement in distant markets where information is scarce and costly is difficult. An additional problem may be represented in the higher unit costs of information that a SME has to face *ceteris paribus* relative to a large company, and the ensuing diminished propensity to get involved directly in foreign production, in particular in the presence of higher cost of collecting information.

This obstacle may be overcome if we consider the case of a 'hierarchical' ID based on the existence of a 'leader firm', which is also already operating (or is ready to begin operating) on international markets. The leader firm may be defined as that firm that, on the basis of past experience, has internalised information and knowledge of the international markets and how they function. Such a firm has a special mastery of the information on foreign markets and can correctly evaluate risks and positive and negative externalities. In this case, the leader-firm would be able to bear the initial cost of the internationalisation project, without sharing it with other firms from the beginning. This firm could prepare a pre-feasibility study of a FDI or joint venture (JV) project and take the responsibility for mobilising support for the project proposal from SMEs located in the 'input' and 'output subsectors' of its production, the service suppliers that are located 'horizontally' to its production activity, and other SMEs engaged in production of the same goods (Figure 1). Such proposal is expected to be more credible and effective if it comes from a leader-firm in the ID which shares with the ID firms common values, norms and attitudes.

If, for example, we take the case of a leader-firm in the machinery industry, it could set up a fruitful interaction with other 'input-' and 'output-firms', and with service suppliers, in order to carry out a FDI or JV project in Latin America. In this case, if local partners operate in the 'output' sub-sector, the 'leader' firm might facilitate the involvement of other Italian firms active in the same ID, thereby supplying not only technology and machinery, but also all the necessary skills and expertise to obtain a competitive product. Initially the 'leader' firm would appraise costs and benefits of the project (and the risks involved). Later, the other firms involved would also participate in the appraisal.

In other words, one could imagine a firm 'attracting' and carrying other firms with it in the process of internationalisation. The final target is a FDI in an area in a foreign country. However, if an ID, or a 'quasi-ID' were operating in the area, it might be that the local SMEs in the ID would resist to the foreign firms trying to get access to the external economies generated within the ID. In

order to avoid a competition that could be damaging for everyone, there is a
need to realise various forms of co-operation among local and Italian enterprises. The forms of co-operation would aim to find areas of common interest
of setting up locally all the flows of information, factors and goods that are
necessary for the existence of a larger and more efficient ID.[16] To summarise,
a 'developed' form of internationalisation of clusters appears to be possible
only if the necessary conditions for the existence of an ID are reproduced
locally.

FIGURE 1

INTERNATIONALISATION OF THE CLUSTER *VIA* A LEADER-FIRM

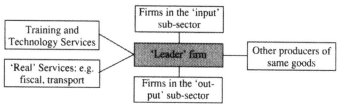

The strategic choice concerning the 'stage' of internationalisation can
be justified by the local availability of at least one source of comparative
advantage (for example, skilled and/or cheap labour, raw materials, access to
third markets and to regional markets or custom unions in the case of
Mercosur and NAFTA in the American hemisphere). In addition, the
availability of some favourable institutional conditions may foster the international expansion of groups of SMEs. Lo Cicero [*1995*] explored the peculiar
function a financial intermediary, such as a merchant bank or a local bank with
knowledge of the socio-economic environment of the ID, may perform. This
intermediary, backed by experience and reputation, could supply not only
financial services, but also real services in support of the international expansion of the ID. It could, using information on the economic and political context in which business takes place, supply services related to three possible
functions, outlined briefly below:

(1) Following one popular line of interpretation, IDs have developed as
organisations to replace markets that do not allow the flow of information,
finance and productive factors necessary for any entrepreneurial activity.[17] The
gamut of inter-personal relationships that preceded the formation of the
ID, and that derive from the common location and productive specialisation,
made possible such flows. The spatial expansion of the ID activities could
strengthen these flows further. The intermediary might facilitate these flows
even if the important advantage of geographical proximity is inevitably

reduced through internationalisation. It has been argued that the international expansion of an ID may 'dilute' the co-operative and community-like relationships central to the success of the ID, and that this may be risky for the future development of the ID [*Becattini, 1993*]. The effectiveness of the intermediary is strengthened if it operates in accordance with a 'leader-firm' as a true 'engine' of the international expansion of the ID. In this case, the support provided by the intermediary may be seen as positive for the project portrayed in Figure 1, and may increase the credibility of the project before other SMEs get involved. This would reduce the risks of the principal–agent relationship.

(2) The intermediary could perform the role of a 'seconding' manager in the design of the strategic international expansion of the ID, and in the monitoring of the implementation of the project in the absence of a leader-firm. In other words, if not locally available, the intermediary could lease the strategic management skills necessary for a developed foreign involvement. This would imply not only assisting in the project design (which normally happens in merchant banking), but also in nurturing its actual implementation, at least initially.

(3) The intermediary, provided that it has sufficient knowledge of the local environment, could link up with another intermediary in the LDC or with an international agent, and act as guarantor in the contractual and post-contractual relationships between parties. In this sense, the intermediary's role would be similar to that of an arbitrator of post-contractual relations between the foreign firms and those belonging to the ID, as well as firms within the ID.[18]

V. POSSIBLE COLLABORATION WITH LATIN AMERICAN QUASI-INDUSTRIAL DISTRICTS

Having defined this theoretical framework, we would like to assess the actual opportunities available to Italian enterprises in IDs to access the advantages of cooperation with similar organisations abroad (this is what we call 'potential' or 'quasi' IDs, those having some essential characteristics). To this end, we have investigated the feasibility of *equity* or *non-equity* agreements with groups of local firms. This follows the hypothesis that the international expansion of an Italian ID would be easier if it could find a similar network and organisation abroad. Therefore, some groups of firms in selected Latin-American countries have been analysed, as they were expected to have some of the features of an ID *alla italiana*.

These studies focused on the three countries that have reached the highest levels of industrial development in the region: Argentina, Brazil and Mexico.

The cases analysed, in spite of their differences, all include SMEs, mostly in the manufacturing sector, which have been remarkably dynamic in the recent past. We overview them in sequence.

The case of Rafaela in Argentina is especially interesting and promising from the viewpoint of the international expansion of Italian SMEs. Rafaela, in the centre-east of the Santa Fé province, is the location of an interesting cluster of firms involved in a variety of manufacturing activities (agro-industry, chemical, industrial machinery, auto components, agricultural machines), and a metal working ID [*Quintar et al., 1995*].

In spite of many differences, an interesting dimension, which makes this area comparable to other Italian circumstances, is the high social homogeneity, made up primarily of Italians which emigrated from Piemonte in the 1870s. This area has recorded a dynamism and an export propensity much higher than the national average. In 1992, the firms located in the 'quasi-ID' exported goods worth US$20 million, this is 20 per cent of total sales, which is a 300 per cent increase relative to 1988. This appears remarkable in view of the average export propensity of Argentinia's enterprises, which was only seven per cent in the 1980s. The increasing openness in the international market for firms in Rafaela is also revealed in the substantial rise of imports, mainly in foreign machinery.

The metal working district (110 establishments in 1990) includes on the one hand, metal and machinery producers, and on the other hand, vehicle components. An in-depth analysis of this case has shown that specific elements have generated an industrial 'climate' conducive to the creation of dynamic comparative advantages, involving a permanent process of technical progress, growing inter-firm linkages, and external economies [*Quintar et al., 1995*]. However, some of the necessary conditions for the existence of an ID *alla italiana* are still missing. The size of the local industrial network is still minimal, and this hinders further productive specialisation and a deepening of labour specialisation. Moreover, inter-firm relationships follow the traditional idiosyncratic modes of Argentina's industry, limiting the development of 'quasi-market' linkages.[19] Nevertheless, a good synergy between the private and public sector has promoted the creation of institutions favouring external economies. Among these, it is worthwhile to mention two institutions: the Association of Metalworking Industrialists and the *Delegación nor-oeste de la dirección de asesoramiento y servicios tecnológicos* (DAT, Direction of Support and Technological Services for SMEs), a provincial support body for SMEs, founded in 1983 and supplying laboratory services geared to quality control, managerial training and technological innovation.

However, in spite of the increase in export and import on the part of the enterprises in Rafaela, other forms of international expansion are still very limited. Certain exceptions can be found. Agreements were signed by some enterprises in Rafaela with enterprises from the US, Germany, Canada, Denmark, Italy, Brazil and India to regulate the exchange of intermediate products and components for the automotive industry, and the provision of specialised technical assistance. Moreover, the *Cámara de Comercio Exterior* (Foreign Trade Chamber) and the *Municipalidad* of Rafaela have created a *Fundación para el Desarrollo Regional* (Foundation for Regional Development) which carries out training programmes and fosters the exchange of technological information and the improvement of inter-firm co-operation.[30] In October 1992, in order to strengthen the relationships with the Italian economy, an agreement was signed with the Modena Chamber of Commerce, within the framework of the 'Tratado de Relación Asociativa Particular' aiming at promoting economic, industrial and technological co-operation between enterprises in Modena and Rafaela. This agreement related to industrial co-operation and technology transfer, exchange of information on sales markets, training and exchange of professionals and specialised engineers, diffusion of information on subcontracting and joint ventures.

From the perspective of the Italian SMEs, the positive interaction between Argentina's enterprises of a 'quasi-ID', and their interest in international co-operation, may offer some favourable conditions for further international involvement on the part of the Italian IDs. In other words, the supply of real services, the opportunities for external economies of scale, of scope and the existence of organisations in that area, given the active and effective interaction between local firms, might encourage an expansion of groups of Italian SMEs internationally to Argentina.

The case of a 'quasi-ID', analysed in Brazil, differs from the previous experience for two main reasons: the greater productive specialisation in the furniture sector, and the simultaneous presence of SMEs and medium-large enterprises in the same location. In São Bento do Sul, Santa Catarina State, in south-eastern Brazil, are located 120 furniture plants employing about 6000 workers, almost one half of the urban population [*Bercovich, 1995*]. This pole has been developing since the early 1970s, and at very high rates: in 1992, São Bento do Sul produced five per cent of the Brazilian furniture, and exported US\$60 million, the equivalent to half of the country's total. The study revealed that medium-size, vertically-integrated enterprises (with about 200 workers) coexist with many SMEs. The number of SMEs has been growing at a high rate during the past few years in response to the low entry-barriers, the considerable external economies made possible by the presence of medium-size enterprises, and a growing demand. Remarkable external economies are related to: good markets for raw materials and for second-hand equipment, efficient services for foreign trade, a high mobility of specialised manpower, a technology institute set up by the entrepreneurs themselves in 1978 (*Fundaçao de Tecnologia, Ensimo e Pesquisa*, FETEP), and an extended network of micro-enterprises supplying specialised services in some stages of production. However, the export expansion of the São Bento do Sul cluster is still mainly due to the exports by larger firms. A few agreements with foreign firms have been signed, mainly for the purchase of machinery, related technical assistance, and for some occasional subcontracting. The tendency to set up more complex and multi-dimensional agreements with groups of SMEs appears to still be very limited.

Rabellotti [*1995*] recently made an effort to look systematically at the experience of two areas densely populated by SMEs in Mexico. About 60 per cent of the country's total, 1,200 and 1,700 shoe manufacturers are located in the regions of Guadalajara and Leon, respectively. These firms, after the trade liberalisation of 1988, opened up to international relations and increased their exports. Among the factors that explain their good performance are: good inter-firm co-operation, mostly of an informal nature and among very small firms, and a good institutional assistance.[21]

The analysis of this Mexican experience has shown the SMEs in the area have an interest in developing an improved and long lasting relationships with Italian shoe manufacturers. One reason for this is that their products are considered worth imitating. What would be the interest of Italian SMEs in establishing commercial, technological, and productive linkages with the shoe manufacturers from Guadalajara and Leon? NAFTA (the North American Free Trade Agreement, linking Mexico, United States and Canada in a custom union) offers new opportunities for firms operating with Mexican partners. The co-operation with Mexican shoe manufacturers may provide Italian SMEs with an interesting chance to break into *niches* in the North American market, otherwise impossible due to the competition from other producers from Brazil, Mexico, and East Asia. Moreover, a strategy of international decentralisation of production is already being implemented by competing firms from South Korea and Taiwan, which have moved their plants to cheap labour locations like Thailand, Indonesia and the Philippines. A closer co-operation with Mexican firms and IDs might offer Italian SMEs the opportunity to exploit the advantage deriving from their advanced know-how, and face the emerging trend of a shift in shoe productions to LDCs. To this end, the agreement between the Association of Brenta Craftsmen (*Associazione Artigiani del Brenta*) and the Employers' Association of Guadalajara and Leon looks very promising. The target pursued with the agreement is not confined to the transfer of an entire plant or some phases of the production process to these areas, but also extends to the transfer of some elements of the Italian industrial organisation and production.

VI. SUMMARY AND CONCLUSIONS

The hypothesis that SMEs face substantial difficulties in their international expansion, in particular beyond the simpler and less risky exports, has been confirmed by much empirical analysis. Among the obstacles to a more 'developed stage' of SMEs internationalisation (inter-firm agreements or FDI) in developing countries are: the market failures related to risk and uncertainty and the economies of scale and scope necessary to operate at an international scale, both for the manufacturing and distribution of all product varieties demanded by export markets. In addition, the alternative option of internalising transactions within the borders of the firm is not open to the SMEs.

However, in spite of these difficulties, a more 'developed' foreign involvement by the Italian SMEs may be fostered through various forms of inter-firm agreements, in particular if they derive from a long tradition of co-operation based on such elements as a common social and human base, a geographic proximity, and the same productive specialisation. These are some of the basic characteristics of the Italian IDs, which have contributed a great deal to their success. The essential experience with inter-firm co-operation and collaboration may represent a key determinant in the further development of the Italian SMEs' international expansion towards newly emerging economies.

In some Latin American countries, where forms of industrial organisation that have been defined as 'quasi-districts' already exist, some of the conditions are also present for generating external economies and favouring the international expansion of Italian IDs to those areas. The presence of quasi-IDs observed in Latin America may attract the Italian IDs, given the high level of organisation observed and the high propensity to collaborate. Support of these forms of international expansion may come from numerous institutional agents, for example, from a specialised financial intermediary or a 'leader-firm'. Further research is needed to address some of the specific issues outlined in this paper, and to test empirically the validity of the hypotheses proposed.

NOTES

1. Becattini identifies two main categories: 'commercial' and 'productive' (or 'developed') internationalisation [*Becattini, 1993*]. Writing of 'stages' of internationalisation does not necessarily imply a pre-defined and identical sequence. Thus, FDI does not always need to be preceded by exports, although exporting to a country often allows valuable learning.
2. Among the main 'intermediate' forms of internationalisation are: joint ventures, trade and production licensing, management contracts, 'turn-key' and 'ready-made' contracts, production-sharing contracts, international sub-contracting [*Oman, 1984a*].
3. By 'strategy' we mean the purposeful action of an agent aiming at the acquisition of power over other agents, even at the cost of giving up present profits in exchange for future

(expected) profits [*Acocella, 1989*].

4. Angori [*1995*]; Bagarani [*1994*]; Becchetti [*1994*]; Bercovich [*1995*]; Carisano [*1994*]; Feistein [*1994*]; LoCicero [*1995*]; Pietrobelli [*1994b; 1992*]; Quintar *et al.* [*1995*]; Rabellotti [*1995*].

5. For the sampling technique and other specific aspects of the questionnaire, see Carisano [*1994*] and Pietrobelli [*1994b*]. In 1989 the average sample firm employed 69 workers, had sales for L.It. 14 billion (about US$8.7 million) and exports for L.It. 6 billion (about US$ 3.7 million). The sample mainly included northern Italy firms.

6. Only two examples of technology transfer agreements have been recorded. These results confirm what had already been discovered in other surveys on the international agreements of Italian firms [*Cespri-Bocconi, 1988*].

7. Evidence from a sample of SMEs from Tuscany (Italy) confirms the conclusion that Italian SMEs mainly expand internationally by exporting rather than investing abroad [*Manuelli, 1994*].

8. The information available on Latin American markets appears to be, perhaps surprisingly, as scarce as information on South-East Asia, which is geographically and 'culturally' further away from the Italian business community. Services providing information on the markets and on the procedures to get access to them have not been available in sufficient quantity/quality.

9. The sample firms rely primarily on local importers (50 per cent), and secondarily on sale agents (33 per cent) for their exports.

10. In addition, the treaties with Brazil and Venezuela, after promising declarations of all partners, have never been actually implemented.

11. 'Group' of SMEs is a broader and looser concept than ID: the latter is a group of SMEs with also special characteristics, including a common location and productive specialisation. Cluster emphasises physical proximity, not necessarily identical productive specialisation.

12. Essential references to the industrial districts are Becattini [*1979; 1987*], and Pyke, Becattini and Sengenberger [*1991*].

13. This is consistent with Paganetto and Scandizzo [*1992*].

14. Hart and Holmström [*1988*] and Nalebuff and Stiglitz [*1983*].

15. Work in progress by the authors includes an analytical model portraying the hypothesis that the activity of a 'leader-firm' may enable the other firms operating in the ID to reduce their risk and transaction costs, that may be especially heavy in an internationalisation project.

16. The advantages from co-operation have been analysed by the so-called models of 'coordination failure', see Cooper and John [*1988*].

17. The prevailing conditions also inhibited the growth of a larger company capable of internalising markets.

18. These proposals for a possible role for credit intermediaries, like for example a merchant bank, all stem from the hypothesis, that is common to the new theories of the firm, that a firm is a network of contracts, more or less explicit and formalised, to manage complex production processes profitably [*Lo Cicero, 1995*].

19. Sub-contracting is seldom used (41 per cent of the local firms never sub-contract anything), and the observed tendency to the increase of vertical integration, has been partly due to the prevailing macroeconomic conditions of uncertainty: in these conditions, the internalisation of a good share of the production process and of the market-linkages was a rational and inevitable response.

20. To this aim, the Foundation signed two co-operation agreements with Spanish institutions: the Asociación de Investigación Tecnológica TEKNIKER at Eibar, and the Centro Tecnológico de Materiales INASMET in San Sebastián.

21. The Istituto Tecnológico del Calzado, created in 1984 in Guadalajara, is a good example of effective institutional support to technology training and R&D.

REFERENCES

Accocella, N. (1989): 'Efficienza e strategia nel processo di multinazionalizzazione: verso una teoria più generale', in N. Acocella and R. Schiattarella (eds.), *Teorie della internazionalizzazione e realtà italiana*, Napoli: Liguori.

Angori, E. (1995): 'La funzione svolta dagli accordi bilaterali: il caso Italia-Argentina. Aspetti istituzionali.', *Studi di Economia e Diritto*, 3/95.

Bagarani, M. (1994): 'Metodologia per rilevare l'esistenza di un distretto industriale: indicatori significativi per l'internazionalizzazione', Working paper CNR-PFI.

Bagella, M. (ed.) (1992): 'Politiche ed interventi per l'internazionalizzazione di imprese medio-piccole italiane in America Latina', 2 volumes, mimeo, Dipartimento di Economia ed Istituzioni, Università di Roma 'Tor Vergata'.

Becattini, G. (1979): 'Dal settore industriale al distretto industriale. Alcune considerazioni sull'unità d'indagine dell'economia industriale', *Economia e Politica Industriale*, 1.

Becattini, G. (ed.) (1987): *Mercato e forze locali: il distretto industriale*, Bologna: Il Mulino.

Becattini, G. (1993): 'Presentazione a "Distretti industriali e mercato unico europeo" di M.Mistri', Milano: Franco Angeli – Ist.Tagliacarne.

Becchetti, L. (1994): 'La grande impresa pubblica in America Latina: l'esperienza IRI, l'offerta endogena di servizi reali, la dimensione degli investimenti, il project financing', *Economia, Società e Istituzioni*, Vol. VI, No. 1.

Bercovich, N. (1995): 'Analisi dell'internazionalizzazione del settore del mobile di Sao Bento do Sul (Santa Catarina, Brasil) alla luce dell'esperienza dei distretti industriali italiani', *Economia e Diritto del Terziario*, 1.

Carisano, R. (1994): 'La piccola e media impresa in America Latina. L'assetto attuale dei rapporti e problemi di inserimento: un'indagine sul campo', *Economia, Società e Istituzioni*, Vol. VI N. 1.

Cespri-Bocconi, (1988): 'La cooperazione internazionale delle imprese italiane: analisi generale e prospettive degli accordi delle PMI in Europa', report for the Task Force on SMEs for the EEC, Brussels.

Cooper, R. and A. John (1988): 'Coordinating Coordination Failures in Keynesian Models', *Quarterly Journal of Economics*, 103, Aug.

Cortellese, C. and C. Pietrobelli (1993): 'La strategia per la ricostruzione economico-sociale nei PVS: quale ruolo per la cooperazione internazionale?', *Studi di Economia e Diritto*, Vol. XXXXIII, No. 3.

Dei Ottati, G. (1992): 'Fiducia, transazioni intrecciate e credito nel distretto industriale', *Note Economiche*, Vol. XXII, Nos. 1–2.

Feistein, H.A. (1994): 'L'indagine campionaria sui progetti di cooperazione presentati alla CGI argentina nell'ambito dell'Accordo italo-argentino', *Studi di Economia e Diritto*, Vol. XXXXIV, No. 3.

Hart, O. and B. Holmström (1988): 'The Theory of Contracts', in T. Bewley (ed.) *Advances in Economic Theory*, Econometric Society Monographs No. 12, Cambridge: Cambridge University Press.

Leibenstein, H. (1966): 'Allocative Efficiency vs. X-efficiency', *American Economic Review*, 56.

Lo Cicero, M. (1995): 'Internazionalizzazione dei distretti industriali: un ruolo possibile per il merchant banking', *Economia e Diritto del Terziario*, 1.

Manuelli, A. (1994): *Internazionalizzazione e trasferimento tecnologico in aree a minor sviluppo. Le problematiche nei sistemi locali di piccole imprese in Toscana*, Firenze: IRPET.

Mistri, M. (1993): *Distretti industriali e Mercato Unico Europeo*, Milan: Franco Angeli and Istituto Tagliacarne.

Nalebuff, B.J. and Stiglitz, J.E. (1983): 'Prizes and Incentives: Towards a General Theory of Compensation and Competition', *Bell Journal of Economics*, 14.

Oman, C. (1984a): *New Forms of International Investment in Developing Countries*, Paris: OECD.

Oman, C. (ed.) (1984b): *Les nouvelles formes d'investissement international dans les pays en developpement. Perspectives Nationales*, Paris: OCDE.

Paganetto, L. and P.L. Scandizzo (1992): 'Quality, International Trade and Endogenous Growth',

Internationalisation: Theory and Practice

Rivista di Politica Economica, 11, Nov.

Pietrobelli, C. (1990): 'Italia-Brasile: Logica di un accordo', *Andes*, 9.

Pietrobelli, C. (1991): *Tecnologia e Sviluppo. L'inserimento internazionale di un'economia emergente*, Roma: Edizioni Lavoro.

Pietrobelli, C. (1992): 'Il ruolo del progresso tecnologico nei processi di internazionalizzazione delle imprese', *Studi di Economia e Diritto*, Vol. XXXXIV, No. 3.

Pietrobelli, C. (1994a): 'Technological Capability and Export Diversification in a Developing Country: The Case of Chile since 1974', unpublished D.Phil thesis, University of Oxford.

Pietrobelli, C. (1994b): 'Internazionalizzazione delle PMI italiane in America Latina e progresso tecnologico: una nota da un'indagine empirica', *Economia, Società e Istituzioni*, Vol. VI, No. 1.

Pietrobelli, C. and R. Rabellotti (1992): 'Relaciones extramercado entre firmas y sus efectos en el desarrollo industrial de los países de menor desarrollo. El caso de un Parque Industrial en Santiago de Chile', *Revista Latinoamericana de Estudios Urbanos y Regionales – EURE*, XVIII, No. 54, and *Economia, Società ed Istituzioni*, IV (1).

Pietrobelli, C. and C. Cortellese (1994): 'Joint Ventures e relazioni economiche internazionali: l'esperienza del Trattato tra Italia e Argentina', *Studi di Economia e Diritto*, Vol. XXXXIV, No. 3.

Pyke, F., Becattini, G. and W. Sengenberger (eds.) (1991): *Industrial Districts and Interfirm Cooperation in Italy*, ILO, Geneva.

Quintar, A., R. Ascua, F. Gatto and C. Ferraro (1995): 'Rafaela (Argentina): un quasi-distretto italiano alla argentina', *Economia e Diritto del Terziario*, 1/95.

Rabellotti, R. (1995): 'Distretti industriali in Messico: il caso del settore calzaturiero a Guadalajara e Leon', *Economia e Diritto del Terziario*, 1/95.

Ramazzotti, P. and R. Schiattarella (1989): 'Investimenti diretti ed esportazioni tra mercato ed impresa', in N. Acocella and R. Schiattarella (eds.) *Teorie della internazionalizzazione e realtà italiana*, Napoli: Liguori.

Rullani, E. and S. Vaccà (1983): 'Oltre il modello classico di impresa multinazionale', *Finanza, Marketing, Produzione*, 1–2.

Sforzi, F. (1987): 'L'identificazione spaziale', in Becattini (ed.), reprinted as: 'The Geography of Industrial Districts in Italy', in E. Goodman and J. Bamford (eds.), 1989, *Small Firms and Industrial Districts in Italy*, London and New York: Routledge.

Vitali, G. (1994): Paper presented to the Conference CNR-PFI, Università Tor Vergata, Roma, 24 March 1994.

EADI BOOK SERIES

For Product Safety Concerns and Information please contact our EU
representative GPSR@taylorandfrancis.com
Taylor & Francis Verlag GmbH, Kaufingerstraße 24, 80331 München, Germany